Magazine Article
Writing

Second Edition

Magazine Article Writing

Betsy P. Graham
Georgia State University

Harcourt Brace Jovanovich College Publishers
Fort Worth Philadelphia San Diego New York Orlando Austin
San Antonio Toronto Montreal London Sydney Tokyo

Publisher	Ted Buchholz
Acquisitions Editor	Stephen T. Jordan
Developmental Editor	Cathlyn Richard
Project Editor	Barbara Moreland-Gee
Production Manager	Kathleen Ferguson
Book Designer	Priscilla Mingus
Photo/Permissions Editor	Greg Meadors/Barbara McGinnis

Cover photograph by Robert LaPrelle.

Credits and sources continue on page 233.

Requests for permission to make copies of any part of the work should be mailed to: Permissions Department, Harcourt Brace Jovanovich, Publishers, 8th Floor, Orlando, Florida 32887.

Address Editorial Correspondence to: 301 Commerce Street, Suite 3700, Fort Worth, TX 76102.

Address Orders to: 6277 Sea Harbor Drive, Orlando, FL 32887
1-800-782-4479, or 1-800-433-0001. (in Florida)

Printed in the United States of America

ISBN: 0-03-0750091

3 4 5 6 7 8 9 0 1 2   0 3 9   9 8 7 6 5 4 3 2 1

To Ralph,
my kind and careful critic

❏ PREFACE ❏

Revising a book is like raising a second child. You have the exhilarating opportunity to benefit from experience. Indeed a better product may result, still recognizable as your child with many of your values and mannerisms, but nevertheless a new individual.

Such was my experience in completely revising and rewriting the first edition of *Magazine Article Writing: Substance and Style*, published in 1980. The new book still consists of complete step-by-step instructions for writing a magazine article without burying the reader in too much detail. Examining the specific techniques that give good writing power and grace, it still places strong emphasis on reading good writing as the best way to improve one's own work. And it insists that significant content and appropriate style are complementary: Lively content can drown in a murky style, yet a pleasing style alone cannot resuscitate a lifeless subject.

Nevertheless, major changes and additions were made to this edition.

❏ Ninety percent of the former examples of various writing techniques have been replaced by new ones.

❏ The new book includes many more examples of writing by students.

❏ A new chapter describes and illustrates five of the most popular types of articles.

❏ The chapter on queries is now nearer the beginning of the book, and a short section on phone queries has been added.

❏ More emphasis has been placed on querying local, regional, and specialized magazines instead of going for the big ones that rarely consider freelance material.

❏ A new section on computer research brings the book up to date without ignoring paper research, which is still essential.

❏ New suggestions on establishing good relationships with editors show novices what to do after a query has been sent or a phone call made.

❏ Many more subheads improve readership and learning.

❏ A brief section on avoiding sexist language helps solve the he/she problem.

❏ A few examples of bad writing show some of the techniques to avoid.

Perhaps the most important section in the book is Chaper 2, "Good Writing from Good Reading." A humorous new article in this chapter demonstrates analytical reading by a process that is entertaining as well as instructive. It provides an excellent example for beginners who want to convert dull, earthbound writing into prose that soars.

One of the most practical chapters deals more fully than other textbooks with the difference between topic and thesis. Without thoroughly understanding this distinction, students may embark on a writing project without any idea of the port they wish to reach. Chapter 7, "Making a Significant Point," shows that a finely focused thesis can keep them on course.

Although the book encourages novices to experiment with using fictional techniques while adhering to fact, the central advice is to write naturally and clearly.

A helpful feature of every chapter is a summary and a set of exercises, "From Principles to Practice." Beginners who apply the recommended principles and follow the exercises can learn how to analyze articles and magazine markets, how to conduct interviews and other kinds of research, how to write a rough draft quickly, and how to revise slowly and systematically. Some of the exercises involve close analysis of the articles in the Appendix.

The Appendix itself is a useful addition to this edition because it gives unpublished writers some complete articles to study. Those written by students will give beginners an idea of what is possible for them to produce, and those by professionals make excellent models for beginners to emulate. The annotated bibliography will be helpful for those who want to do more reading on the various aspects of magazine article writing.

Critics have said the book's greatest strength is its contageous enthusiasm for writing and its informal style. About the original version, a student said to me (possibly with an eye toward an A), "I like this book because it doesn't sound like a textbook. It's fun to read." For readers at all levels of expertise, I hope this new version will be even more fun.

I would like to express my thanks to all who have helped me in the revision of this book: Cathy Richard and Barbara Moreland-Gee, editors, for constantly encouraging my efforts; my husband for patient listening, reading, and judicious suggestions; Ginny Moreland of the Georgia State University library for editing the new chapter on research, and reference librarian David Burke for showing me how to use the computer for research; Greg Hutchinson, reference librarian at the Sue Kellogg Library in Stone Mountain, Georgia, for willingly giving me miscellaneous bits of information by phone; Jean Peterken for reading a majority of the chapters and her excellent suggestions for improvement; and Edith Kilgo for sharing much of her extensive knowledge about selling to "small" markets.

To the following former students I am especially grateful for their generosity in giving me permission to use their work: Jennifer Cogelia, Richard Daigle, Nancy E. Davis, Hank Ernest, Jr., Helen Friese, Frida Ghitis, Chantry S. Heard, Leigh Hilliard, Edward Coleman Hosch, Elfriede Kristwald, and Beverly Levine.

I would also like to express my thanks to the following who read the manuscript at various stages and made constructive suggestions. Their help made this a better book than it would otherwise have been: Lee Brown, San Diego State University; Sandy Hall Chiles, Dallas Independent School District, Talented and Gifted Magnet High School; Robert McClory, Northwestern University; Gene Meyer, Ohio State University; Judy Polumbaum, University of Iowa; Carol Reuss, University of North Carlina, Chapel Hill; and Nancy Roberts, University of Minnesota.

CONTENTS

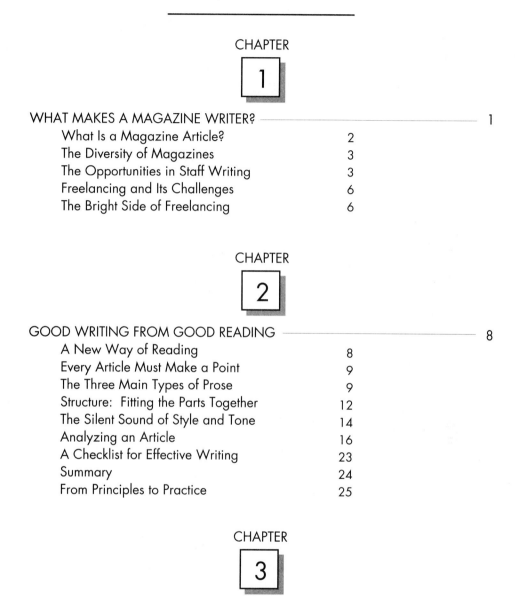

CHAPTER

4

CHAPTER

5

CHAPTER

6

CHAPTER

7

CHAPTER

8

CHAPTER

9

CHAPTER

CHAPTER

CHAPTER

CHAPTER

CHAPTER

CHAPTER

CHAPTER

16

CHAPTER

17

Magazine Article
Writing

CHAPTER

1

WHAT MAKES A MAGAZINE WRITER?

Capable, creative, and perhaps idealistic individuals are often drawn to magazine writing by its vigor and freedom and by the important role it plays in influencing the affairs of a democratic society. They respond to flashy four-color magazines and to the flourishes of writing that seem to put a sheen on the plainest of facts. But before attributing too much glamour to a craft that can be excruciatingly difficult, aspiring magazine writers should look closely at the requirements and realities of the field.

Magazine writing is exciting and adventuresome, but nationally distributed publications such as *People* and *TV Guide* have a relentless thirst for new article ideas and for writing that is riveting. Selling articles to such magazines, therefore, is brutally competitive. Local and regional markets (described in Chapter 3) are much more available to young writers, but their standards, too, are high. In addition to writing skills, most magazines want writers with imagination, resourcefulness, persistence, and a knowledge of the needs and interests of people.

A final quality basic to success in magazine writing is a reverence for the power of words. The poet Dylan Thomas, for example, was awakened to their charm even as a very young child when he first heard Mother Goose rhymes. "I tumbled for words at once," he wrote. "There they were, seemingly lifeless, made only of black and white, but out of them came the gusts and grunts and hiccups and hee-haws of the common fun of the earth; and though what the words meant was often deliciously funny enough, so much funnier seemed to me, at that almost forgotten time, the shape and shade and size and noise of the words as they hummed, strummed, jigged and galloped along."

If you're serious about writing, you, too, will need a similar awareness of the almost magical power of words. At the same time, William Zinsser injects a cold splash of realism when he says in *Writing to Learn*, "Writing isn't a special language that belongs to English teachers and a few other sensitive souls who have a 'gift for words.' Writing is thinking on paper. Anyone who thinks clearly should be able to write clearly—about any subject at all."

If, then, you know that thinking and facing blank sheets of paper or blank computer screens is hard enough to bring sweat to your brow—and you still want to write nonfiction articles for magazines—you may have found your field.

WHAT IS A MAGAZINE ARTICLE?

In considering magazine writing as your life's work—or as a satisfying hobby—you should examine the magazine article as a special kind of writing, unique in some ways but flexible enough to include many different styles, treatments, and subjects.

Most articles are designed to satisfy the modern craving for information and entertainment. They convey knowledge, interpret events, and, as a result, improve lives. Matching the tempo of today's lifestyles, some are fast-moving and factual. Others entice serious readers with longer, more reflective articles about social, scientific, and political developments. Modern magazines are highly specialized, reflecting the diversity, individualism, and independence of the American people. According to their particular readership, they amuse, inspire, challenge, or shock, and even as they inform, they entertain. Enlivened with anecdotes, quotations from experts and celebrities, and vivid language, they borrow some of the hype of advertising, some of the literary qualities of good fiction, and some of the research techniques of investigative reporting.

Partly because of this wide diversity in readers and magazines, it is difficult to define the chameleon nature of magazine articles. Although they are classified as nonfiction, they contain some of the qualities of fiction. They interpret, comment, analyze, and provide insight into the various facets of society. Their writers tackle every imaginable topic from the most trivial to the most serious in a style that, depending on the subject and the magazine, can be formal or informal, aloof or personal, highly literary or perfectly plain.

The truth is that no one has ever satisfactorily defined the magazine article. In his introduction to *The Best American Essays, 1990*, Robert Atwan says articles have become "literary hybrids." Indeed, "hybrid" seems a good term for the offspring that has resulted from merging many disparate kinds of writing to produce the modern magazine article. Typically, it is a mix of carefully researched information and personal opinion.

Journalism students may be shocked at the phrase "personal opinion." While magazine articles are generally not sprinkled with such expressions as "I think," the chief quality that distinguishes them from newspaper features is a more obvious point of view. The authors' ideas and attitudes are much more palpable in magazine writing. For example, if an intimate style is appropriate to the magazine that freelancer George Leonard is writing for (and in his case that usually means *Esquire*), he can bare his soul on the page and no one will object or even find it odd. Newspapers, on the other hand, strive for an impersonal, more objective tone and, in most cases, confine opinion to editorials and signed columns.

There are other differences between magazine articles and newspaper features. Although they are more similar today than they were at one time, good magazine pieces usually exhibit greater depth and polish because their writers are free from the time and space constrictions of newspapers. This privilege gives the magazine writer more time for research, for reflecting on the long-range significance of the material, and for attention to a pleasing style. Moreover, because the magazine writer often writes to a highly specialized audience with specific tastes and interests rather than the general public with its huge range of ages, educational levels, and lifestyles, an article can be more precisely focused.

THE DIVERSITY OF MAGAZINES

The first periodicals were published in England and France, but Americans are the quintessential magazine readers. Far more magazines are published in the United States than in any other country in the world. In fact, thousands are being published today that the average reader never heard of.

Like Americans, magazines are constantly changing due to finely focused demographic research that defines potential readers with specific interests and lifestyles. Dozens fail each year as new ones spring up to fill a specific niche in the curiosity of an extremely heterogeneous society.

The magazine writer writes in a style and uses a particular level of language that is appropriate to a narrow audience. The *National Review*, for example, with its particular political slant and highly educated readers, publishes writing that is opinionated, analytical, and intellectual. In contrast, articles written for *Bicycle Guide* feature physical activities such as racing, touring, and mountain biking described in plain but highly evocative language. The specialized nature of today's periodicals means that an article must be custom-made for a particular magazine.

The scope of magazine articles is as wide as the American landscape. They can be literary and elitist, homey and unpretentious, or highblown and controversial in their alternative viewpoints. Direction is dictated by subject, audience, and, above all, the writer's taste, beliefs, and curiosities. This diversity suggests that many different people with wildly differing interests can succeed as magazine writers.

THE OPPORTUNITIES IN STAFF WRITING

Because thousands of magazines of every conceivable kind are published every month, they offer many job opportunities, but requirements of the well-known ones are stiff and the competition is formidable. They vary enormously in quality, circulation, pay, size of staff, and in the experience and talent required of employees.

Since large-circulation, well-known magazines are the most demanding, a good place for beginners to apply is to the small specialty magazines, particularly local business or in-house publications. (Huge numbers of these public relations magazines are unknown to the general public; they will be discussed further in Chapter 3.) All of them—from newsletters to slick four-color magazines—need multiskilled persons who can write, use word processors, edit, and help with layout and design. Working for these smaller magazines will give a beginner experience in all phases of publishing: planning future issues, coming up with ideas for covers and getting to know local photographers and artists who can produce them, even writing feature articles or possibly a column. In this environment a new writer may be asked to propose ideas for effective page designs or layouts, taking the photographs himself. And he will almost certainly have to do his own word processing and even occasionally run errands. The work is hard and the deadlines are constant. Still, in most cases there is opportunity for creativity and satisfaction in seeing issues one has helped to produce and in knowing other people will read and enjoy the product.

In contrast, most of the consumer magazines (those subscribed to or seen on newsstands) have much larger staffs. They tend to hire experienced specialists in one or more areas of publishing: editing, writing, research, fact-checking, circulation, advertising sales, or graphic design.

Business Week's Guide to Careers says this about staff writing: "Magazine writers often begin as researchers, working under a senior writer or editor. (At many magazines, all the writing staff members are called editors.) Magazines usually have a mix of short news articles or departments and feature stories. The usual progression is to move from a researcher-type position to one of the departments with increasing responsibility for feature writing after several years."

Do You Have the Right Stuff?

Most magazines hire college graduates with degrees in English or journalism. A degree in another area may be acceptable if you can demonstrate the ability to write well. It always helps, of course, if you exhibit a cooperative spirit, convince the employer that you can take the pressures of deadlines, and are willing to start at a rather menial level if necessary to learn the business from the ground up. One essential, though, is to ensure that the job offers advancement opportunities if your performance is impressive. Without such assurance, it might be better to look elsewhere for an entry-level position.

To get a job in the editorial department of a magazine, you'll need a neat, carefully prepared portfolio that displays samples of your work, preferably published articles. Employers who pay good salaries want evidence that you write well and that your work will benefit their publication. So begin now to compile a portfolio of clippings. Write for your school magazine or newspaper, or for your alumni magazine. Write some features for the local newspaper or for an organization to which you belong. Best of all, freelance some of your work to a local or regional magazine. Do whatever you can to get work published under your byline for your portfolio. Even unpublished work done in writing classes is better than nothing at all.

Folders or notebooks for displaying your work are available at office supply or art supply stores. Like most photograph albums, they contain double transparent pages into which you can insert your material. The folded pages of long articles can easily be slipped out for closer examination.

If you land the job, try to complete every assignment, no matter how trivial, cheerfully and efficiently. Keep your eyes open to the way the business operates. Look for opportunities to volunteer help with a project that requires more skill than your present one. If you can prove that you're capable of handling more responsibility, you're almost certain to receive it. Higher pay and recognition, unfortunately, do not always come with more responsibility, but if you got the promise of opportunity to advance when you took the job, you can always remind the boss of that commitment when you're sure you've earned it.

Some Problems to Anticipate

For a beginner, one of the disadvantages of being on the staff of a magazine rather than being a freelancer is the lack of freedom. Even if you become the editor-in-chief, there's almost always someone else whose whims (or superior experience or clout) affect your work. If you do a variety of jobs in publishing a magazine, you often have to submit your opinions and recommendations to several other people for approval. You would like to develop an article a certain way, for example, but your superior insists on another approach. Or you come up with the concept for a handsome illustration and the graphic artist calls it impractical. These situations are frustrating to new staff members, but with added experience your ideas will be sought and used more frequently.

Members of in-house corporate magazine staffs have to cope with a special kind of frustration because they stand between employees and management; they have two masters and it's almost impossible to please both. Sometimes they cannot be completely honest in print because heads of corporations don't like to pay for publications that criticize their policies.

As for your future prospects, you can always look forward to moving to a larger, more prestigious periodical. On a large-circulation magazine, if you're hired at a low level—and that's almost certain if you can get such a job at all—you can strive for eventual promotions and better pay, all the way to editor-in-chief. Moreover, magazine jobs are good stepping stones to other kinds of work: in public relations, advertising, television writing, or book publishing.

It's not too difficult to move on to other jobs if you're good with people and very good with words.

FREELANCING AND ITS CHALLENGES

The other route to magazine writing—freelancing—offers much more freedom but much less security. Only exceptionally prolific and self-disciplined freelancers earn a good living, and it can take years to become established. Pay for an article may be no more than $25, but it can be as much as $4,000 or even more for big-name writers.

Most freelancers launch their writing careers while holding a full- or part-time job. This arrangement pays bills and allows them to write at night and on weekends. It also tests their stamina and persistence.

Remember that if you freelance full-time, you will have to provide for yourself all the fringe benefits that are guaranteed staff writers: an expense account, costly medical insurance, office space and equipment, a paid vacation, and retirement income. There is no gang at the office to joke with or to learn from, so most inspiration and all motivation must come from you alone. Benjamin Stein stresses the gloomy side in an article for *The Wall Street Journal* entitled "Nothing Concentrates a Worker Like Living on the Edge." He says, "If you are a civil servant at the Federal Trade Commission or the White House—both of which I was before I became a freelance writer—you can sit at your desk and shoot the breeze with your boss and get paid. You can have sick days and get paid. . . . Freelance writers get paid absolutely zero if they do not produce. (They often unfortunately get paid zero or close to it if they do produce, as well.) They do not stand a chance of paying the mortgage, feeding the kids and paying the all-important phone bill if they have not ground out the pages to sell. . . . When the freelancer walks into an office and sees the abundance of pens, Xerox paper, folders, extra lightbulbs, etc., all available to the lowliest worker at no charge, why, it's like a kid at a candy store."

THE BRIGHT SIDE OF FREELANCING

But there is a bright side. Successful freelancers say it's the best job in the world. They insist they could never go back to working nine-to-five for a boss. In fact, they claim they have no boss. And it is true that if you are a freelancer you can work at home or wherever you choose. Between assignments you can coast for a while, not working at all. At other times, you may be paid to fly to Japan to interview a fascinating businessman. Or you may be a participatory journalist like George Plimpton. In that case, you would deepsea dive—and write about it. Or work in the kitchen of the fanciest restaurant in New York—and write about it.

As a freelancer your earnings would be limited only by your talent, energy, and luck. Perhaps the highest goal to aim for would be to develop some of your magazine articles into lucrative books and then to progress from books to screen writing and huge financial rewards.

Like most freelancers, you might dislike the isolation, but you would often be absorbed in learning about the lives and accomplishments of extraordinary people. Every day you would be engaged in discovery. In T.H. White's *The Once and Future King,* the young Arthur confesses to Merlin that he is depressed. Merlin quickly advises him of the cure: "Learn something new." If you become a freelancer, you will seldom be depressed. Every day you will learn something new.

Magazine journalists—both freelancers and staff writers—enjoy rewards that, for them, are more attractive than fame or money. They cover exciting and sometimes bizarre events; they enjoy the stimulation of contact with creative minds; and they stay in touch with the mood and tempo of the day.

Not a bad way to live.

CHAPTER

2

GOOD WRITING
FROM GOOD READING

One habit all serious writers share is reading. Some read books and articles of every kind: the intellectual, the spiritual, the trivial. But most are discriminating because they know that reading imprints their minds with a variety of words, ideas, styles, structures, and writing techniques of all kinds. In their apprentice days, some have even practiced by copying passages from a favorite classical author in the hope that a graceful style would rub off.

A NEW WAY OF READING

You, too, can understudy the experts by reading good books and articles. From them you can learn much about sentence structure, about word order and the subtle cadences of prose, about the parts of speech that communicate most vividly. You may learn the effectiveness of rhythm, whether it comes from the emphatic repetition of words, from the repetition of structure in parallelism, or from repeated sounds in alliteration. No matter what you want to learn about writing, you can profit immeasurably from reading the kind of writing you admire, provided you take the time to analyze it. If you want to improve your prose, the best method is to learn to read analytically. All the elements of writing referred to in this chapter—thesis, varieties of prose, structure (or organization), style, and tone—will be studied in detail later, but it is important for you to begin at once a new kind of reading. As a student of writing you should learn to look behind content into the ways words are combined to convey meaning.

First, choose an article you read last year and still remember, preferably from a magazine you would like to write for. If a particular article comes to mind, it should make a good model to be analyzed and perhaps emulated, for the impact of excellence lingers. Or in your current reading, if you find an article that seems compelling or persuasive, if it favorably impresses you for any reason, close the magazine and ask yourself which part of it is memorable, whether that is a page or a paragraph. That is the part to analyze in detail, but you should also study the piece as a whole. Read it again, this time noting not so much its content as the writing techniques used.

EVERY ARTICLE MUST MAKE A POINT

First of all, note that the article has a **thesis**: it communicates a message, or idea, or impression. It states a fact, a proposition, or a theory that will be proved in the body of the article. It makes a point. Its early statement in an article leads you to expect that the writer will stick to this particular aspect of the subject and that by the end you will understand exactly what the author is saying about the subject.

Next, examine in what form the thesis appears. Is it stated clearly, even bluntly, in one or two sentences? And is it paraphrased at intervals throughout the article? Or is the idea merely implied? Then try to determine the mode of writing used to support or develop the thesis. Prose is either expository, narrative, or descriptive. Scholars of rhetoric usually include a fourth category described as argumentative or persuasive. But since all writing has at least a mildly persuasive quality, for our purposes argumentation need not be distinguished from exposition. To read analytically, it's important to understand the difference between these forms.

THE THREE MAIN TYPES OF PROSE

As a writer you will need to choose the kind of prose that is most effective for a particular subject. **Exposition** is the prose of informing, explaining, clarifying. You write expository prose (this chapter is an example) to make a point understandable and clear. It is an intellectual form of discourse. **Description** and **narration**, by contrast, engage the emotions as well as the mind. All three are effective forms of communication and most good article writers use each—even within the same piece—instead of relying solely on exposition.

Although it may also appeal to the senses of sound, smell, touch, or taste, *description* commonly paints a picture of something seen or experienced. Although adjectives are generally associated with description, the experienced writer often strikes out several adjectives and inserts instead a precisely chosen noun or verb. For example, instead of "A beady black sinister-looking bug flew quickly past my ear," the sentence might be "A hornet zoomed by." To describe is to render, to evoke, to make real. In a famous passage about how he tried to write, the great novelist Joseph Conrad said, "My task which I am trying to achieve is, by the power of the written word, to make you hear, to make you feel—it is, before all, to make you *see*."

A good example of description is the following lead from an article in

Newsweek, February 4, 1991, about prisoners of war in the Persian Gulf. You may notice that, although the paragraph is primarily descriptive, it nevertheless contains bits of exposition and narrative, proving that the different modes of prose often overlap. Still, the writer is mainly describing, painting a picture for the reader of a situation few people will ever experience. He chooses details to make the reader feel what it was like to have been thrown from an exploding plane over Iraq and into a terrifying plunge to the desert below.

Note especially the surprising but accurate noun *crump*, the visual verbs— *cartwheels, hurls, tears, floats, shudders*–and the quote at the end containing an unexpected analogy about the fall from power to helplessness.

The top gun never believes it can happen to him. Not when the engines of his F-14 are roaring in his ears, his instruments all check out and the smart bombs and missiles are ready at his fingertips. Not when the enemy won't even come up to fight. Not even when the antiaircraft batteries open up around the target and the night lights up with tracers. Then suddenly he sees a blinding flash and hears the crump of an explosion. Black smoke fills his cockpit. The plane cartwheels out of control. With a sharp bang the ejection seat hurls him into the darkness at 600 miles an hour. Icy wind tears at his face, and his bones shudder with the jolt as his parachute opens. Then down, down he floats, right into the hands of that enemy he was just trying to kill. "One minute you're a hawk in the skies," shudders an old POW who has made the tumble, "the next you are an ant on the ground."

Narration which is usually entwined with description, tells a story. For that reason it is a valuable device for enlivening an article that would otherwise consist mostly of factual information. For example, in a reminiscent article describing his forty-year career, *New York Times* reporter A.M. Rosenthal tells about one of his first assignments. If he had merely explained what he had learned about the First Amendment in pure expository prose, the result might have been a dull article. But he wisely put most of what he had to say into story form. Narrative is a major part of the article's structure, although there are short paragraphs of exposition between the long, fictionlike episodes. Sometimes, however, in a primarily expository piece, writers do just the opposite. They will interrupt a long flow of facts with a short illustrative anecdote.

Here is the episode mentioned above from an article that appeared in *The New York Times Magazine*. Note the suspense and humor that narrative can create.

The very first day I was on the job as a reporter—a real reporter, with a press card in my pocket and a light in my heart—I learned all about the First Amendment. It was a Saturday and I was sitting in The Times's newsroom when an assistant city editor walked over, told me that there had been a murder or a suicide at the Mayflower Hotel in midtown and why didn't I go over and see what it was all about. Yes, sir! I rushed out, jumped on a bus, got to the hotel, asked an elevator operator where the trouble was. Ninth floor, he told me, and up I went. A push of the buzzer and the door opened. Standing there was a police detective. He was twelve and a half feet tall. I started to walk in and he put his hand into my face. That hand was just a bit larger than a basketball.

"Where are you going, kid?" he said.

"I'm a reporter," I said. "Times. I want to see the body."

He looked at me, up and down, slowly. "Beat it," he proposed.

Beat it? I hadn't realized anybody talked to Times reporters that way. I knew there had to be some misunderstanding. So I smiled, pulled out my press card and showed it to him. He took it, read it carefully front and back, handed it back and said: "Shove it in your ear."

Shove it in my ear? I could not comprehend what was taking place. "But I'm from The Times," I explained. "A reporter from The New York Times. Don't you want me to get the story right?"

"Listen, Four Eyes," he said, "I don't care if you drop dead." Then he slammed the door in my face and there I stood, staring at that door. I slunk off to a pay phone in the lobby and called the special reporters' number that had been confided to me—LAckawanna 4–1090, I've never forgotten it—and confessed to the clerk on the city desk that I had not only been unable to crack the case but had never even seen the corpse.

"Don't worry about it kid," he said. "We got it already from the A.P. They called police headquarters and got the story. Come on in."

Right there at the Mayflower I learned my first lesson about the First Amendment. The First Amendment means I have the right to ask anybody any question I wish. And anybody has the right to tell me to shove it in my ear.

After you have analyzed the mode of discourse used by the author of your admired selection—whether expository, narrative, or descriptive—turn your attention to another important element of writing: the structure or skeleton of the piece.

STRUCTURE: FITTING THE PARTS TOGETHER

Structure applies to the organization of an article, the arrangement of its various sections, or bones, into a logical, dramatic shape. The muscles and tendons that hold it together are its transitions.

But first, the large elements of the piece must be arranged according to some kind of pattern; the organizing plan may be chronology, relative importance, cause and effect, comparison and contrast, analysis (division and classification), and so on. The final choice is dictated by the thesis, the readers, and the purpose of the article. For example, if you're writing a personal experience story, you will be using narrative and description, and your first impulse may rightfully be to tell the entire story in strict chronological order. But maybe not. It might be better to start with a very dramatic episode in the middle of the story to catch your reader's interest, and then go back to the beginning for background and explanations. Sometimes you may complete an article before realizing that you could rearrange paragraphs or large sections into a more effective pattern. Organizing information gives rise to an overall structure.

Wise handling of structure will result in better management of your readers' attention; you must keep them eagerly reading from one paragraph to the next. And a logical structure with appropriate transitions will provide coherence, the quality that makes an article easy to read. Sentences and paragraphs will flow smoothly and logically, with the idea of each sentence growing out of the preceding one, thus making comprehension swift and pleasurable. A coherent, carefully crafted article has a silken, almost sinuous texture and movement. It's seamless, streamlined, and sleek. No sudden turns, disconcerting detours, or unexpected leaps of thought. Its form and flow are predetermined, with sections seemingly arranged according to an inherent logic embedded in the subject and thesis, and with transitions that make the logic perfectly clear.

The following excellent example of coherent writing is from the editorial page of *The New York Times*. Its material is arranged in order of increasing importance.

When Fred Astaire Leaves the Room

First, there were his looks. In truth, they didn't amount to much: medium height, skinny build, a longish nose, thinning hair. But in top hat, white tie and tails he was champagne to everybody else's beer.

Next there was his voice. That didn't amount to much either. It was dry, astringent really, and its range was narrow. But once he sang a song he owned it. And what songs they were! "Night and Day," for instance, and "Begin the Beguine" and "The Way You Look Tonight" and "I'll Go

My Way by Myself"—all rueful, all romantic and, no matter how skillful their other interpreters, all his.

Finally, there was his dancing. That amounted to great art.

What images he leaves behind. He and Ginger Rogers face each other, turn, then slide effortlessly into a quick scatter of steps. Backed by an army of dress-alikes, he puts on his white tie, dudes up his shirtfront, polishes his nails and takes millions of people out of a Depression and into an atmosphere that reeks with sophistication. Partnered by a hat rack, he skims about a dimly lit stage; firecrackers snapping at his feet, he taps a counterpoint.

He danced with some marvelous people, but his only real peers were the composers with whom he worked. Tapping to "Half of It Dearie Blues," he called out "How's that, George" to his accompanist, George Gershwin. "That's fine, Freddie!" Gershwin called back. They sounded joyous.

Once a little girl was allowed to stay up late to watch one of his movies on television, and cried when it ended. "It's so sad," she exclaimed, "when Fred Astaire leaves the room." It is indeed.

In examining the structure of an article, first identify the thesis. Sometimes it's stated in a sentence that you can underline, but it's often merely implied. And take a critical look at the title. It may give a hint of the thesis or the tone of the piece. At any rate, before deciding whether the writer has arranged his material in the best possible way, it's helpful to know what point he wanted to make. In this case, he simply wanted to say it's sad that Fred Astaire has died.

When you're reading analytically, it's also helpful to ask yourself how *you* would have written an article on this subject, in this case a brief tribute to Fred Astaire. What would you have wanted to say, what images would you try to evoke, and how would you have arranged it all? Could you include some narrative? How about quotes? Knowing that it's hard to avoid gushing or being overly sentimental in writing about such a beloved person, could you be subtle? How could you conclude without saying something trite?

Let's see what the *Times* writer did. He probably began scribbling some thoughts down on paper or on his computer. Wild, random thoughts. But as the list grew, he might have begun to see a pattern in the chaos. Perhaps he remembered the incident of the little girl and what she said. Ah, there's a bit of narrative! And that also gives him his conclusion. Then he decides to begin with Fred's looks and end with the most important part, his dancing. So now the troubled writer feels a sense of direction and is on his way. He has a skeleton.

The completed article has a typical three-part structure: a beginning, a middle, and an end. The lead consists of three paragraphs beginning with helpful transitions: *first*, Astaire's looks, *next* his voice, and *finally* his dancing. There is a satisfying rhythm in the parallels between the second sentences in each of the three paragraphs: "they didn't amount to much," "that didn't amount to much either," and "that amounted to great art." The middle section is the development part of the piece; it conveys a series of images or pictures of Astaire's dancing and singing. Then the conclusion—the graceful, subtle echo of the title that makes the thesis clear at last. The three parts of the structure are logically organized and appropriate transitions stitch it all together.

THE SILENT SOUND OF STYLE AND TONE

Style results from the language characteristically used by a writer: the kinds of words and sentences preferred, the way words are arranged into patterns or grammatical structures, the ornamentation or literary devices used or avoided. Has the author chosen short or long words, abstract or concrete words, formal words or slang, long and complex sentences or short ones? Style in writing is similar to style in dress. Clothing reveals personality and projects a particular image. It may be plain or flashy, conservative or trendy, flamboyant or subdued. So it is with writing style.

Tone is the element of writing that indicates the author's attitude toward his material and tends to infect the reader with similar feelings. Its equivalent in speech is tone of voice. Tone in writing arises primarily from word choice or from the combinations of words. For example, *father* and *dad* have entirely different connotations and a different "sound." *Father* is a more old-fashioned word, suggesting respect and yet affection, too. It implies a certain distance in a relationship. *Dad*, on the other hand, is less formal, a modern parent, a pal.

The tone of an article is usually described with an adjective: satiric, reverent, scornful, awed, sentimental, angry, nostalgic, admiring, amused, objective, intense. The list could go on and on to cover the entire range of human emotion.

Consider the following two selections with contrasting styles and tones, studying them as examples of how language reflects personality and how it emits a sort of silent sound. You can almost hear the writer's tone of voice. The first is by the late Welsh actor, Richard Burton, from *Meeting Mrs. Jenkins*; it was later published in *Vogue*. He is describing his first sight of Elizabeth Taylor, at a Hollywood party.

I smiled at her and, after a long moment, just as I felt my own smile turning into a cross-eyed grimace, she started slightly and smiled back.

There was little friendliness in the smile. A new ice cube formed of its own accord in my Scotch-on-the-rocks.

. . . . She was unquestionably gorgeous. I can think of no other word to describe a combination of plenitude, frugality, abundance, lightness. She was lavish. She was dark, unyielding largesse. She was, in short, too bloody much, and not only that, she was totally ignoring me.

. . . . Eventually, with half-reasoned cunning and with all the non-chalance of a traffic jam, I worked my way to her side of the pool.

The Welsh are known for seldom being at a loss for words and for having a tendency to exaggerate. And indeed, verbosity and hyperbole are both evident in this selection which could never be described as being pale or bland. It is an emotional outpouring from a man whose speech was surely influenced by the superb language of Shakespeare and other classical authors whose lines he knew by heart. In this particular excerpt, however, he uses a great many abstract words, some of them fairly unfamiliar, but he brings them all down to earth with an occasional bit of slang (too bloody much, for example). One of his best techniques is to render very concrete the icy reception he receives from Elizabeth Taylor. He does it with a symbol: the forming of ice cubes in his Scotch.

His tone is unabashedly breathless and adoring, but his attitude toward himself is wry and self-effacing. The pervading tone is one of smoldering emotion.

The tone of the next selection—also about a first encounter with an exceptional person—is extremely admiring, even awed, but the emotion is held in check. Without gushing, Annie Dillard gives specific and very visual details that are grounds for her admiration. Her subject is a stunt pilot, Dave Rahm. Note the control of her precisely constructed sentences. Thought is uppermost here, rather than emotion run wild. Her similes are, appropriately, from the world of art. "The Stunt Pilot" was published in *Esquire*.

The black plane dropped spinning, and flattened out spinning the other way; it began to carve the air into forms that built wildly and musically on each other and never ended. Reluctantly, I started paying attention. Rahm drew high above the world an inexhaustibly glorious line; it piled over our heads in loops and arabesques. It was like a Saul Steinberg fantasy; the plane was the pen. Like Steinberg's contracting and billowing pen line, the line Rahm spun moved to form new, punning shapes from the edges of the old. Like a Klee line, it smattered the sky with land-scapes and systems.

Dillard's language is much more figurative (note the three similes in the last three sentences) and more visual than Burton's. Every word seems exact; she rigorously shuns hyperbole. The two different styles reflect two entirely different personalities and different ways of communicating admiration.

ANALYZING AN ARTICLE

The following article and analysis will give you an idea of how to go about looking beyond the content of an article to the techniques involved in its composition. Analysis of thesis, types of prose, structure, style, and tone will be discussed following the sections of the article examined. Each of these elements will be explored in greater depth in subsequent chapters.

Stalking the Wild Orthographers
Henry Woodhead

Of the 50 words on the list, *umlaut* drew the most resounding chorus of jeers.

"It ain't even English," an irate contestant screamed at the enunciator, whose facial muscles at that point seemed on the verge of spasm as he stood alone in the hostile crowd. "Definition!" another speller demanded. The situation was tense.

The sergeant at arms, an elfin man in a white turtleneck, graduate of a military school, was poised and ready. The committee had picked him for the job because he was the least among them, and they figured a little fellow would be more immune to physical attack. Unfortunately he had a voice to match his size. He let fly. It was a strain. "Quieeeeeeet," he said. The ascending vowel lifted him to his tip-toes and then dropped him, spent. From behind the bar came the crash of a bobbled beer glass. The roaring subsided and broke into spasmodic yammerings. The contestants bent once again over their legal pads in woozy concentration, trying to take the measure of *umlaut*.

A great deal takes place in this three-paragraph lead to which most readers will respond, possibly without an awareness of *how* their thoughts and emotions are being kindled. First of all, note the rather scholarly sounding title; perhaps it makes the reader wonder what an orthographer is but decide to read a few lines to see what the stalking is all about.

One word in the first sentence hooks you: *jeers*. And because it is the last word, you cannot miss it. (The two most important words in any sentence are the first and the last.) If you reverse the word order, for instance, to "Umlaut drew the most resounding chorus of jeers of the 50 words on the list," the emphasis of the sentence is deflated. *Jeers* deserves the spotlight because it lets you know that, despite the formal-sounding title, something rowdy is going on. Ending the first paragraph with *jeers* gives the jolt that propels you to the next paragraph. Then, another jolt: "It ain't even English!" By now you realize you have been playfully deceived by the title.

There's irony here—and humor.

And so you settle back for the ride, caught up in a story that already has lively characters, realistic dialogue, and action that borders on violence, though what the battle is about is not yet entirely clear. By the end of the third paragraph the scene has been set, and your interest snared. At this point the narrative pauses for an expository section that will explain the furor, identify the setting, and imply the point of the piece.

It was the 5th Annual Open Orthographic Meet, a spelling bee for grown-ups. It began five years ago as a game among a handful of friends and if spelling was ever a game, it developed into the hardest hardball in town. The setting was the taproom of one of Atlanta's few remaining bona fide neighborhood taverns, a place with a clientele ranging from leftover street people to high-salaried professional people, who in this particular setting seemed to resemble leftover '40s Bohemians.

You may remember the spelling bees of your adolescence in the public school system, squirmy debacles in which students were lined up against a wall, firing-squad fashion, while the words ricocheted between teacher and victims, and the losers fell into their seats grinning like baboons from embarrassment. (These were the days when blackboards were still black, not green, and the emphasis on education was such that the World Series was broadcast live during class over the public address system.) If you were a boy among the dwindling number of survivors, you found yourself on the horns of a dilemma; if you didn't try to win you knew in your youthful soul you were selling yourself short; if you won, you were in for a full day's worth of hazing from your noaccount ringwormed companions, along with painful armfrogs. This dilemma was always resolved when the buck-toothed girl was the only one left standing. The proceedings were accompanied by distressing urinary urgency which always seemed to disappear when you succumbed to a word and gained the safety of your warm desk.

The 5th Annual Open Orthographic Meet, however, was not kid's stuff. It had teeth. There was a 50-word list, beginning with *backgammon* and ending with *myrmecophagous*. There was a five-word sudden death play-off list—unneeded, as it turned out—composed of five rounds during which the 100 or so contestants were pared down to three finalists. For the winner, there were the spoils: $24 in cash and an inscribed silver medallion suitable for wearing around the neck on a silver chain. There was one contestant who became so frustrated he began eating his test sheet. He resembled the Cookie Monster on Sesame Street.

The smoke of battle has lifted long enough to let you know the thesis of the article—that *this* spelling bee is serious business. The contest has been placed in perspective with a nostalgic look at the spelling bees of childhood, thus arousing a half-forgotten memory (an effective technique writers use for evoking emotion). "The meet had teeth" echoes the thesis, and more details explain how the contest is conducted and, in a humorous bit of hyperbole, how difficult the words are (Webster himself could not have spelled them).

Wisely, this writer does not begin the article, as an inexperienced one might, with this expository section. Its essential information is tucked in after your attention has been caught. Then the narrative begins anew with some reminiscences about how the 5th Annual Open began and a description of the frenetic preparations that preceded the event.

Instead of giving the dry facts of exposition, you listen in on the spelling bee's pioneers as they reminisce and the present participants as they fret over the coming battle. Quotation marks are doubly effective because few of us can resist eavesdropping, and quotation marks highlight whatever falls between them.

First some background, from Tom Couch, one of the founders and a long-standing member of the committee: "Five years ago a group of us were sitting around arguing about who could spell the best. I don't know how the subject came up, but we decided to have an orthographic meet. None of the good spellers wanted to conduct the thing, so several of us who knew we could not spell worth a damn took it on as a lark.

"We had no rules, just made up a list of words and passed out some pencils and paper. It was surprising. It got scary. People were shouting and swearing at us: 'You fool, you can't even pronounce the word!' and things like that. It was serious business.

"It turned out a minor success, but it was clear that by the next year the committee would have to get it together. We hammered out some rules and regulations that have stood to this day," Couch said, with a touch of pride.

Levi Terrell had a sore throat. This he revealed to the rest of the committee as it met for the third and final session in the dining room of the Couch home just prior to the event itself. Terrell's sore throat was crucial to the success of the evening, for he was one of the two enunciators. There was a standby enunciator but no one can pronounce a word like Levi Terrell, with such elegance and grace, in such a husky, healthy baritone. He had come straight to the meeting from the airport and a business trip to Louisville, where he had sought out a doctor for his sore throat.

"The doctor was looking down my throat, and I said, 'Do you know what you see?' and he said, 'Why, yes.' And I told him, 'You can look but please leave it alone. Don't bother it; let me take it back with me, because I need it.'" Terrell related to the group. His voice, while stable, had a lilting rasp to it, as if the vocal chords had been lightly sanded but the final coat of varnish had not yet been applied. At any rate, he would go on.

Tom Couch, the other enunciator, was having trouble with *cunctator,* the pronunciation of which—kung-tater—connotes the image of a potato skilled in the martial arts. He couldn't get it down. He had it once but lost it. He and Terrell went over and over the word, trying to iron out the creases. Everything else was ready. The three dictionaries—the *American Heritage,* the *Oxford Universal,* the *Webster's New World*—were stacked and waiting. They would be used to check alternate spellings in case of a challenge. "We've been asked, but we just don't feel like bringing all 13 volumes of the Oxford English Dictionary," Couch remarked. "These people can be so testy."

The Leonidas Trackmaster stopwatch was in its case next to the dictionaries. The spellers would have exactly 20 seconds to ponder each word. There was still a little time to kill before the committee left for the scene. Remembering past events, they began to get edgy.

"The first year they were at each other's throats," recalled Marianne Fluehr, a committee member.

"It got so bad I had to leave," remarked Beverly Couch, Tom's wife.

"Last year there was a guy who was taking an acid trip, a real trip, and you couldn't read his hand. The t's weren't crossed, the i's weren't dotted, and he insisted that every word was correctly spelled," Marianne said. "Even with the benefit of a doubt, he didn't make it."

The acid-head aberration notwithstanding, the ability of some of the serious contenders borders on the surreal, Marianne indicated. "One year a girl won it by spelling—nobody else could come close—the word *phthisic.* I asked her later how in the world she knew that word and she told me, 'I didn't. It just sounded like a PH-TH word to me.'

"Another year the winner was a ringer brought in by the Legal Aid clique. Guy named Levin. First-class speller."

Levi and Tom were smoothing the rough edges on *poinsettia* and finding the right handle on *bechamel.*

"We'll be all right," Levi said. "It's going to come down mellow. . . ."

"This is the same thing I wore last year," Tom said, pulling a sleeveless sweater over his shirt.

"But the sweater didn't have a hole in it last year," Beverly pointed out.

"I can't spell them," Levi said, "but I sure can say them. . . ."

Tom was back wrestling with *cunctator* again. He pronounced it over and over. "I'm losing my cool," he said, waving his arms. Finally he pronounced it three times in a row correctly.

"Out of sight," Levi cried. "We are fired up."

The above section illustrates the value of short paragraphs and short quotations. Both make the printed page look attractive and easy to read. And the content is equally enjoyable. You relish the irony of the spellers' reminiscences about old times, and the dialogue is so real you "hear" it. Every detail reinforces the thesis that, to these contestants, this spelling bee is Armageddon.

Standing room only, and the place looked like somebody touched off a smoke bomb. The big round table in the corner was commandeered for the committee against the wishes of its four occupants, who cooled down and entered the contest and made it past the first round of words.

"Welcome, strangers, to this event!" said the master of ceremonies, Richard Hatcher, who was standing in a chair in his conservative gray suit with red tie. A kid who had been selling pornographic magazines on the curb outside the tavern wandered through the door. "This is fantastic!" he said. "Let me get rid of these things," he continued, meaning his stack of magazines under his arm, "and I'll be right back. I'll be right back," he promised.

In the back room someone put his quarter into the pin ball machine. It meant bells dinging when the contestants needed total concentration. "I'll give you two dollars not to play that thing," said a concerned customer nearby. The pin ball player didn't accept the money, but entered the spelling contest instead.

Pencils were passed out from a Woolworth's bag, and shirt boards for writing on, since the table surface was occupied by beer. The noise sounded like the collapse of a small Central American government.

"SHADDDDDDUP," the sergeant at arms managed. The twenty-eight spellers were silent and serious and alert. This was no joking matter. Rules which sounded no more complicated than advanced geometry were outlined by the master of ceremonies in a series of shouts, and the meet commenced.

"The word is *aflutter,*" Tom Couch announced, with resonance. "*Aflutter,*" Levi repeated, hoarsely.

"That's a silly word," one contestant remarked.

"Atwitter," another commented.

At the end of the first round the correct spellings were called out. A man in a tight gray T-shirt, who resembled John L. Sullivan the boxer, said, "I missed that one" after the first word. After the second word, he said, "Missed that one, too." The third: "Missed that one." On hearing the fourth word spelled, he uttered a four-letter word of his own and stalked out of the tavern. Another contestant devoured his list, which was on a napkin.

Two cultivated ladies talked. "Is Jonathan still in it?" the first asked.

"No," said the second. "He's out by one. It must have been that cocktail he had before dinner."

Donna Brown, a secretary who didn't make it either, allowed that she had been practicing for a full year, albeit informally. "My boss is a professor of management, and I've been typing all those manuscripts of his. Mostly it's all 'vis a vis' and 'ergo' but sometimes he'd come up with a pretty heavy word and I'd look it up to make sure of the spelling. And of course, as you get older you run across more words."

And on it went, through *smorgasbord, persnickety,* and *baize,* past *vigesimal, bijouterie,* and *onomatopoeia,* with spellers falling by the wayside until finally only six have survived. They are clustered at one end of the room at the same table. Two of them are wearing the medallions which identify them as former winners. As each impossible word is pronounced, they look up and blink, like owls awakened at high noon.

We have a winner, whose name is John Peek, and who designs the interiors of banks for a living. Peek's victory is received with much fanfare. Amid cheering, he stands on a chair and throws the old Nixon victory sign with his arms. There are hugs and kisses all around. His is a popular victory since he has come within a hair's breadth of winning before, and because he is a regular customer of the tavern. He bends forward to receive his medallion, and then submits to an interview. He has spelled 36 of the 50 words correctly. He notes that he was a Phi Beta Kappa at Georgia.

"On the night of the first annual meet I had a business-related cocktail party and couldn't be there. A friend of mine won, and I knew damn well I could spell better than him," Peek says. "I've been trying four years to prove it. I've come in second or third. Last year I was overconfident and blew it."

Peek's thoughts on spelling: "Spelling, in English, is primarily a visual phenomenon. If you've seen a word before you should be able to remember what it looks like and spell it. Now I've never heard of any of the last five words on the list, so I asked for definitions of each one, and in that way I knew whether the roots were Latin or Greek or whatever, and that helped immensely."

Peek marches to the bar, receiving congratulations along the way, and approaches the barmaid, who is busy filling a pitcher from the tap. "Look, sis, look!" he says, flapping his medallion joyfully.

"You finally did it, didn't you," she says, watching the beer rise to the top.

The war is finally over, the victor has made an acceptance speech, he has been interviewed, and he proudly shows his medal of honor to the barmaid.

How does Woodhead put it all together?

Note his manipulation of structure to create the suspense of the article, to keep you reading: He aroused curiosity in the narrative and descriptive lead, and he gave the facts you were curious about in an expository section. Next he heightened the suspense with a long section of dialogue about preparations for the event. Then came the excitement and tension of the combat itself (at the very end he moves into the present tense). And finally, he slows the tempo and mutes the tone for a low-key conclusion: the waitress gives the victor an absent-minded congratulation, but her focus has turned from conquered empires to the beer she is pouring, to business as usual.

"Stalking the Wild Orthographers" has all the elements of a humorous, entertaining article. It smiles at the irony of the adult spelling bee, but its tone is gentle, nostalgic, and amused, never sarcastic or scornful. Primarily narrative, the article shows rather than tells. Specific, visual details, actions and dialogue, put you there in the tavern. You see it and hear it and smell it. You feel the intensity of battle. You warm to the mix of humanity here. If indifferent people were present, Woodhead ignores them. Relying on the prerogative of all writers, he chooses only those details that enable him to show the point: this spelling bee was an intensely competitive battle.

One of the most enjoyable facets of this piece—one that you react to without always being conscious of its presence—is the military imagery that unifies the article, lights up the thesis, and contributes to its tone. Woodhead enjoys every minute of the bloodless battle and the fierceness with which its participants enter a contest as harmless and childlike as a spelling bee. That enjoyment affects the words he chooses and therefore his style and tone.

Look, for example, at the martial terms he uses: bomb, commandeered, ricocheted, sergeant at arms, sudden death, spoils, firing squad, physical attack, victors, survivors. In the first sentence of the fourth paragraph his sense of humor and relish for irony compel him to follow the comically pretentious "5th Annual Open Orthographic Meet" by "a spelling bee for grown-ups." He doesn't hesitate to use hyperbole in comparing the noise in the tavern to the collapse of a small Central American government, or to tell the anecdote about the kid abandoning his pornographic magazines to enter the spelling bee. Woodhead also uses the rhythm of alliteration to create emphasis: urinary urgency, hardest hardball, firing-squad fashion, husky and healthy.

Metaphors and similes make his abstract ideas concrete and visual: losers grinning like baboons, he resembled the Cookie Monster on Sesame Street, his voice sounded as if the vocal cords had been lightly sanded but the final coat of varnish not applied, spellers blinked like owls awakened at noon, smoothing the rough edges on poinsettia, an elphin man, the words ricocheted. Woodhead seems to enjoy personification (the ascending vowel lifted him to his tip-toes); onomatopoeia (the crash of bobbled beer glasses); and an oxymoron (woozy concentration).

A CHECKLIST FOR EFFECTIVE WRITING

From the specificity of Woodhead, let's turn to a general checklist of the elements or qualities that make magazine writing effective. Woodhead, who is now an editor with Time-Life Books, must have, at least subconsciously, used such a list.

1. The use of narrative. Facts can be dull, but few people can resist a good story.
2. Emphasis on irony. Surprise, the unexpected, and incongruity give writing depth, intellectual challenge, and sometimes humor.
3. Visual detail. Movies and TV are fierce competitors with print journalism because they are so visual, but they have limitations. Good writing, on the other hand, invokes the imagination, which has no limits.
4. Quotations. Who can resist gossip or hearing what other people, especially celebrities and experts, say?
5. Contrast. In situations, in people, in words, in images.
6. Variety. In word choice, sentence structure, sentence length, paragraph length. A three-word, one-sentence paragraph can give bracing relief from the monotony of long paragraphs.
7. Figurative language. The use of simile, metaphor, personification, or hyperbole gives strength and freshness to expression.

8. Humor and wit. See "Stalking the Wild Orthographers."
9. Warmth and intimacy. Not all subjects will call for these qualities, but the human element is essential in most writing because people are more engaging than things.
10. An intelligent or unusual point of view. Good writing reflects an interesting mind and personality.

The qualities listed above are admired by a great many successful writers, and you will begin to notice them as you learn to read in this new way, the analytical way. But the real beauty of analytical reading is that it will enable you to make your own list of admired qualities, perhaps deleting some of those mentioned here, but adding others.

In your everyday reading, as you note the presence of the items on your list, you may also note their absence. A great deal of prose today sounds as though it sprang into being from a robot. Bland and bloodless, it is as impersonal and as unclear as an income tax form. Analytical reading will help you discover the characteristics of limp writing, the kind you want to avoid, as well as the techniques that produce the elegant kind you hope one day to write.

SUMMARY

Here are some of the lessons that may be learned from this analysis of a magazine article:

1. Every magazine article must make a point. Without an easily recognizable thesis, an article will give the impression of aimless wandering and the reader will be confused.
2. For coherence and emphasis, at intervals throughout the article the thesis should be repeated, elaborated, or stated in different terms. An article should have a logical plan of organization with all its units linked together by smooth transitions.
3. Exposition explains, informs, clarifies. Narration creates suspense and illustrates. Description combined with narration renders dialogue, scenes, or impressions with cinematic force. It makes us "see." According to the subject or purpose, a writer chooses the appropriate mode or blends all three.
4. Although style is an author's characteristic manner of expressing thoughts in language, it can vary with the subject and purpose of the article, and careful handling of style can produce the desired effect. A student of writing can strive to develop a pleasing style by studying the effects created by rhythm, metaphor, understatement, and appropriate word choice.
5. The careful handling of tone is a persuasive rhetorical device since it reveals the author's attitude about the subject and tends to produce the same attitude or feelings in the reader.

FROM PRINCIPLES TO PRACTICE

1. Xerox a magazine article you have recently enjoyed and read it again, this time analyzing it carefully. Underline the first statement of the thesis and each successive variation. Next, bracket passages of exposition, description, and narration, labeling each according to type. Look also for passages that combine the three modes of writing. What words would best describe the tone of the article? For example, does the author's attitude or "tone of voice" seem matter-of-fact, satiric, amused, contemptuous, or something else?

2. Select a familiar spot in your community—a snack bar with coin-operated food machines, for example—that seems to you to be a lonely place. Communicate this impression of loneliness in three different ways:

- Write an expository paragraph stating that the snack bar is a lonely place. Develop the paragraph by giving factual evidence to prove your point.
- In another paragraph describe the snack bar's physical details and atmosphere that show its loneliness.
- In a third paragraph tell a brief story from your own experience or imagination that will illustrate the loneliness of the snack bar.

Make no attempt to connect your three paragraphs. This exercise is meant to help you learn the differing modes of communicating an idea or making a point. Note that though the subject matter is the same, the effect and length of each paragraph will be different.

CHAPTER

3

THE MARKET FOR MAGAZINE ARTICLES

In the preceding chapter, we dissected a magazine article to study its anatomy: how its parts are put together to make it clear and unified and interesting to read. To write an article that will sell, a similar analysis must be made of the magazine market.

ANALYZING THE MARKET

Beginning writers may think a freelancer produces an article on inspiration and sends it off to a magazine by intuition. Not so. Marketing an article is a competitive business transaction. Before you begin to write, therefore, you will increase your chances of selling if you find out what customers want—what the readers want to read and what editors want to buy.

Your success will be affected by your shrewdness in assessing the demands and the diversity of the magazine market. Which editors accept freelance material? What kinds of articles are selling? What subjects do editors consider compelling enough to lure the reader away from the television set, a current novel, or the golf course? Can you find a magazine you would especially like to write for because its values and interests match your own? Equally important, do these subjects interest you enough to spend weeks researching and writing about them?

Choosing a market and a subject forces you to think in two directions at once. You get an idea for a topic and then you think ahead to a magazine market for it. Or you find a magazine that publishes the kind of article you think you could write. At that point your mind searches and considers any hobbies, experiences, travels, unusual theories, and so on that may lead to an appropriate subject.

One vital suggestion: Begin with small, less familiar magazines and build toward the big newsstand attractions as your skills mature. Don't begin with *Smithsonian, Harper's,* or *Fortune* unless you have an introduction from one of their writers and a spectacular article of particular interest to that market. Try instead a college magazine that accepts nonfiction by unpublished authors. Also investigate state, regional, or city markets such as the Sunday magazine section of your newspaper.

Local publications make good markets for beginners because they seek articles on the subject you know best and because they attract fewer submissions from established writers. That means less competition for you. If you have lived in your present community for a long time, you are probably familiar with the city, state, and regional magazines that feature material on your locale. If not, begin your search in the yellow pages of the phone book under "publications." This list will by no means be complete, so ask next at the chamber of commerce and state offices that deal with tourism or conservation. The local librarian can also help you compile a list.

Regional and corporate publications are difficult to find because of the lack of satisfactory directories and because they seldom are carried on newsstands. But if there are any large business firms, manufacturing plants, or insitutions near you, their publications might become outlets for your work. Such magazines may include a few articles of general interest in each issue even though the bulk of their material is company-related and staff-written. At any rate, when you phone to ask about publications from any source, ask for a copy to analyze.

THE NATURE OF MODERN MAGAZINES

In getting a feel for the market for articles, you first need to understand the general nature of magazines, how they compete with other forms of communication and with each other.

Go to a large library or newsstand and study the characteristics of the publications you see. Published weekly, monthly, or quarterly, magazines contain a variety of materials, informative and entertaining articles, short stories, poems, and pictures. Those that consist of more advertisements than editorial matter are called consumer magazines. They are supported primarily by the income from ads but also from subscriptions and newsstand sales. Another general category is made up of trade, technical, and professional magazines whose readers subscribe to them for new information about their work. Some corporate publications have no ads and are distributed free to employees or customers.

Magazines are called periodicals because they are published periodically rather than daily. In contrast to books, they are not intended to be saved; there is an impermanence in the look of magazines that symbolizes the ephemeral quality of their contents. A magazine usually deals with the here and now and thus is soon outdated. It lacks the newspaper's bustle of daily events or the more nearly timeless content of a good book. In depth and scope of information, magazines stand between newspapers and books. In entertainment, they compete with all other forms of the media.

Since each of its competitors has advantages, the magazine has had to find and focus on its assets. Traditionally, such highly respected magazines as *The Atlantic* have excelled at commentary and interpretation of political, social, and cultural issues, at placing events, people, and trends in perspective. Such publications have had an important role (and a long history) in molding the attitudes and tastes of American readers. At the opposite end of the spectrum are dozens of junk magazines that are lacking in taste, restraint, and even correct information. As competition among magazines has intensified in the last decade, some editors have catered to the crasser appetites of their readers. As television, a major competitor, has featured more and more sexually explicit material, they have followed suit. When such magazines as *Psychology Today, Business Month,* and *Savvy Woman* fail within one year, alarmed editors begin to lose sight of their loftier goal of leading, inspiring, educating. Their top priority becomes survival, even though that entails stooping to a lower level of values. The debate will continue over whether magazines should strive to lead society to higher cultural standards and better ways of living, or merely reflect the dangerous changes that are taking place. Uncertain market conditions, increased competition from more kinds of magazines, and rising production and distribution costs will have profound effects on these problems. Magazines are striving to maintain their aura of leadership, to find their finely tuned niches, but advertisers' demands to influence editorial decisions are more strident than ever before.

Though it displays dozens of magazines, a typical newsstand's selection is a very small sample of the thousands published each week or month. Even a large library's periodical collection gives only a glimpse of the market's scope. There is actually no one place, no library or distribution center, that contains a complete collection of American periodicals. Seemingly, a magazine has been created to satisfy every human curiosity and taste. Here are a few, chosen merely to illustrate their diversity: *The Diver, Utne Reader* (a magazine for alternative viewpoints), *Gay Sunshine, Forests & People, Gun World, Mother Jones* (features liberal investigative articles), *The Church Musician, Cat Fancy, Careers, Remodeling, Black Belt, Tattoo Advocate Journal,* and many more. There are "skin" magazines, men's and women's magazines, sports and hobby magazines, news journals, and magazines for the professions. *Writer's Market* lists fifty categories in its consumer magazine division and more than sixty under "Trade, Technical, and Professional Journals." Because they typically have smaller circulations and therefore smaller budgets, the latter are ignored by established writers who can earn bigger fees elsewhere. As a result, some of these magazines are willing to work with new writers.

Due to the diversity of the market, a principle of freelancing for beginners is never to write an article for some "typical" magazine. It does not exist. Effective freelancing is a custom-design enterprise. Your chances for selling are best when you write for a specific magazine with specific readers in mind. A famous writer can produce a good article with some assurance that one of several potential markets will buy it. But as a beginner, you should "custom-write" to enhance your chances of selling. And that means pinpointing a suitable market, preferably only one magazine, within your capabilities.

Freelancer Edith Kilgo, who has sold hundreds of articles, most of them for small specialized magazines, told in an interview how she learned to succeed as a freelancer: "I started writing for minor markets because the big guys wouldn't buy my work. But I soon found that I could make more money writing lots of 'small' articles for the $200 market than I could by selling an occasional $1,000 article.

"I also learned that if I was to make money by this method I would have to allot one day only to write one article. The fees simply didn't justify the painstaking research and highly polished style necessary for selling to a slick national magazine.

"Here's the way I worked. I began by writing for magazines that would pay $100 for an article. I scanned *Writer's Market,* looking for magazines that were eager for material by new writers. When I had sold a few articles of that caliber, I queried some $200 markets, emphasizing to the editors that I had recently published three articles. (A query letter proposes an idea for an article you have in mind. Chapter 9 tells how to write them.) I did the same thing when I moved up to the $500 group, never totally abandoning the $100 markets. The most I was ever paid was $1,000 for an article that appeared in *Good Housekeeping.* At that point I queried a book publisher about a book on household money management, including in the letter a list of all the articles I had published and some tear sheets of the best ones. She was impressed with what I'd done, and subsequently gave me a contract.

"Sounds like the end of the story? Not at all. When the book came out, I returned to magazine writing, finding that editors were impressed that I had published a book. My sales mounted. Meanwhile I began to concentrate on selling excerpts from the work I'd already published. For one of them—and this took no effort at all—I was paid $400.

"To sum it up, I still think the best markets are those that make up the bulk of the entries in *Writer's Market.* You might think they would be tacky little magazines cheaply produced. But that's not the case at all. *Today's Christian Woman,* for instance, is well edited, beautifully designed, and is comparable in content to *Good Housekeeping.* Its articles are wholesome but certainly not fanatically religious. The editor describes them as relational, psychological, or spiritual, and I've enjoyed writing some of them."

In choosing markets, think small, Kilgo said, and you'll make more money than if you think big. The small successes will spur you on to bigger and better markets later. She calls her method Kilgo's Law of Moving Up.

Perhaps you are already familiar with a "small" specialty magazine because of your hobby or profession. If so, you may already have a potential market and topic. Do you have an idea for an article that seems suitable for this magazine? Are you capable of writing in the style it favors? Can you create an article of the quality and depth it demands? A former student, Julie Scoggins, discovered that because of her profession, nursing, she had the perfect market at her fingertips: *RN Magazine*. (RN stands for Registered Nurse.) She knew it usually contained serious, rather dry, technical articles. But she thought it needed something juicier and more entertaining. So she wrote a humorous article on how she had personally handled an obstreperous patient. *RN* snapped it up immediately.

Not everyone is quite this fortunate, of course, but Scoggins' strategy was destined for success: she chose an appropriate market, she wrote from her own experience about a common problem, she wanted to help other nurses solve this kind of problem, and she lightened it all with laughter.

MARKET-INFORMATION SOURCES

There are two easily accessible sources for information about magazine markets: *The Writer's Handbook* and *Writer's Market*. Each year both directories (available in most libraries) catalog and identify the hundreds of magazines that buy freelance nonfiction. *Writer's Market* claims to list 4,000. Many of these will at least consider the work of unpublished writers. They include the addresses of editors who should be queried and a general description of the articles they seek. When you find a few that are appropriate for your purposes and compatible with your skills, write to the editors, requesting "writer's guidelines" and copies of the magazines.

For example, suppose you are an avid sailor and want to write an article on some aspect of sailing. The article is only a vague idea at this point, but you think you would like to write about some of your sailing adventures. *Sports Illustrated* as a potential market occurs to you at once, but you wisely move on to something more modest and less competitive. *Writer's Market* lists two other more realistic outlets for your work: *Sailing World* and *Sail. Sailing World* is inappropriate, you discover, because it features racing articles. But *Sail* sounds promising. Here is what the directory says about it: "50% freelance written. Works with a small number of new/unpublished writers each year. Monthly magazine that wants articles on sailing: how-to, personal experience, profiles, historical, and new products. Generally emphasizes the excitement of sail, and the human, personal aspect. No logs. . . . Buys 100 mss/year (freelance and commissioned). Length: 1,500–2,800 words. Pays $300–800. We sometimes pay the expenses of writers on assignment."

Ideally you should scan a year's issues of any magazine you're seriously considering writing for, noting especially the subjects of their articles and checking to see whether your idea has already been used. Even though you may write a brilliant article in January, an editor will reject it if the magazine carried a similar story in October.

HOW TO ANALYZE A MAGAZINE

With your potential markets eventually narrowed to one, two, or three small-circulation or regional magazines, analyze each one carefully. Study the cover and illustrations, contents, advertisements, and the articles themselves. You should then be able to answer these questions:

❑ What is the magazine's slant? (Conservative, liberal, feminist, antiestablishment? What way of life, philosophy, or stance does it promote? What seems to be its mission or purpose?)

❑ What is the personality or overall tone of the magazine? (Humorous, cheerful, intellectual, satirical, wholesome, spiritual, hedonistic?) Slant and personality somewhat overlap because both reflect the editors' and readers' attitudes toward life.

❑ What general topics are regularly covered? (Family activities, politics, sex, religion, beauty, foods?)

❑ What are the favored treatments given these topics? (Are the articles factual with a high number of how-to stories or think pieces, or is the prevailing treatment anecdotal and entertaining as well as informative?)

❑ How long are the articles? (Length is indicated in number of words, not pages.)

❑ Does the magazine have a characteristic style of writing? (Is the language sophisticated, plain, ornamental, conversational, formal, or flashy? Are the sentences simple or complex, short or long? Or do the articles display a variety of styles that reflect the personalities of many writers?)

❑ What is the typical reader like in terms of age, sex, occupation, lifestyle, income, education? A close examination of the articles, illustrations, and advertisements should enable you to draw up a profile of the typical reader. If not, write to the magazine's advertising department for information on reader demographics.

Some of these questions will already have been answered for you in the descriptions editors write for *Writer's Market*. But you need to see for yourself that they truly publish what they claim to be seeking.

Analyzing the market, the panorama as well as the close-up, is a time-consuming process. But it is essential if you're serious about selling.

SUMMARY

1. Because modern magazines are tightly focused on specific audiences and therefore have contrasting editorial requirements, a freelance article should be written for one suitable type of publication and, ideally, with one specific magazine as a target.
2. To reduce the competition they must face, beginning freelancers should be willing to write for modest markets and modest fees.
3. A target magazine should be analyzed for slant, tone, typical reader, favored topics, treatment of topics, style of writing, and average length of article measured in number of words.

FROM PRINCIPLES TO PRACTICE

1. Spend at least two hours browsing through *The Writer's Handbook* and *Writer's Market* until you are familiar with the variety of magazines that seek freelance articles. Look for possible markets for your work, eventually narrowing the possibilities to one or two magazines.
2. Choose the one whose style, format, and subject matter qualify it as the most suitable market for your writing. Analyze a recent issue as suggested in this chapter.
3. If past issues are available either in a library or private collection, study your chosen magazine over the past twelve months. Note especially the range of subjects covered, the presence of seasonal material, the number of issues built around a theme, and any exceptions to the expressed or implied philosophy of the magazine.
4. After completion of your analysis, write the results in paragraph or outline form, assessing the suitability of the magazine as a market for you.

CHAPTER

4

CHOOSING
A TOPIC

Before ending the analysis of the magazine market, an important point to remember is this: Choosing the right magazine to sell to and selecting the right topic to write about are twin endeavors. They must take place at the same time. You may have a spectacular idea for an article, but if you try to sell it to the wrong magazine, failure is certain. Compatibility between reader, writer, and topic is essential. In the process of matching your topic to a targeted audience, you engage in a tentative try-it-on process, testing an article idea for a specific magazine and trying another combination if it doesn't fit.

WRITE FROM PERSONAL EXPERIENCE

No matter whether you begin with the article idea or with market selection, you may freeze when the time comes to settle on a topic. You have nothing, you insist, to write about. Invariably you've been advised to write about what you know, but you're inclined to think that what you know is dull. The trouble is that, in searching for an interesting subject, you try to recall the whole panorama of your life. But as long as you dwell on so wide a horizon, the task seems too huge to tackle. It's true you need to survey the meadow, but ultimately you must concentrate on one sturdy dandelion. Learn to think small, to think specific. It is in the particular, in the complex arrangement of the petals so to speak, that you will find a subject worthy of your gaze, and much more likely to interest your reader. When you begin to consider the specific experiences of your life, topics bloom.

In a recent magazine article writing class, the eleven students, after much doubt and deliberation, finally settled on the following subjects. Each one chosen would be explored from the writer's unique experience or knowledge:

❑ A ten–week journalism internship in New York

❑ What it's like to be a female deputy sheriff

❏ A summer job in Yellowstone National Park

❏ The myth of plastic surgery hazards

❏ Kids who kill and their treatment in the courts

❏ What hospitals are doing about the nursing shortage

❏ Staying in a German home during a trip to Bavaria

❏ Scuba diving to see Florida's manatees

❏ The huge granite carving on the face of Georgia's Stone Mountain

❏ A controversial local radio personality

❏ The exorbitant cost of medical care for pets

All were excellent topics, and you may be thinking "I can't imagine coming up with such interesting things to write about." But the truth is that neither could these students until they quit thinking about the blur of their whole life and focused instead on specific experiences they had had or interesting people they knew. Five of them wrote about personal experiences (the internship in New York, the female sheriff, the summer job in Yellowstone, the trip to Bavaria, scuba diving). The other subjects arose from knowing an interesting person (a plastic surgeon, a mother who is a nurse, a veterinarian, a juvenile court judge, a talk-show host) or from work connections (a job in Stone Mountain State Park). Even then, they had to decide on the point they wanted to make about these topics, a task covered in Chapter 6.

There is one danger, however, in writing a personal experience piece. If, in telling your story, you seem too self-absorbed, you may lose your readers. Every article must offer some kind of benefit to them. Does it give them a vicarious adventure they might otherwise never have? Does it contain a touch of humor in showing the folly of your misadventures? Or does it help readers decide whether they should vacation in Mexico? Readers are busy and the TV beckons, so your article, like every article, must either inform or entertain.

On the value of writing from personal experience, the editor of *Air & Space/Smithsonian Magazine* says, "Our writers' ideas come from anywhere and everywhere, but I can't help noticing that their best stories are usually those that are linked to their own lives in some way." And Tom Clark of *Writer's Digest* says, "You'll still have to do research on the topic but your experience gives the article reality, insight."

Consider a very personal source of ideas for articles: a diary or journal. If you don't keep one, it's still not too late to begin. Such a habit will flex your writing muscles and preserve subjects for your writing that you might otherwise forget. Using a journal as a stream of consciousness record the way writer/editor Amy Greene does will occasionally reveal a subconscious concern that may prove to be valuable in your life and in your writing. For example, Greene says she recently found a recurrent thread in her journal: her yearning for meaningful work. Those last four words about meaningful work contain an excellent germ for an article about the difficulties of finding it.

Another journal writer asks, "Why do I write? For clarity about my life. I write to see what will come out of the end of my pen. Sometimes I am amazed at what appears on my written page." You will almost certainly experience such epiphanies, and some of them will contain the germ of an article.

MAKING A "WANT" LIST

To generate some personal ideas with universal application, try this experiment. Make a list of the things you are concerned about and therefore like to read about. Your list may go something like this:

1. I want to be sure I'm getting the most out of life, that I'm not missing something within my grasp.
2. Within my limited time, I want to know practical ways to help others or improve the environment.
3. I want to be able to keep up with what is going on in a complex, swiftly changing world.
4. I want to know how to maintain my health: to exercise and eat properly.
5. I want to know how to improve my relationship with my family.
6. I want adventure, real or vicarious.
7. I want to better understand human behavior.
8. I want to keep my friendships alive and healthy, and to learn to make new friends in a highly mobile society.
9. I want to continue to grow by learning new things.
10. I want to read about the lives of accomplished, active people, described in tough, unsentimental language.
11. I want what I read to help me put my life in better perspective.
12. I want to laugh more often.

Your "want" list will help you discover facets of your life or interests that you can write about to help other people cope with their problems. For example, after a period of moody introspection about what was wrong with her relationships with men, a former student began to realize she was afraid of sex. She also discovered that, contrary to expectations raised by the sexual revolution, many of her friends had the same fear. As a result, she wrote a moving article on this subject.

Much like learning a new way of reading, writers must learn a new way of observing and thinking. They must carry a new consciousness with them: that literally everything in life has in it the core of an article. Edith Kilgo, for instance, says her southern husband brought home a "mess" of collards one night, hinting broadly that she cook them for dinner. Edith had never cooked collards before in her life, but she was game to try. In the midst of washing the curly greens and becoming frustrated by the sand hidden in the crevices of the coarse leaves, she suddenly realized she had come upon an idea for an article. Soothing her husband with a promise to cook the collards later, she quickly dried her hands, rushed to her typewriter, and wrote an entertaining piece about this nutritious but daunting southern dish. No doubt she had to do some research to find an authentic recipe, but that was a small matter and was quickly done. The article sold to a women's magazine.

From now on, try to observe, read, listen, and experience everything with the constant question in mind: Is there an article idea here? As this habit forms you will learn that there are seldom brand new ideas but always new refinements of old ideas, new uses for them, and new ways of expressing them. And there is always *your* way. In addition, new discoveries and products are changing our lives, young people are growing to a maturity of new achievement and adventure, and every twenty-four hours a new day brings unique problems, progress, and events.

Christmas is a good example. Written about to the point of exhaustion, Christmas can still be the subject of a fresh and interesting article. For the Christmas that is coming this year has never occurred before. You can write about its uniqueness. Remember, though, the more a subject has been written about, the fresher your style and slant must be.

THE IDEA FILE

Although some editors seek intimate, personal articles, others prefer strictly informative stories based on in-depth research. If you lean toward that kind of writing, begin reading newspapers in a new way, with scissors in hand. Newspapers systematically investigate almost all aspects of our society with a large network of reporters who spend their working hours looking for something new. Consequently, newspaper articles report all kinds of discoveries and developments that help define our society. But because of reporters' limited time and newspapers' limited space, the stories are sometimes brief and superficial. When you find such a story, you can investigate the situation involved, conduct a series of interviews and other forms of research, and write an in-depth article on the subject. By thoroughly reading and clipping newspapers, you will gradually build a valuable idea file.

Another source for topic hunting is scholarly journals, master's theses, and Ph.D. dissertations, all available in college libraries. Such publications contain valuable information, but their academic language cries out for "translation" for the average lay person. Cultural anthropologists, for example, have written about some of the negative attitudes and images Americans hold about retirement and the effect they have on older Americans. Psychologists have explored the effects of humor on aggression and the therapeutic value of dancing. The general public will never benefit from such research unless some freelancer makes it available in popular magazines.

If you write well, scholars and busy professionals are often glad to collaborate on an article or to give you facts for an article publicizing their research and ideas. For example, a student writer once read a graduate student's research paper on mental golf practice. No need to bury this useful idea within academic circles, she thought, and promptly wrote an article on the subject, giving credit to the physical education student for his original idea. A fresh idea thus got double exposure.

If you live near a large city, you can get excellent ideas by attending conventions such as the American Medical Association, the National Hair Dressers Association, the American Association of Juvenile Court Judges. When professionals meet, they share ideas, discoveries, problems—many of them good subjects for magazine articles. Permission to attend most meetings of this kind should require no more than a phone call to the press office of the association (usually in the hotel or convention hall where the meetings are held). Introduce yourself and explain why you would like to attend. If you have a specific article idea in mind, you will be welcomed, but even if you're just shopping for ideas, you will usually be invited to attend on an informal basis.

If you drop by the press office instead of calling, follow the same procedure. In addition to the information or inspiration that may accrue from such encounters, you may make useful contacts with professionals who will be willing to give you helpful information on their specialties.

For other topic ideas, read the *Congressional Record* or the *CQ [Congressional Quarterly] Weekly Reports* for accounts of what Congress does each week. *The National Journal* tells what the executive branch of the government has done in the past week. Another good source for new developments is encyclopedia yearbooks, which yield authoritative information on recent achievements, discoveries, events, trends, and issues.

Read old magazines (six or seven years old) looking for articles on subjects that need to be updated, refuted, or given better treatment. You cannot steal the words of the author, but subjects cannot be copyrighted. Be fair, however, by giving credit for any original ideas that have been useful to you.

The yellow pages of a metropolitan phone book sometimes yield good subjects. For example, the listing of watchdog-training schools could suggest several different articles: how the dogs are trained and how reliable and effective their protection is; an article on the kinds of people in our society who are buying watchdogs; a survey article on other security devices, their costs, unique features, and ease of use.

Simply reading *Writer's Market, The Writer's Handbook*, and *Reader's Guide to Periodical Literature* can be helpful when searching for topics. *Reader's Guide* indexes all the subjects that have recently been written about.

Every time you read *anything*—comics, classics, billboards, bottle labels, best sellers—you should be thinking: Does this suggest a topic for me? A poorly researched article published in one magazine could be well researched, written with a different angle, and sold to another magazine. If you find yourself disagreeing with an author, write a rebuttal in an article of your own.

Still another way to find something to write about is to browse through the material in a good library's vertical file. It contains pamphlets and booklets from businesses or the government on subjects you may find surprising and therefore interesting enough to write about. You may prefer to consult the *Vertical File Index*, a subject and title index to selected pamphlets published monthly. For example, this index refers to a pamphlet entitled "Pan for Gold on Your Next Vacation: A Guide to Low-Cost, Unique Adventure," a topic that presents several different article possiblities. For a local magazine you could do your own version, featuring nearby sites for gold prospecting. Or you might write about another kind of prospecting, searching for crystal formations.

College students and people who live near a large university have a community of experts as neighbors, most of whom are willing to share their knowledge and ideas with freelancers. Accessible for interviews, they are usually articulate and enthusiastic about the subjects they are researching.

It is not essential, however, to live near an intellectual or artistic center to find good topics or sources for articles. Wherever human beings are, interesting activities or careers or hobbies or theories are being explored. Try to look at your community from a new perspective. Every day editors assign New York writers to cover events, to write about interesting people, or to rediscover historical spots all over the United States. Don't be scooped in your own home town.

The final suggestion for topic searching, then, is simply to see your environment with new eyes from new angles. Artists have always used this technique, as anyone knows who has watched one before an easel: cocking the head, squinting the eyes, standing back, moving close. The subject matter, like yours, is familiar and close, but the artist is trying to see it with new-found wonder.

No subject has ever been exhausted, but many seem dull or dated because the words that describe them are sluggish. Get an old idea up out of its rocking chair, dress it in new flamboyant clothes, wind it up with robust verbs, and thrust it into action. It's true that the key word in describing a good subject is *new*, but editors also like articles on old topics rendered with a fresh slant and an energetic style. Though you may not find a new subject, you can make an old one dance.

TESTING THE TOPIC

When an idea occurs to you that you are vitally interested in, how can you test its worth? Answers to these questions should give you a valid assessment:

1. Is the topic appropriate for the magazine market you have chosen? If not, can you find a topic that fits?
2. Is it of compelling interest to a large number of people, not merely to you? Can you state specifically why other people would want to read an article on the subject? In what way would it benefit them?
3. If it is so broad that only a book could deal with it, can you narrow your focus to one small aspect of the subject?
4. Is the idea too familiar? If so, can you find some element that has not been written about? In other words, can you give it a new angle or explain a new development?
5. Can you research the subject without incurring too much expense?

The first few topics you think of may not pass this test. In case a more systematic search is needed, remind yourself that writing a magazine article is a form of communication. Where do you get the ideas you spontaneously share with friends? In most cases, inspiration comes from the things you do: observations about your family, your town, your region, your experiences at work or leisure, and from reading or listening to the ideas of others.

SUMMARY

1. To write a compelling article, choose a subject you find exciting. Then check it out with friends to be sure they, too, find it meaningful and significant.
2. Remember that selecting a topic and a suitable magazine market must be undertaken simultaneously. Professionals don't begin to research a subject until they have chosen at least one magazine to query.
3. Be doubly sure if you choose an old subject that you can give it a new slant with an engaging style.
4. You must find a narrow focus if you're interested in a broad topic.
5. Look for potential topics in newspapers, in conversations with friends, in old magazines, in observations of your changing environment, in unusual people, in the experiences you've had, in scholarly journals and other reading. Work to develop the habit of looking for topics everywhere.

FROM PRINCIPLES TO PRACTICE

1. Read an assigned issue of a good local newspaper, listing all the possible topics suggested to you by the news stories, features, ads, or cartoons. Compare your list to those of the other class members.

2. Go through some six- or seven-year-old magazines and list the subjects that could be updated or developed in a different manner.

3. Find your library's vertical file, go through some of its material, and list topic ideas you may like to develop.

4. Using the test offered in this chapter, check the feasibility or value of your best two or three potential topics.

CHAPTER

5

TYPES OF ARTICLES

Wherever else you may look for ideas to write about, there is no substitute for extensive reading: newspapers, advertisements, signs, and especially magazine articles of all kinds. The idea is to keep in step with the dazzling changes taking place in society and to note the kinds of material editors are buying.

By reading articles of all types you will gain a broader perspective of the potential open to you as a freelancer. Because articles can be classified in so many different ways (according to subject, treatment, or purpose), a comprehensive list would be impractical for our purposes. The types discussed in this chapter, therefore, comprise a highly selective but helpful group. Those most popular are: personal experience articles, how-to's, profiles, reports or information articles, and essays. Ultimately you may decide to specialize in one of these types, but for now, use the categories as a final aid in selecting a good topic and learning the characteristics and requirements of each kind of article. The list can show you possibilities and prime the pump of your imagination.

This chapter, then, will examine the characteristics of five different kinds of articles; a sample of each is included to inspire you. These five types, of course, are not entirely pure and separate. Because writers make their own hybrid genres, some of them overlap. Still, those listed and exemplified here will give you a menu to search in trying to find a viable subject.

PERSONAL EXPERIENCE ARTICLES

Articles based on your personal experience probably promise a higher degree of success for a beginning writer than any other type, provided you're certain there's a reason for readers to be interested in your experience. What's in it for them? Is it something they might like to try, or to experience vicariously if not directly? Is it unusual? Is the story enjoyable, suspenseful, amusing?

This type of article must give readers a sense of participation in your experience. All the while they're reading, they will be thinking: What would I do if I were in this situation? How would I feel? Should I try it myself? And if you give enough details about the setting, the characters, and the conflicts or action in the story, they will have a sense of being there with you. Your story should be emotional and dramatic.

Not all magazines publish personal experience articles, so search through *Writer's Market* for an editor who seeks them.

The following excerpt is from a personal experience article written by a student, Hank Ernest, Jr., after he had spent ten weeks as a journalist intern with *Newsday* in New York City. It was his first visit to New York, and he was apprehensive about his performance at work and his ability to find his way around in such a strange and overwhelming place. Here's how he begins:

I had imagined myself pushing papers or, at best, doing a couple of feature stories on the Boy Scouts. But I was in for a surprise. The interns were given maps of Queens, Manhattan, and Brooklyn and sent packing, practically from day one. We were told we would be replacing vacationing staffers and given general-assignment stories, and to expect little supervision from editors.

The Brooklyn map should have come equipped with a bullet-proof vest.

Working a story from Brooklyn almost always turned out to be a harrowing experience. One particular story involved a woman who was assassinated in her apartment in apparent retaliation for her anti-drug activism. The people of the poor, mostly Hispanic neighborhood in the Bushwick section of Brooklyn were to hold a candlelight vigil to mark the first anniversary of her death. When I arrived at the scene, at about six in the evening, little kids were playing in the street. I parked on a harmless-looking side street and ran off to cover the event a couple of blocks away.

Prayers of hope and peace rang out in the simple ceremony as a large crowd of police stood ominously by. But my mind was at ease, thinking the area had been purged of the drug trade that had ravaged it just a year ago. My premature relaxation would be short-lived, however.

After gathering my story and calling it in (newspapers call this a "phoner") for the next morning's edition, I rushed off to find my car. But the neighborhood where I had parked was transformed. As I walked down the block, I overheard a guy complaining about the police and how they had hurt his drug business that night.

"Man, I can't do nothin. Cops everywhere," he said in total disgust.

I kept walking, but now at a faster clip. I began to notice that the children on the streets had grown up. Drug dealers and prostitutes were hawking their wares to passing motorists. I suddenly realized I was in one of the most dangerous, drug-infested areas of New York City. I speculated that the cops had assembled as a show of force just for the media. The publicity generated by the murder over a year ago caused the police to temporarily clean up the neighborhood. But after several months they disappeared, causing the area to be taken over once again by drugs and prostitution.

Fear was my worst enemy. I just wanted to make it out of there alive. I had quickened my pace once more before turning the dark corner to my car. There I found three of the meanest looking characters I had ever seen sprawled all over my car. Somehow I managed not to break stride as I approached my little Festiva. To make matters worse, there were two cars parked adjacent to mine, effectively blocking my departure.

My mind raced. I could only think of all the reporters in Beirut and other U.S.-hating countries who file stories in the middle of mobs yelling anti-American slogans. They usually got away without a scratch. I was hoping journalistic immunity was a worldwide phenomenon. The fact is, I thought my life had come to an end. I was thinking about the headlines my death would make in the New York tabloids: NEWSDAY INTERN MURDERED IN COLD BLOOD; FAMILY IN ATLANTA OUTRAGED; NEWSDAY OFFERS REWARD.

Back to reality, the first words spoken were those of one of the men relaxing on my car. He said, "Aye mane, this your car?"

Take it, I thought to myself. Go ahead and take it. I'll walk the Brooklyn Bridge back to Manhattan. I'll swim.

"Yeah, it sure is," I said, trying desperately to conceal any trembling that must have been apparent.

With that, they jumped off my car and summoned the drivers of the other cars to move so that I could get out. I said "thanks" and never looked back.

The student author begins with his Boy Scout expectations but quickly mentions bullet-proof vests. From that point on, the drama deepens, and our identification with the young journalist never stops. Fear keeps the reader hurrying breathlessly from one paragraph to the next until the very end. Then, surprise and relief. Pleasure comes from the story's contrasts: prayers and violence, success and failure, vulnerable youth and hardened age, a touch of humor and paralyzing fear.

ESSAYS

Essays are difficult to define because they are such slippery chameleons. Rather than being entirely based on research, they spring from the writer's mind and experiences. They can be narrative, philosophical, satiric, personal, humorous, or political. The essayist chooses a topic most of us are concerned about in our private, and sometimes public, lives, and then turns on it the prism of a discerning eye. With wit and imagination, the writer examines, contemplates, dissects, and reflects, somehow giving meaning to the confusing details of daily living.

In her Introduction to *Best American Essays: 1988*, Annie Dillard writes an insightful essay on the essay itself as a versatile and valuable literary form. In her view, the essay is more valuable than the short story or even poetry. Here are a few excerpts: "The essayist does what we do with our lives; the essayist thinks about actual things. He can make sense of them analytically or artistically. In either case he renders the real world coherent and meaningful, even if only bits of it, and even if that coherence and meaning reside only inside small texts."

By "small texts," she means such things as being a parent, making friends, preparing a meal, finding an unusual shell, going to the grocery store—ordinary things that on the surface may seem dull or trivial. But when thoughtfully and imaginatively explored, they reveal themselves as "sermons in stones."

Almost every article of depth today contains an element of the essay. As you read through the following examples of some of the most common types of articles, you will be aware of this ubiquitous quality. It reaches over into other genres with its discursive curiosity, informal but graceful style, wit, and insight—qualities to be sought in any kind of writing.

The essay chosen to illustrate this category was written by a former student, Elfriede Kristwald, who wrote and sold it in various versions to four different publications. This version appeared in *The Boston Globe* as a Valentine's Day feature.

What's Love Got to Do With It?

They used to call it love. Now, it's co-dependency.

Love—the living for, in, through, of, and with another—was once a godly emotion, worthy of the poet's labor, the artist's creation, the philosopher's brooding. Wars were fought in the name of love, civilizations destroyed, nations founded.

The only history lessons I recall that no one in my class ever slept through were those in which our teacher explained the mess Paris and Helen caused to the city of Troy or how Rome changed forever through Antony and Cleopatra's torrid affair. Tristan and Isolde's love story made studying the boring medieval bearable, and even the little megalomaniac Napoleon looked more attractive through his devotion for Josephine.

Compared with the emotions that inspired the Taj Mahal, "The Rubaiyat" or the "Mona Lisa," what we now call love seems sanitized, debugged, and plastic-coated. We are proud of having demystified love. We now sell it, neatly packed and labeled, as "commitment" or "communication" in group sessions, private counseling, or at the local bookstore. What doesn't fit this mold is simply diagnosed as "addictive," "compulsive," "dysfunctional," or "pathological." The only "healthy" form of love we are taught today is *self*-love.

Best sellers tell us that "Women Who Love Too Much" end up with men who suffer from the "Peter Pan Syndrome" or "Men Who Can't Love." We learn that "Learning to Love Yourself" helps to avoid making "Wrong Choices" and that "Understanding the Psychology of Romantic Love" is the map to finding "The Road Less Traveled." In all these books, love—as glorified by Dante, Shakespeare, Goethe, or Elizabeth Barrett Browning—doesn't fare too well.

The buzzword is co-dependency. Family counselor and PBS television host John Bradshaw believes that the relationship of two "inseparable" people who feel that they *must* be together is "co-dependency," which—among other scary things—is a "symptom of abandonment" often coupled with "sexual addiction." The "most common of addictions," Bradshaw defines co-dependency in terms that would put Emily Dickinson or the great bard right out of business.

But it is difficult to think of the quintessential lovers of literature as "co-dependents." Despite pop psychology, group sessions, and Bradshaw shows, I wonder, did Juliet really just suffer from mankind's "most common addiction"? Was Romeo only a neurotic "relationship junky" in need of a good shrink?

I have trouble thinking of Mozart's Constanza and Verdi's Aida as "dysfunctional co-dependents" who must learn to nurture the "inner child." And it is difficult to imagine anyone telling Orpheus that losing his Eurydice in Hades "may have been a blessing in disguise" that will allow him to "focus on himself."

In this sensible, self-sufficient and salubrious world of ours, the existence of another as the reason for our own is no longer necessary. We grow babies in test tubes, see and hear ourselves in movies and on tapes, and proudly satisfy our needs and wants alone. We no longer see ourselves reflected in the soul of another. A mirror does just fine.

Walking units of emotional health who have successfully rid ourselves of addictive-compulsive feeling, severed the dysfunctional ties of
co-dependency, and are no longer in danger of loving another, we can
proudly ask ourselves:
"How do I love me? Let me count the ways. . . ."

Essays are for insight and delight. Good writers love them because, like
jugglers, they enjoy challenges. They try to fling one more perfect, surprising
word into the air to float with the six that are already there, hoping to give their
work the wit and distinction they seek and knowing that style is all important
in essays.

HOW-TO ARTICLES

The high number of instructional articles in magazines shows that
Americans constantly seek to develop new skills and to live fuller lives. They
have a craving for learning how to do almost anything or how to improve themselves in some way. And so, depending on the specialization of the magazine,
editors seek articles on how to lose weight, excel at almost any sport, be a better lover, manager, student, writer, cook, counselor, sportsman, conversation-
alist, or mother. The list is long and the demand is high. The how-to article,
then, in response to a broad spectrum of human needs and desires, provides a
good way to begin freelancing. You may already have a skill that qualifies you
as an expert in some field, or you can interview authorities and thereby spread
their knowledge to the popular market.

Such articles are comparatively easy to write if you have a logical mind
and a gift for empathy. Logic enables you to arrange the information with no
confusing gaps; empathy helps you put yourself in the readers' place, thus
anticipating their questions and knowing what they need to know first, then
second, and so on. In a how-to article, the meaning of every word must be
clear, all technical terms defined. Aware of the importance of tone, the best
writers avoid being condescending or preachy by maintaining a helpful rather
than a dictatorial attitude. They strive for a conversational intimacy, partly by
addressing the reader directly as "you." And they never assume that the reader
knows everything *they* know. This means, unless their audience is fairly knowledgeable, they must begin their instruction at an elementary level.

In writing a how-to article, it's imperative to write an alluring lead.
Convince readers that they will profit from your article and even have some
fun with it. Let them know what problem you will help solve or what you're

going to teach them, and why. Here is your chance to strut your stuff with words and wit.

The following is a sample, a mere taste really, of a different kind of how-to writing that will give you an idea of the wide-ranging versatility of this genre. It's from an *Esquire* article, "The Case for Pleasure," by George Leonard. The article begins with a history of mankind's search for pleasure and the dulling of the capacity for joy brought about by civilization and today's frantic hedonism. Then Leonard tells us how to turn away from "the modern route to pleasure (that) confronts us with a maze of wrong turns, leading far too often to burnout, addiction, spiritual emptiness, and financial ruin." His first suggestion is unusual:

Avoid the quick-fix route to pleasure. Learn to love the plateau. Driven by the needs of our consumerist-credit economy, Americans have created a powerful media image of happiness and success that, for all its glitter and appeal, is impossible to realize. According to this image, life at its best consists of an endless parade of climactic moments. On the TV screen you see men working for about two seconds—then it's Miller time. Touchdowns, taste thrills, ecstatic rendezvous, successful business meetings, and instant vacation crowd your consciousness. Life moves from one peak to another. There are no plateaus.

Two years ago in the *Esquire* fitness issue, we demonstrated that the mastery of any skill—in fact, the development of almost everything in life—involves working diligently for extended periods of time without seeming to get anywhere. Now and then you enjoy a spurt of progress, of easy success—the occasion for celebrations. But there's an inescapable rhythm of existence that demands that, for lasting success and satisfaction, you have to spend most of your time on a plateau.

. . . . Life is not an endless series of climaxes. You can't go straight from one high to another all the time or even most of the time without eventually crashing.

The first step toward long-term pleasure lies simply in understanding that plateaus do exist. Say you've been working for quite a while on something—learning tennis, improving a relationship, starting a new business—and you seem to be getting nowhere. It might be that you're doing something wrong, that you're on the wrong track—you always have to consider that possibility. But even if you're doing everything perfectly, even if you're exactly on track, you'll probably end up spending most of your time on a plateau. Just knowing and accepting that can soothe the mind and inspire the heart.

The next step involves learning to love the plateau. Improbable?

Maybe. But you'll find that the people we call masters in almost every field are likely to be the ones who not only practice most diligently but also enjoy it the most. It may take a while, but sooner or later you'll discover a certain pleasure in just hanging in there, day after day, month after month. . . . The joy is precisely in the practice itself, in the continual unfolding of the ancient rhythm—as inevitable as the beating of your heart—that finally leads to mastery. For one on this path, the moments of triumph are pleasant, nothing to scoff at, but they are essentially incidental.

Adopt the Zen strategy of finding joy in the commonplace. You might think that the value of Zen practice lies in the unwavering apprehension of the present moment while sitting motionless. But a visit to a Zen retreat quickly reveals that, potentially, *everything* is meditation—building a stone wall, eating, walking from one place to another, sweeping a hallway.

The secret is all in the way you approach the matter of time. Since earliest childhood, most of us have been taught to direct our attention to the past and to the future. Those are nice places to visit—necessary, in fact, for survival and success. But they are not where pleasure resides. If you're really interested in finding pleasure, start by directing your attention to the present.

Take walking, for example. It's a marvelous thing in itself, but we tend to squander it, merely as a means of getting somewhere. Try changing the context: let the very act of walking be the main event. Be aware of every step, the feel of your feet on the floor, the rotation of your hips, the swing of your arms, the soft breeze on your face. . . .

This is old stuff, as ancient as human consciousness. But we have to keep reminding ourselves to cherish the moment, especially in a society that stokes our craving for objects and experiences out there in the future or back in the past. . . .

Don't be a loner. Do things with and for people. If there's anything that studies on health show, it's that man is a social animal, that good health involves loving, caring connections with other people. This doesn't deny the joys of solitude—a sojourn at some Walden Pond, a retreat to the fastness of your own room, a long, lonely walk. There's an old tradition that enlightenment requires a withdrawal from daily entanglements, a period of time in a literal or figurative desert. But even for a saint, there's the return to the family of humanity and a chance to do service for others.

If you have no family or friends nearby, you can still get involved in volunteer work, which is strongly linked to both good health and pleasure. In an era when cynicism is increasingly equated with wisdom, it's easy to overlook the fact that human beings are genetically disposed to altruism and that there's intrinsic pleasure in responding to a cry for help.

But it's not just giving that brings pleasure; it's also receiving. In concert, these two essential human acts join in a circle of interaction that expands with use. When the circle is complete, the more you give, the more you get, and vice versa.

In addition to being a good example of a serious and almost spiritual kind of how-to article, George Leonard's writing illustrates the personal and self-revealing aspect of today's magazine articles. Reading his writing is like having a conversation with him. It reveals a great deal about his character and values.

PROFILES

The American public is fascinated with **profiles** of celebrities, partly because they appeal to the gossip instinct, to curiosity about famous people's private lives and minds. But despite the softer demand for them, articles about extraordinary unknowns are probably more practical for beginning writers to tackle. Understandably, a check of market directories will reveal hundreds of markets for celebrity profiles, but you'll also find some magazines that welcome stories about ordinary people who are in reality anything but ordinary. Profiles of both kinds are usually written about people who are extremely successful in some way, financially, professionally, romantically, parentally, and so on. We like to identify with such people or to get new ideas about how to be successful ourselves.

To write a revealing profile requires a tremendous amount of research, but the resulting article should never be a chronological account of a person's life. It may probe a baseball player's childhood for clues that explain his character and personality today, but the best profile would begin by *showing* him in some recent characteristic scene with actual dialogue between him and some other person. Good writers use every cinematic device possible to show how the person looks, talks, moves, suffers, or rejoices—everything that we see in real life when we are with someone. They don't *tell* us that the person is kind, insecure, competitive, sarcastic. They *show* these qualities instead, in technicolor action and lifelike dialogue.

The following example of a profile was written by a student who turned in this portrait for a class assignment with no intention of ever making money on it. He had very little time to spend with his subject, a homeless man who maintained self-respect and a sense of humor despite the tragic circumstances of his life. But in the following excerpt note how the student, Edward Hosch, catches the idiosyncrasies of the man's dialect to make us hear and see him and feel that we know him.

Rocky Road

Every major city has a skid row with multi-million dollar business complexes frowning down disapprovingly on society's misfits as they wander through their aimless lives.

Rocky Miller can tell you all about it. Rocky's a wino. He's called Atlanta's skid row "home" for nearly a decade, he says. He claims to be fifty-nine years old, but that's just if you count the years, not the hard living carved into his modeling-clay face, abused body, and cracked, grubby, calloused paws.

Everything he owns is on his back and in a green plastic garbage bag never far from his side. A heavy, incredibly soiled ankle-length overcoat covers several layers of faded, frayed clothing down to a tattered undershirt, yellowed with age and sweat. Other bits and pieces of ragged cloth peek out from his "suitcase," crammed tightly under several bundles of newspapers—his "blankets."

You can sit and talk to Rocky, naturally friendly and gregarious despite his less than lofty position in life. He doesn't ask for change or a handout of any kind—a definite point of pride with Rocky.

"Ain't no way. I ain't no beggar. I got my pension money. I earned it (in the Army). I paid for it with half my damn hip and don't you forget it. Ain't never asked nobody for nothin' and won't never. I'm my own man, always have been. That might get me in a little jam ever' now and then, but a body's just gotta follow his own trail, y'know what I'm sayin'?"

Did he ever have a family?

Animated mock misery flows laughingly from his voice. "Hey, listen—I had me a wife once, back when I was in the Army. Oh, mercy—that woman could talk the ears off a wooden rabbit. I mean, her lips was looser'n a ten-cent pair of socks, I ain't kiddin' ya. Had me 'bout all I could take one day and just got my pore ears AWAY from there—up and left! 'Bout two more minutes worth of her voice and I prob'ly would've ended up loony as she was! Thank goodness we didn't have no kids for me to worry over. Well, truth is, I couldn't hardly ever get the old crow to shut up long enough to even think about gettin' romantic. Lord. I'm gettin' a headache just rememberin' on her."

Rocky's lifestyle has been the same for so long that he doesn't give much thought to changing any more. He has his "nappin' places" around: behind a dumpster in an alley between a restaurant and a loan office on

Ivy Street; the back of a $2-per-day parking lot in a pile of lumber and junk; and once in a while he'll sneak into an abandoned or seldom-used warehouse, where a broken window offers easy access.

Doesn't he ever go to the Union Mission on Ellis Street?

"Listen, I'll tell ya 'bout sleepin' at the mission. Now don't get me wrong—them people runnin' the place, I'm sure they got good hearts and they mean well, but you ain't gonna find a whole lotta high-class people stayin' around there, ya know what I'm sayin'? What I mean is, some of them beggars sleepin' there next to ya would steal a tired man's snore if they got half a damn chance, I ain't kiddin' ya. Now, they ain't all that way, of course—most of 'em is just as regular as you and me. But I just don't need the extry aggravation 'bout havin' to worry is there gonna be more fingers than mine investigatin' my pants pockets some night, don't ya know? If it looks like I'm fixin' to get snowed on or somethin' I'll head on down there, but I ain't gonna make me no holiday reservations or nothin'."

Listening to him now, you can ignore the grimy face and filthy clothes, the red, watery eyes that have seen so much, and the body odor that takes your breath away when the wind shifts. Buried deep inside, you can still discover parts of what must have been a fine man once. Now he's got his wine, his stories, and his songs. Just like Rocky Miller says, he's his own man—and don't you worry about it.

This article contains a great deal of information, all of it from the talk with Rocky. Ideally, with more time the student writer would have found out even more about Rocky's past—especially how he became homeless. He could have observed him in as many different situations as possible, using only the most pertinent and dramatic of the information he had gathered. But Hosch did the best he could after one long and startling interview in a McDonald's restaurant where the sociable Rocky came in for a cup of coffee and, sharing a table, they struck up a conversation.

INFORMATIVE ARTICLES

A huge number of articles are informational—on science, history, finance, sports, careers, medicine, new products, politics, education—but they are often entertaining as well.

If you find facts more fascinating than how-to's or portraits or essays, you might like to specialize in writing informative articles. They require painstaking research, in the library and talking with authorities, but the market for them is good.

One warning: The subject matter of such articles may be intrinsically engrossing, but sometimes mere facts can seem tiresome. So informational writing needs more art than you might think. Even in complex, scientific articles, the famous naturalist Loren Eisley uses figurative language to give his work more depth and greater clarity. He compares "the unpitying eye of science," for example, to the eye of a lighthouse. Just because you're writing a strictly factual piece you need not leave the realm of literature. While you may not aspire to such a lofty level, you can still focus on people rather than laboratories, statistics, or objects. And you can turn whatever you're writing about into a story. If you tell how a new discovery or product or idea evolved, you're telling a story, and your reader will "listen."

The key word in this kind of article is *new*. If the world remained the same, there would be little to write about. Change keeps life everlastingly interesting. And change in any aspect of our existence can keep us writing. Do you know a scientist who is on the brink of a new discovery? Have you heard about a new product that will soon be on the market? Are the kids in your town beginning to use a new gadget or toy that may become a fad? Is there a change in the mood of college students or a new trend that others would want to hear about? These are the kinds of topics that generate informational articles.

The following excerpt from an article in this category is from *Discover*. Written by Shawna Vogel, "Lighting Up the Body Clock" is about new discoveries in what happens when our biological clocks become confused and we experience, for example, jet lag. Note that it's told as a story.

On May 23, 1989, Italian interior designer Stefania Follini climbed out of the cave in Carlsbad, New Mexico, in which she had spent the past 130 days. Follini had been the willing guinea pig in an experiment to determine what would happen to her mind and body when she was deprived of all time cues. In the secluded recesses of the cave she had no knowledge of the daily rising and setting of the sun. Her living area was constantly though dimly lit, and there was no social contact with the outside world except for messages left on a computer at irregular times by the project researchers.

The experience made Follini's body clock go haywire. When she was asked, four months into the experiment, how long she had been underground, she replied that about two months had passed. Follini had been counting off the days as she whiled them away, but for her the time from morning to morning had stretched considerably. At times her 24-hour sleep-wake cycle would extend to 44 hours, and she would stay up for 30 hours, then sleep for the next 14.

Follini's experience underscores the crucial role that daylight plays in keeping our biological clocks synchronized with Earth's cycle of night and day. But you don't have to spend four months underground to throw your internal clock completely off. According to a recent study by sleep researcher Charles Czeisler at Brigham and Women's Hospital in Boston, you can reset your clock to any new schedule within a mere two or three days, simply by exposing yourself to bright light. The new clock-setting, however, depends on the exact timing of the exposure.

When light hits our open eyes, it initiates nerve signals that travel to a cluster of cells within the brain's hypothalamus called the suprachiasmatic nucleus. These cells in turn transmit signals throughout the body to maintain a host of rhythmic cycles—not only events such as sleeping and waking but also the regular rising and falling of core body temperature.

Three paragraphs follow in which the author explains some experiments with bright sunlight to reset the "clock." Then she concludes:

For more than a decade veteran biological-clock watcher Arthur Winfree of the University of Arizona has been easily adjusting his own timekeeper when traveling from one time zone to another. Any traveler, he says, can do the same.

For example, to reset his clock after flying from New York to Paris—where the sun rises six hours earlier—Winfree exposes himself to some Parisian sunlight at a time equivalent to early morning in New York. That's about 2 P.M. Paris time. So by spending a late lunch hour reading the newspaper outside on a park bench, he can help keep jet lag from ruining his trip.

With or without active sun-seeking, however, everybody's clock will eventually catch up to a new time zone. Even the cave-dweller Follini, whose periods of sleeping and waking bounced around chaotically for months, would have resumed a normal sleep-wake cycle after about a week above ground—had she not immediately embarked on a time-zone-hopping publicity tour.

This article is tightly condensed because it appeared in a year-end issue of *Discover* that summarized the top science stories of the year. Consequently, many details have been omitted, and only an excerpt is included here. But note how the writer concentrates on the human element and uses narrative at every opportunity. Then she refers to jet lag with which most people can identify. Both techniques are effective lures to keep a reader reading.

This completes a sampling of five popular types of articles for you to meander through in your search for the perfect topic. These general categories should stir your imagination and give you some ideas for the kinds of subjects being explored today.

SUMMARY

A final suggestion for choosing a topic is to review a list of some popular types of articles and their requirements. Examine them in the light of your writing aptitudes and interests.

1. Personal experience stories are probably the best bet for beginners. Be sure that your experience has significance for others and that you don't appear too self-absorbed.
2. The broadest category is the essay. It allows you to express your opinion and to concentrate on style and wit. The essay is elastic. It can be stretched to deal with any subject so long as it amuses or gives insight.
3. How-to articles are comparatively easy to write if you have a skill or know an expert, or if you have some ideas on how to live a better life. Clarity is of critical importance, as is the arrangement of your instructions in logical order.
4. Good profiles require painstaking research, including excellent interviewing skills and shrewd judgment of human character.
5. Success in selling informational articles depends not only on clarity and coherence but on an interesting style and timely subject matter.

FROM PRINCIPLES TO PRACTICE

To help you choose the most practical subject for your article, ask yourself the following questions:

1. Have you recently had an *unusual experience?*
2. Do you have some strong convictions about a current issue that you would like to air in an *essay?*
3. Do you have a skill you could teach (or wisdom you could share) in a *how-to?*
4. Would you like to do research on some discovery for an *informational article?*
5. Does an extremely interesting person live in your community—a celebrity or an unknown—who would make a good subject for a *profile?*

CHAPTER

6

THE QUERY
LETTER

Now that you have chosen an appropriate market and sharpened your conception of what you want to say in your article, it's time to tackle an important but challenging part of the freelancing process: proposing and selling the central idea of your article to an editor. There is no point in writing an article unless you can find a potential market for it. Students are sometimes dismayed to learn that successful writing demands successful salesmanship. But the truth is that having an agent to sell for them is impractical at this point. Agents like to represent established writers whose works will produce hefty commissions.

If you're a novice, the alternative is to learn how to make your own sales, either by persuasively describing your article idea by phone or by writing an effective query letter. A query is really a sales letter for an article that does not yet exist. Still, proposing an idea to an editor before writing the article saves a great deal of time and effort. The idea may not fit the market you have in mind, or you may encounter a dozen other obstacles that you can't control. Your concept may need to be refined or shifted from its original shape before an editor will give you a contract to proceed with the writing.

In fact, for every article idea you submit, the editor has four potential reactions: 1) enthusiastic acceptance, 2) strong interest but no guarantee to buy, 3) guarded interest if certain changes are made, or 4) flat rejection. Your next move depends on which of these reactions you receive.

If you decide to call rather than to write, the editor may either reject your idea and give you some reason for doing so, or react with interest and tell you that the idea has possibilities and the submission editors would like to hear more about it. In that case, you respond at once, giving details about your concept, how you plan to develop your ideas and conduct your research. Such a letter should be a tempting sample of the article you have in mind.

Whether you call or write, immediate acceptance is probably years ahead for you. Editors will agree to buy articles sight unseen only from writers whose work they know well. But it is not unusual for editors to like your idea and encourage you to complete the article **on speculation**. That means they make no promises to buy it; they will merely consider it. In that case, if you are willing to gamble, you can complete your research and write the article, fired with the thought that at least your work has potential.

If the editor likes your subject but suggests a different slant, your willingness to write to his specifications will enhance your chances of success. Unless he has asked you to change your concept beyond recognition or to make a point you don't believe in, a different direction is worth trying.

If you receive a flat rejection, of course, you must query another carefully chosen magazine or abandon the project.

No matter what the reaction, you're better off for having queried.

EFFECTIVE QUERY LETTERS

The query letter may be the most difficult writing you have ever done. A showcase for your skills, it must be clearly and gracefully written. Its organization, word choice, sentence structure, and mechanics must be impeccable. It must be obvious that you know the magazine target well: Don't propose an article to *Ms.* magazine on how to prepare a souffle; you will only irritate the editor. Without gushing, the query letter must sell your idea. Without rambling, it must pinpoint your thesis and describe how the idea will be researched and developed. Without exaggerating, it must tell why you are qualified to write on your subject.

Before you begin, check the masthead of a recent issue of the magazine for the name of a specific editor to address but steer away from the editor-in-chief or the managing editor: they seldom read queries. *Writer's Market* usually lists the correct person to contact, but turnover is high in the magazine field and you want to be sure you're writing to someone still on the staff. Avoid having to say "Dear Editor."

It will help to think for a moment about the editors' state of mind when they read through the queries that have accumulated while they labored to put the last issue to bed. The deadline pressures are relentless, so the pile of letters is probably high. Magazines like *Cosmopolitan* receive hundreds each day. Still, article editors approach their desks with certain expectations. They are as eager to find a good new writer as you are to be discovered. But experience has taught them that most of these letters will be poor indeed. Consequently, they scan each one with faint hope, probably glancing first to see if any *look* professional. A well formatted letter, preferably typed on a computer and printed on good quality paper with the highest resolution printer you can find, is guaranteed to get a closer reading than one that looks pale and shabby.

Oblivious to the competition in freelancing and ignorant of the editor's expectations, novices often submit letters with misspelled words, cliches, incoherent organization, and too little concrete detail about the article idea. Any one of these errors may lead to a rejection slip. Editors tend to be perfectionists who are convinced that a carelessly written letter indicates a muddy mind.

Make it a pleasure to read your query by limiting it to one page or a page and a half. And either keep your paragraphs short or compose a one-sentence paragraph to open up the page with white space. For correct form, see the sample queries at the end of this chapter. (Include your address, phone number, and date even though they were omitted from the samples.) It's a good idea to type QUERY above the salutation, and it's a *must* to include a self-addressed stamped envelope (SASE).

The first sentence has to shine. It must either be written with flair and imagination or propose a striking new idea. For example: "Would you be interested in an article on five surprising ways to make a million dollars?" After this opener, the letter could plunge into a specific description of how you will develop the topic. If you know a brief anecdote about how one person, to everyone's astonishment, made a million dollars, include it in your description. Some writers compose the lead of the article and use it as the first paragraph of the query. In that case the second paragraph should begin with the explanation that the preceding one is the tentative lead of an article for *Money* magazine. Succeeding paragraphs should describe how you plan to continue the article, including the people you plan to interview and indicating the article's tone (humorous, satirical, authoritative, or straighforward).

Your letter must be specific rather than vague or general. It must show that you know exactly what you want to say in the article, and it should show energy and enthusiasm without going overboard.

If you have published before, list the best-known publications in which your work has appeared, and include a clipping of your best piece. If you're a beginner, make no apologies. Think of yourself, and conduct yourself, as a professional.

Avoid implying that the article has already been written. You are proposing an *idea* for an article. And end the letter with a request for the editor's reaction to that idea.

These instructions may sound as though the query letter is written to a formula. Not so. The less like a formula it sounds, the better. It should be as fresh and personal as you can make it without being chatty. In addressing it to a specific editor you are showing that you want to speak to him personally about a subject of mutual interest. Try to see him as a human being who wants to find good material for his magazine.

If your proposed article is long and complex, an outline query may be more suitable than a brief letter. This kind of "outline" does not have Roman numerals and subheadings. It is simply a much more complete description of your article, detailing the information to be covered in each of its sections. You might fill in the details for the following hypothetical divisions: The article will begin with a story of how one woman made a million dollars with a mail-order business operated out of her kitchen. The next section will discuss the characteristics millionaires share and the principles they follow in making money. The third section will tell the stories of how four other people have used those same techniques and how the reader also can use them for financial success.

Remember, the preceding sentences are merely the skeleton of an outline for a hypothetical article. In actuality you would fill it in with many details, ending up with several pages in contrast to the usual short query letter.

Finally, you would enclose a brief letter saying that you are including an outline for a proposed article on five ways to make a million dollars, and ask for a reaction to it.

THE QUESTION OF SIMULTANEOUS QUERIES

Controversy has arisen about one area of proposing an idea for an article: Should you send out simultaneous queries? The temptation to do so is strong because editors are sometimes extremely slow in responding. Some freelancers complain that they can not make a living if they are confined to sending out one query at a time. They insist that simultaneous submissions are perfectly fair if they inform editors of what they are doing. Acknowledging that they could receive more than one acceptance which would place them in a dilemma, they say that such success is too rare to prohibit the practice.

There are, however, real objections to simultaneous queries. Some edtiors resent them and refuse to consider such proposals. Other editors say this practice gives them an initial negative reaction to the idea unless it is exceptionally appealing. And if they discover that you have queried other editors about the same idea, they may put you on their black list.

Your choice of the best process will probably depend on the geographic separation of your potential markets. If they are not considered competitive with each other, simultaneous submissions would be all right. But most people would consider it unprofessional and self-defeating to send proposals to two similar magazines with a near identical readership.

TELEPHONE QUERIES

Instead of writing a letter to sell an article idea, you may prefer to make a telephone call. If you're better at expressing yourself orally than in writing or if you're acquainted with the editor, this might be the best approach. Or if you have several ideas for a particular magazine in your locale, by all means call the editor and make an appointment to discuss your ideas. Phone calls are ideal for writers who have established a professional relationship with an editor. But some of them are irritated by phone calls from strangers, especially beginning writers. They want something in writing that they can think about and show to their colleagues in editorial conferences. And most of all, many editors want to see a sample of your writing. That's what a query letter gives them.

HOW TO REACT TO REJECTION

The most common response, the one you dread but should be prepared for, is a printed rejection slip. Even worse is no answer at all. In either case, your only consolation is that you wrote a query rather than the whole article. But don't give up so soon. Revise your letter for another suitable market. In fact, you should repeat this process many times.

Recognize that luck is almost always a part of selling. What one person finds distasteful, another gulps hungrily. But elements other than differences in taste sometimes determine your luck. On the day he reads your query, the editor may be in a sour mood so that nothing sounds interesting to him. Or he may simply overlook your letter and inadvertently put it in the reject pile. An article very similar to yours may already be scheduled for publication; there is no way you could have known this from your study of *Reader's Guide* or *Writer's Market* or from your examination of recent issues of the target magazine.

Another consolation in the face of rejection is to remind yourself that not all famous writers were immediately appreciated. You must be persistent enough to continue querying editors until you find one who likes your work. You must be ambitious enough to continue to learn by writing and rewriting and tough enough to take rejections without giving up.

It's difficult to know what to do if you hear nothing from an editor you have queried. Most beginners wait for three or four weeks before sending a polite reminder that they want to be sure their letter has been received and that they would appreciate a decision as soon as possible. If there is still no response, they feel free to query another magazine.

Sometimes you will receive a printed rejection slip with a handwritten note on it. If a busy editor takes the time to write even one sentence, you can take it as a slight encouragement.

Or rejoice if you receive a cautious reply to your query that says your idea has possibilities and that if you care to complete the article, the editor will look at it on speculation. To this reaction, write a gracious response immediately and, if you're willing to write without a guaranteed sale, say that you will begin to work on the article at once.

Suppose an editor responds with a personal letter to you rather than with a printed thank-you-but-no form. It may include suggestions about changing your slant to make the proposed article more compatible to the magazine's readers or other editorial needs. Such a response is cause for celebration, and it's probably worth going to the trouble of writing the article according to the suggestions, although you have no contract. Answer promptly and appreciatively and say when the completed manuscript, revised as suggested, will arrive. Under these circumstances your chances of making a sale are fairly good. Even if the article doesn't sell, the editor will most likely remember your work, and you may make the sale with another story in the future.

What if an editor gives you a contract to write an article you have proposed but decides not to publish the completed article? Most reputable magazines will pay a "kill fee" in this case, usually a percentage of the fee originally offered.

ONE EDITOR'S RARE RESPONSE

It's extremely rare for an editor to take the time to write a long personal letter to a beginner, but on the following page is an example of one who did. The student queried *Southern* (no longer in print), proposing an idea for an article on the effect of imprisonment on mothers. The editor's response contains many concrete suggestions for writing effective queries, and it vividly shows "how an editor's mind works." It deserves careful study by ambitious freelancers.

Unsolicited Manuscripts

Although editors insist that they spurn unsolicited manuscripts, once in a while they do buy them. Occasionally freelancers sell articles, especially short or humorous ones, by sending them unannounced to carefully chosen magazines along with a self-addressed stamped envelope and a brief cover letter. But by far the more professional and practical sales method is to write a deftly worded query letter that blooms with fresh ideas.

SUMMARY

1. The query letter should be written (or the phone call made) after background research has been done but before writing the article.
2. Addressed to a specific editor by name, a good query is a sales letter showing that you write well, that you have a fresh subject, and that the slant and treatment are suitable for the editor's magazine.
3. The first sentence of a query is crucial. If it's drab, many editors will read no further.
4. The letter should include your qualifications for writing the article and show that you are fully familiar with the editor's magazine.
5. To make a favorable impression, a query must look professional: mechanically perfect with no strikeovers or mistakes in spelling, grammar, or form.
6. It must enthusiastically but realistically describe your idea. A conceited tone could be fatal.
7. The letter should include your name, address, telephone number with area code, and date.

SOUTHERN
MAGAZINE

Dear Vickie:

Thanks for sending me your query about women in prison, but I'm afraid it doesn't sound to me like a story that's exactly right for SOUTHERN. I understand you're a student of Betsy Graham's, so if you're game, I'll try to tell you why the story doesn't strike me as right for us. That might give you a sense of how an editor's mind works, and help you in future queries - though I caution that all editors, like all people, are individuals, and what appeals to one may not appeal to all. Still, you can take the following for what it's worth.

The main problems I had with your query are that (1) it didn't tell me why your story was unique and (2) it didn't tell me why your story should be done _now_. On this specific point, since we cover 13 states, I have to have some reason for doing a story in one state over another. Why should I be interested in mothers in prison in Georgia more than mothers in prison in Kentucky or Louisiana or Virginia? For ATLANTA or a Georgia magazine, the Georgia specificity makes sense; people want to read about their neighbors. But for a national magazine (which is basically what we are) you have to make some sort of case for your choice of locale. Is Georgia a leader in brutality/reform/interest/lack of interest? Do you know a specific case there that, while not unique, illuminates the broader regional/national story? Is there something about the story in Georgia that would make someone who doesn't live in Georgia care what that state's officials have to say about the issue? That's the sort of thing you need to consider.

Then there's the question of "Why now?" The women/mothers in prison is actually a pretty old story. Newspapers and TV stations have dealt with it time and again until it's almost become cliche. That doesn't mean it isn't important, but it does mean that you have to have a way of grabbing a reader's (or editor's) attention, and the topic alone won't do that. You either have to have a story that is so humanly compelling that it overwhelms all argument, or have a new angle/event/attitude that justifies taking a new look at an old situation. Granted, sometimes magazines and newspapers revive old issues for no reason other than an editor somewhere has become interested in it again, but you can't really depend on catching an editor just at the time he/she is mulling over your topic. If you do, you may run into the problem of the editor already having chosen a writer for the topic.

What you need to do as much as possible (and it's easier to say it than do it) is make your query seem urgent/on the edge/immediate. If you have a very specific story to tell - one person's tragedy/adventure - that matters less, but if you're querying on what is basically a broad topic, then that matters more. You have to explain why people should/would care about the topic, and especially why _now_. That can be hard to do, and that's why the more specific a query can be, the better. If your query, for example, had started out detailing the plight of a woman arrested and jailed for stealing money to buy her kids a bike, only to find out she could have no contact with her infants, and then finding further that her problem was not a unique problem - well, you'd have more of a story to grab with, and less need to strike an editor at just the right time. It still wouldn't have sold to me simply because I'd still think women in prison is an old issue, but it would have caused me to contemplate the possibility of a story more.

Hope this helps more than intimidates; it's meant in that spirit, anyway. And one final bit of advice - if you can find a typewriter that types in other than script, I'd use it. A script letter just looks frivolous, and your letter makes clear that you aren't frivolous. A script query won't be rejected out of hand, but it will start you off on the wrong foot, sort of like going to a job interview in a prom dress or a tuxedo. That doesn't mean you won't do the job marvelously well, but it's not necessarily the best first impression. Be informal and friendly in the content of the letter, not the look, and you'll probably get a slightly better first reading.

Yours,

Mitchell J. Shields
Senior Editor

FROM PRINCIPLES TO PRACTICE

1. Analyze the sample query letters that follow to assess their strengths and weaknesses.
2. Which letters would you respond to positively as an editor? Explain the reasons for positive as well as negative reactions.
3. Write a query letter for the article you are planning and researching. Use the above summary as a checklist for its effectiveness before submitting it. Be especially careful to delete all clichés, thus showing that you value variety and freshness and that you write with simplicity and clarity.

Mr. Marion L. Salzman
<u>Career Vision</u>
600 Madison Avenue
14th Floor
New York, New York 10020

Dear Mr. Salzman:

When summer rolls around, many young people seek boring summer jobs in department stores or fast food restaurants. But not all of them. Some young adults attempt to combine travel, adventure, fun, <u>and</u> work by applying for a job in a national park. I know from my own experience what a wonderful opportunity this is, and I would like to tell your readers about it.

I spent two summers in Yellowstone National Park making friends from all over the world and physically working harder than I ever have in my life. The hard work was worth it, though, for the opportunity to live in such beautiful and peaceful surroundings.

I am drawing on my experience in Yellowstone to write an article that informs young people of this excellent job opportunity. I'll offer them tips on where to get applications and what to expect should they apply and get hired.

I believe that your readers would benefit from my experience, and I would like to submit the article to you on speculation. I look forward to hearing from you soon.

Sincerely,

Leigh Hilliard

At first glance Ms. Hilliard's letter looks as if she has done everything right: editor addressed by name, correct form, no mechanical errors, article described, value to readers pointed out, freelancer's credentials given, willingness to write on speculation stated. But if you were the editor looking for exciting new material, would you respond positively to this query?

The letter needs a big shot of adrenaline to give it drama, uniqueness, concrete detail—in short, energy and enthusiasm. It sounds bland, careful, almost bored. Look at the cliché in the first four words. Are any of the words really arresting? Does the writer *show* the fun and adventure such an exotic setting would provide? Does she show that she has thought deeply about this valuable experience? Does she show her individual style or outlook?

The writer was capable of bringing this letter to life, but in writing the first draft of her first query letter, she seemed too inhibited to let her idea leap off the page. But leap it must.

Mr. Jeff Fellenzer
Travel Department
Los Angeles Times
Times Mirror Square
Los Angeles, CA 90053

Dear Mr. Fellenzer:

Have you ever wondered if there was a suitcase junkyard? A final destination for all the unclaimed baggage rotating around those airport carousels? If you've ever lost baggage on an airline flight, have you asked, as I did, where does it all go?

One place it lands is Scottsboro, Alabama. In a store called Unclaimed Baggage are the piles of old suitcases that could not be traced - also their contents. Here, one might find a wedding gown, a designer sweater, or Aunt Agatha's brooch. It's all there at Unclaimed.

I've visited Unclaimed many times and have made some dandy purchases (it's cheap!). Are you interested in an 800+ word article on this fascinating place?

I am a widely published travel and food writer, based in Atlanta. A weekly cuisine column under my byline is also published by Creative Loafing in Atlanta. My credits and clips are enclosed.

I'm looking forward to hearing from you.

Sincerely,

Helen M. Friese

Helen M. Friese

Enclosed: clips

This successful query led to the publication of Friese's article in the *Los Angeles Times Magazine*.

Ms. Lisa Bain
Articles Editor
<u>Glamour</u>
350 Madison Avenue
New York, NY 10017

QUERY

Dear Ms. Bain:

After having lived with my boyfriend for two years I remember the excitement and newness of discovering his habits. He loved to read in the bathtub in the morning and he went through a funny ritual of styling his hair. But there were disturbing discoveries too: He smoked marijuana before he went to work in the morning and again when he returned at night.

All along he insisted he was just a casual user: it "helped him to relax." To him it "was no big deal." But I watched this "no big deal" and "harmless" drug sap his energy and motivation, give him a hunger that made him balloon from 190 pounds to 265 pounds, and trick him into forgetting career goals and focusing only on the present.

I felt powerless.

He didn't want to admit he had a problem, and I felt too foolish to seek help. After all, I reminded myself, it's only marijuana. But the more I watched him sitting on the sofa, smoking joints and stuffing his face, while I cooked and cleaned, did my school work, and prepared for work the next day, the more angry, disgusted, and bitter I became.

He refused to discuss his problem or do anything at all to change. So I decided to do something. I left. Those who say casual drug use is harmless are only kidding themselves. I watched it slowly suck the life away from someone I loved.

I believe that my article "The Casual Killer" would interest your readers, and I'd like to send it to you - on speculation. I look forward to hearing from you.

Sincerely,

Jennifer A. Cogelia

Jennifer A. Cogelia

A college magazine would have been a better target for this query than *Glamour,* but the letter is a good sample of the article the student had in mind. Note, however, that a justified right margin creates distracting gaps between words and sentences.

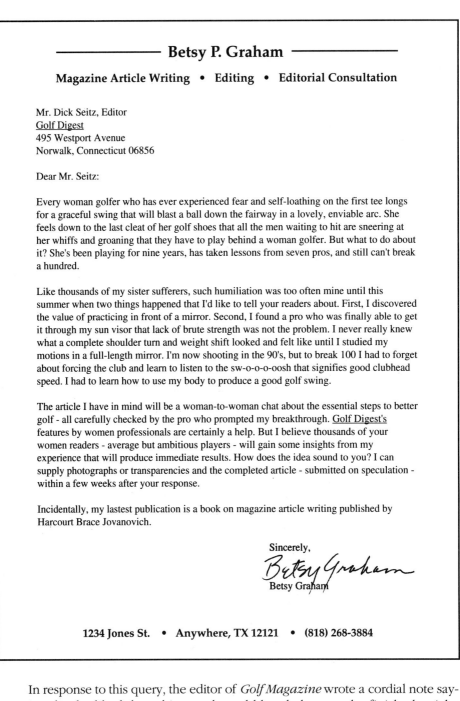

————— **Betsy P. Graham** —————

Magazine Article Writing • Editing • Editorial Consultation

Mr. Dick Seitz, Editor
<u>Golf Digest</u>
495 Westport Avenue
Norwalk, Connecticut 06856

Dear Mr. Seitz:

Every woman golfer who has ever experienced fear and self-loathing on the first tee longs for a graceful swing that will blast a ball down the fairway in a lovely, enviable arc. She feels down to the last cleat of her golf shoes that all the men waiting to hit are sneering at her whiffs and groaning that they have to play behind a woman golfer. But what to do about it? She's been playing for nine years, has taken lessons from seven pros, and still can't break a hundred.

Like thousands of my sister sufferers, such humiliation was too often mine until this summer when two things happened that I'd like to tell your readers about. First, I discovered the value of practicing in front of a mirror. Second, I found a pro who was finally able to get it through my sun visor that lack of brute strength was not the problem. I never really knew what a complete shoulder turn and weight shift looked and felt like until I studied my motions in a full-length mirror. I'm now shooting in the 90's, but to break 100 I had to forget about forcing the club and learn to listen to the sw-o-o-o-oosh that signifies good clubhead speed. I had to learn how to use my body to produce a good golf swing.

The article I have in mind will be a woman-to-woman chat about the essential steps to better golf - all carefully checked by the pro who prompted my breakthrough. <u>Golf Digest's</u> features by women professionals are certainly a help. But I believe thousands of your women readers - average but ambitious players - will gain some insights from my experience that will produce immediate results. How does the idea sound to you? I can supply photographs or transparencies and the completed article - submitted on speculation - within a few weeks after your response.

Incidentally, my lastest publication is a book on magazine article writing published by Harcourt Brace Jovanovich.

Sincerely,

Betsy Graham
Betsy Graham

1234 Jones St.   •   Anywhere, TX 12121   •   (818) 268-3884

In response to this query, the editor of *Golf Magazine* wrote a cordial note saying that he liked the subject and would be glad to see the finished article. Unfortunately, the writer was too busy teaching magazine article writing to do her own homework, and she never wrote the article.

McCall's

Dear Contributor:

Thank you for your article suggestion. It has been read by members of our staff, and we regret that it does not meet our current editorial needs. We are sorry that the large number of queries we receive makes it impossible for us to offer individual comment.

We wish you success in placing your proposal elsewhere, and appreciate your interest in <u>McCall's</u>.

Sincerely,

The Editors

Your Query inspired such interest that it did make the rounds of editors, but was unfortunately vetoed by the upper echelons. Thanks, though.

230 Park Avenue, New York, N.Y. 10169

Here is a sample of the kind of encouraging reply that editors sometimes add to a rejection slip.

CHAPTER

7

MAKING A
SIGNIFICANT POINT

When you begin to put words on paper, those words must make a point. In short, you must have a thesis. Unfortunately, the word *thesis* has a poor image: it brings to mind dusty dissertations and hard work. But even more unfortunately, a surprising number of would-be writers do not know what it means. It simply means the *point* of a piece of writing. Every effective article has both a topic *and* a thesis. The two are not the same. The function of the thesis is to narrow the topic for the writer and to hand the reader a road map that will show where he or she is being led.

For example, suppose you've decided to write an article about surfing. You've thereby reduced the field of potential topics to one human endeavor, but surfing is still a broad subject that could lead in a dozen directions. The point could be made that surfing is one of the most dangerous of all sports, or that it is a peculiarly demanding sport to learn, or that there are certain areas in the world's oceans where surfing is exciting because of the kinds of waves prevalent there. Still another possibility would be to tell the reader how to surf or to describe some of today's best surfers. The article might present a psychological profile of a typical person who is attracted to surfing or a personality profile of one particular surfer who has become a legend for unusual courage and skill. Aware of all these possibilities, you might begin by reading up on surfing in a general, almost random, way to get a clearer grasp of what you would like to say. But eventually you must settle on one point. Then, with your destination chosen, you can find the roads to take you there. You can complete your research, looking only for evidence that will help prove your point. No matter how novel or fascinating a fact the research uncovers, if it does not help prove or support the thesis, it will have to be ignored.

To learn to recognize the distinction between topic and thesis, begin now to read with a new awareness of thesis statements, their importance to the reader, the way they are worded, and their location in articles.

PLACEMENT OF THE THESIS

In some cases the first sentence tells what point the author wants to make. Sometimes the thesis will appear in the last sentence of the lead paragraph. In other instances, you will look for it in vain until the fourth or fifth paragraph. And in still others the point will be implied rather than stated. But no matter what the form, it must not be delayed too long. In that case the reader may give up on making sense of the article and stop reading.

Readers will be doubly bewildered if there *is* no thesis. Because of the resulting incoherence, they will soon get the feeling they're reading something like a phone book which contains a list of unrelated names. They will wonder why they are being told these particular facts. Readers usually know what an article's topic is by the title or the illustrations, but before they have read too far they must know with certainty what point the writer is trying to make *about* the topic, and the point must seem significant.

The thesis statements in the following excerpts from articles, some by students and some by professionals, appear in bold type.

The first example appeared in *The New Yorker* under the title "Shanghai Blues." The author, William Zinsser, states his thesis in the place of honor: the first words of the first sentence. The rest of the first paragraph is included here to put the thesis into context.

Jazz came to China for the first time on the afternoon of June 2, 1981, when the American bassist and French-horn player Willie Ruff introduced himself and his partner, the pianist Dwike Mitchell, to several hundred students and professors who were crowded into a large room at the Shanghai Conservatory of Music. The students and professors were all expectant, without knowing quite what to expect. They only knew that they were about to hear the first American jazz concert ever presented to the Chinese. Probably they were not surprised to find that the two musicians were black, though black Americans are a rarity in the People's Republic. What they undoubtedly didn't expect was that Ruff would talk to them in Chinese, and when he began they murmured with delight.

The long but easy to read opening sentence in the paragraph above puts readers perfectly at ease by telling them who, what, where, when, why, and how. It's a little unusual in magazine writing to find, newspaper fashion, the famous five W's in the first sentence. But here these facts serve readers well by letting them know they are about to read an article on what it was like when Chinese students first heard American jazz. Later in the paragraph the significance of the subject is stressed with the words "the first American jazz concert *ever*." And the undercurrent of irony in the situation nudges the reader on: jazz, that most American of all music forms, played for Chinese students by black Americans using a classy-sounding instrument, the French horn. Zinsser is an artist who uses his own instrument—words—with consummate skill.

Here's another entirely different example that contains a two-sentence thesis appearing at the end of a very short lead paragraph. In this instance, the purpose of the piece is purely for entertainment, not for information, and the tone, therefore, is light and playful. No matter how amusing or even trivial an article may be, however, the writer must still make a point. Written by Rick Reilly, this article about the rebirth of golf appeared in *Sports Illustrated*.

Yo, golfers, come out of the sports closet. It's O.K. Bring those saddle shoes and fuzzy head covers with you. No need to hang your visors in shame. We have an announcement to make. **Golf isn't dorky anymore. Golf is cool.**

We're talking pants with actual belts and cotton shirts that won't start a three-alarm polyester fire. We're talking 3 1/2-hour rounds and caddies. Golf carts are out. They're actually building golf courses where you can walk again.

Golf is a trip. Jack Nicklaus is 50 and could leg-wrestle you to death. George Bush plays golf. So does Alice Cooper. Cripes, *Batman* plays golf. Willie Nelson has his own course and his own tournament. Dork has never been within three counties of Willie Nelson.

Tennis? Tennis is over there in the Goodwill pile with jogging and Jazzercise.

Few readers, settled down for an evening of casual reading, will say, "Aha, there's the thesis!" when they come upon the point plainly stated. It is important information they are used to being given. They absorb it and read on. This subconscious awareness of direction or focus is equally true of an implied thesis. A personality profile, for example, may not contain a sentence near the beginning that explicitly states "John Doe is an extremely unusual plumber" or "Reader, this article is going to show you what Meryl Streep is like off camera," but enough carefully selected and obviously related details will be given to show the direction the article will take.

Such is the case with the next excerpt from an article by Gary Smith that also appeared in *Sports Illustrated.* Entitled "Ali and His Entourage," the piece paints a remarkable portrait of Muhammad Ali by profiling the seven people who worked closely with him during his glory days. But no one sentence encapsulates the thesis. Instead, the author begins with a bleak scene that shows Ali as he is now in the grip of Parkinson's disease. Interpreted figuratively as well as literally, the last sentence shown here is really the point.

Around Muhammad Ali, all was decay. Mildewed tongues of insulation poked through gaps in the ceiling; flaking cankers pocked the painted walls. On the floor lay rotting scraps of carpet.

He was cloaked in black. Black street shoes, black socks, black pants, black short-sleeved shirt. He threw a punch, and in the small town's abandoned boxing gym, the rusting chain between the heavy bag and the ceiling rocked and creaked.

Slowly, at first, his feet began to dance around the bag. His left hand flicked a pair of jabs, and then a right cross and a left hook, too, recalled the ritual of butterfly and bee. The dance quickened. Black sunglasses flew from his pocket as he gathered speed, black shirttail flapped free, black heavy bag rocked and creaked. Black street shoes scuffed faster and faster across black moldering tiles. *Yeah, Lawd, champ can still float, champ can still sting!* He whirled, jabbed, feinted, let his feet fly into a shuffle. "How's that for a sick man?" he shouted.

He did it for a second three-minute round, then a third. "Time!" I shouted at the end of each one as the second hand swept past the 12 on the wristwatch he had handed to me. And then, gradually, his shoulders began to slump, his hands to drop. The tap and thud of leather soles and leather gloves began to miss a quarter-beat . . . half-beat . . . whole. All stopped and sucked air. **The dance was over.**

The following excerpt is from an interview with an American who was held hostage in Iran. It was published in *The Retired Officer,* its author a former student, Richard Daigle, who is now director of student publications at Emory

University. This article also begins with a scene, but in this case the narrative is followed by an expository paragraph that funnels down to the thesis.

In a dank, dimly lit room, the torture began. A rubber hose whipped out, biting into the back of the beaten man. Each successive strike stung like a jolt of electricity, raising yet another purple welt on the wounded skin. Stretched and tied face down over a desk with his terrorist tormentors gloating over him, the hardened military man could do nothing but hope to endure the punishment without "snapping."

"We will break you, Colonel Scott," sneered the terrorist that Scott had nicknamed Pig Face. Scott lashed back, cursing him. Instantly he felt a deep pressure penetrating the right side of his face, the first sensation of a heavy blow to the jaw from a steel pipe. The pressure gave way to piercing, knife-like pain. Scott tasted blood and felt pieces of teeth floating like pebbles in his mouth.

Before more damage was done, another terrorist, Hossein, entered the room and chided Pig Face for going too far—inflicting an injury that would be too noticeable and thus reflect poorly on the terrorists should they be discovered. Hossein brought an ice pack for Scott.

The true test of a man's integrity, says Col. Charles Scott, comes when his life is in the balance. Scott's test, which began Nov. 4, 1979, was a 444-day ordeal in Iran that gripped Americans like few modern-day crises have. To Scott the ordeal seems to have happened in another lifetime. But today he claims he is a better man for it. "You reach a point where you pass the limit of fear. **I learned a great deal about myself, but I also learned a great deal about the almost indefinable reservoir of strength each one of us has that we never even know is there until we get into one of these crisis situations.**"

•

The remainder of the article, entitled "A Former Iranian Hostage Looks Back," tells how Scott used that strength to outwit his tormentors and to save his life.

You may have already noted that the thesis sometimes appears or is suggested in the title, as was the case in the above selection. Even so, a hint is not enough. Careful writers rephrase the thesis at intervals throughout their stories. This subtle repetition gives readers the secure feeling that they are in the hands of a pro who is guiding them, logically and coherently, on an enjoyable journey.

The next excerpt to be examined for effective thesis placement appeared in a local publication soon after it became known that AIDS was spreading to the heterosexual community. Knowing that many readers might bypass an article on such a depressing subject, author Frida Ghitis deliberately delayed revealing the point she wanted to make until after arousing the readers' curiosity enough to keep them reading. The title, "Confronting Fear," raises some questions: Fear about what? And who is afraid? Then Ghitis further tantalizes by introducing two women characters without telling why they are significant and by sinking some ominous details into the text. Finally, just to be sure her readers will continue, she inserts the sentence "Life was about to change forever for Nancy and Jenny."

Nancy was careful when she looked for a new roommate almost two years ago. A youthful Atlanta-area divorcee with two small children, she was naturally cautious about bringing a stranger into her home. She finally settled on Jenny, a young woman from California who came highly recommended. It was never a secret that Jenny had used drugs. She had been an intravenous user, but was now clean and intended to continue her recovery from the addiction. Nancy was supportive of Jenny's efforts to make a better life for herself but wasn't prepared for what was in store for her and her new roommate. Life was about to change forever for Nancy and Jenny.

For Jenny, the change would involve a journey of physical and emotional pain both from the disease that was attacking her body and from the way her family and society would respond to it.

For Nancy, the journey would start with near-crippling fear and avoidance of her roommate's pain. **The need to educate herself in order to lessen her own fear would lead to a desire to help in her friend's lonely battle and culminate in a commitment to work in the fight against a modern-day tragedy—Acquired Immune Deficiency Syndrone—and to a new way of looking at life.** Up to this point Nancy had been satisfied to support herself and her children by taking in a roommate and working as a part-time tailor out of her home. She is now one of 500 volunteers working through AID Atlanta, this city's main means of dispensing AIDS education and help to PWAs (persons with AIDS). She speaks on AIDS awareness to groups throughout the city, and she has returned to school in hopes of making the teaching of "wellness" her profession.

The final example of effective thesis placement shows how some writers begin an article with rather general comments on a topic that may seem unrelated to the subject implied by the title. Then, by way of a skillful transition that begins a new paragraph, the writer slides into the thesis statement and all is suddenly clear. The lead paragraph was actually a very carefully designed preparation for the main business at hand. Thomas M. Disch uses this technique in "The Death of Broadway" which appeared in *The Atlantic*.

A city is a machine that works by inertia. By virtue of their solidity and expense, large buildings act as a brake on social change. Each one, from the most squalid tenement to the ritziest hotel, represents a way of life that has jelled into just this form and is jealous of its right to continue as is. Thus neighborhoods in the process of gentrification acquire graffiti threatening death to yuppie invaders, and all bastions of privilege hire doormen to defend them from riffraff. Finally, however, no single building, no street, no neighborhood, can hold its own against the glacial advance of larger, social forces.

Right now such a social glacier is poised at the edge of New York City's already much eroded theater district.

The remainder of the article, of course, is devoted to explaining what those social forces are.

If you have trouble wording a thesis statement, complete this sentence: This article will show that _____. In the preceding selection, the article shows that because of urban decay and unaffordable ticket prices, Broadway theaters will eventually die.

It is also helpful to ask yourself this question: What do I want to say *about* my subject? These suggestions seem almost too elementary to be given, but a surprising number of student writers turn in "completed" manuscripts without really knowing what point they wanted to make.

Another suggestion in phrasing the thesis is to state the point in one short, simple sentence. This does not have to be the final wording. Here it is merely stated for your own benefit.

A thesis may change as you research. For example, you may adopt a tentative thesis while researching your subject but at the same time remain open-minded to other, better directions. By the time you sit down to write the first draft, however, the thesis should be firm.

THE DIFFERENCE BETWEEN THESIS AND PURPOSE

Do not confuse the thesis and the purpose of an article. The purpose may be to inform, to entertain, to persuade, to clarify, to explain, or to stir up a particular emotion such as anger. In contrast, the thesis is a statement or assertion you want to make about the subject.

Having a focused thesis in mind is a crucial step in writing of any kind, even a personal letter. If you write a letter to your parents, the subject is probably you and your life away from home. If you write frequently, the subject may be your life in the last few days. You certainly don't have a formal thesis in mind when you sit down to write, but you do have a few specific things you want to say about your experiences in the last few days. You had two flat tires on the same day, one of your checks bounced, you have three term papers to write, and your throat feels sore. You cannot refrain from making the point, explicitly or implicitly, that life last week was miserable.

A thesis gives your writing a controlling idea. It provides unity, singleness of purpose, coherence. All the materials that you use to flesh out your article such as anecdotes, facts, comparisons, descriptions, and explanations must relate to your thesis. If they do not they must be ruthlessly pruned.

SUMMARY

1. A thesis is the specific point the writer makes about the topic. It provides a focus and guides the reader in a specific direction.
2. The thesis should be stated or implied near the beginning of the article.

FROM PRINCIPLES TO PRACTICE

1. Find and write out the thesis of two articles in the Appendix. Indicate whether you copied the authors' words or whether you had to write in your own words an implied thesis. Is the thesis stated in one sentence or spread out over two or more? In which paragraph does it appear?

2. In one of the articles specified by your instructor, copy each sentence that restates the thesis. Do these restatements seem repetitious or are they done with subtle variation?

3. Do the titles of either of the articles contain the thesis? If so, does this practice heighten or lessen the interest of the article?

4. Write out the name and a brief description of the proposed market for your article, the topic you have chosen, and a single-sentence thesis, all to be turned in to your instructor.

CHAPTER

8

FINDING FACTS
IN THE LIBRARY

One of the differences between a manuscript that sells and one that does not is the amount of authoritative information it contains. As a writer, you must learn how to conduct thorough and efficient research, including the use of electronic databases. If research brings to mind spending beautiful spring afternoons in a musty library while everyone else is picnicking or sunning at the beach, try to change your mindset. Think of yourself as an information detective. Solving mysteries is far more romantic than spading up facts from heavy reference books (though that, too, is part of putting the puzzle together). Tracking down the information you seek is also done in the real world, peering into the psyches of glamorous actresses or motorcyclists or zookeepers, talking with all kinds of people who live passionately. It can be participatory: taking part in an antiwar rally as many writers have done, or substituting for the quarterback in a Detroit Lions football game as George Plimpton has done. Or it can be saturation research as a student once did when he spent two weeks in a mountain commune immersing himself in the lives of believers in a strange new cult. Research is making phone calls and writing letters and visiting the setting of a person or issue you're investigating to give your article a solid sense of place.

Like other kinds of detective work, research has its dangers. It's easy to become addicted, partly because it can be exciting in itself and partly because it delays having to write. The difficulty is not where to find the energy to keep going but how to find the willpower to stop. There is also danger in believing everything you see in print. Many otherwise sophisticated people are inclined to have an exaggerated reverence for the printed word. Avoid this pitfall by double checking your information with knowledgeable people and reputable books and articles.

DEFINITIONS OF TERMS

Before you begin your research, it's important to review the definitions of terms you will encounter. Confusion about any of the following can make the process more difficult.

Abstract: A short summary of an article or other document, provided in some periodical indexes and equivalent databases.

Bibliography: A list of the works of a specific author or the sources about a specific subject, including a description and identification of the editions, dates of issue, and authorship. In other words, a bibliography tells you where to find information about a subject but it doesn't include the work itself.

Catalog: A complete list of items—books, authors, or subjects—arranged systematically (usually in alphabetical order) and often including descriptions of the listed items. A library's card catalog is an example.

CD-ROM: Compact-Disk Read-Only-Memory is an optical storage system similar to audio CDs. It allows large databases to be stored locally and searched with a microcomputer.

Database: An electronic file that may contain information from hundreds of magazines, newspapers, scholarly journals, and government reports. Usually made available to the researcher through a computer-telephone link provided by a public or academic library or through a personal computer with a modem.

Directory: A reference that includes addresses, telephone numbers, and information on memberships, publications, and other data about people, organizations, or institutions.

Index: An alphabetical list of the names and subjects included in a printed or electronic source that tells where the item may be found within that source.

Vendor: A company that acquires and maintains many databases from different publishers and makes them available through communication lines to users worldwide. For example, one of the largest vendors, DIALOG, offers six hundred databases through its large central computer, and more are being added all the time.

The best place to begin research on your topic is in the largest library near you. Get as much information as you can find on your own, consulting encyclopledias, almanacs, newspaper indexes, and indexes to periodicals such as the *Humanities Index* and *Readers' Guide to Periodical Literature*. Although you have probably already checked *Reader's Guide* in selecting your topic, you now need to find and read the pertinent articles themselves.

Then, when you have done as much independent research as you know how to do, introduce yourself to a *reference* librarian, not just anyone behind a desk. Tell this person you are researching a topic for a magazine article, describe your tentative thesis, list the sources you have consulted, and then ask advice on additional ones.

Reference librarians are clever about thinking up the right headings or key words under which to look for a particular piece of information. If you can't think of a precise heading, you may fail to learn about some of the most useful sources. Even the card catalog (some would say *especially* the card catalog) sometimes seems to hide information because of its strange classifications. For example, if you're interested in tombstones you have to look under Sepulchral Monuments.

A reference librarian can solve such mysteries and uncover sources you never dreamed existed.

LEARNING TO RESEARCH BY COMPUTER

The first advice a research expert may give you is to use books and periodicals as well as the computer in your search. Despite what many people think, the computer has by no means replaced paper (more about this later). But if you are writing on a topic of current interest, one that has been written about recently even though it may pertain to ancient history, a reference librarian may take you to a computer and ask you to describe the topic as precisely as possible. Together you will begin thinking of key words and their synonyms that pinpoint your subject and thesis. Computer research involves an electronic search through a huge pool of documents to locate words that match your key words, thus extracting the information you seek. Otherwise, pinpointing facts within a comprehensive bank of national and even international sources could be like searching for a face once seen in the window of a passing train.

Of course, before beginning the search itself, you and the librarian must first narrow the general pool of information. First, you will choose an appropriate database, one that contains material related to your topic.

That was the process carried out recently when a print-oriented freelancer asked a university librarian to lead her through the process of researching a topic by computer. She chose the same subject as the student mentioned in Chapter 4: kids who kill. To begin, she and the reference librarian, David Burke, settled on the following key words placed in two groups as the parentheses indicate: (*kids, children, teens,* or *teenagers*) and (*kill* or *murder*). Burke first chose to tap into one of the largest and most popular vendors, DIALOG, and then to add other databases of different types to the search. In each case, the computer did a lightning-fast search through thousands of documents, looking for a match or a "hit" to some of the key words. The result, which Burke had perhaps anticipated, was too many matches. (In just one database the key words appeared in 1,514 documents!) Finally Burke tried another database called "Magazine ASAP," and at the same time he narrowed the key words to *kids* and *kill*. Using this combination of only two words, the search yielded a manageable number of sources: four articles.

At that point, he gave the computer the command to print abstracts of those four, thus allowing the writer to choose two articles that seemed closest to the target topic. In a few minutes they had printouts of two helpful articles from *U.S. News and World Report* and *Woman's Day.*

The cost for computer research depends on the length of time you're "on line" (actually using a database). For this search, including the printouts, the cost was $47. Without copies of the articles, the cost would have been about $25. If asked, the computer will give you an estimate of the cost as you proceed.

At this particular library, databases for sociology, psychology, and education are available at no cost on CD-ROM, so it is a good idea to ask if your library offers such a useful service.

Note that some databases give you bibliographies only; others can provide abstracts of documents and full texts, usually a far more useful service.

No single catalog lists all the databases now available because new ones are being compiled and old ones updated at too fast a pace to be listed in one publication. The most comprehensive source to date is the *Directory of Online Databases,* revised quarterly and published by Cuadra and Elsevier.

COMBINING COMPUTER AND PAPER RESEARCH

For professional writers, scientists, medical personnel, psychologists, economists, businessmen, lawyers, and people in almost every information-hungry profession, computer research has been a godsend. Yet if it is so wide-reaching, fast, and current, why use those old-fashioned books and the cumbersome card catalog at all?

The answer is that the information stored in databases in most cases goes back only to about 1970. So for now, at least, computer research will yield only part of the picture if your topic has a history that goes back farther than that date. Moreover, even much current information is unavailable through databases. Consequently, you still need to use books and periodicals. And even for conducting paper research, you may still occasionally need the help of a good reference librarian.

Many references described in the remainder of this chapter are available in databases *and* in paper form. Follow your preference as to which you will use, but remember the limitations as well as the benefits of computer research.

WHERE TO LOOK FOR GENERAL INFORMATION

The following list of general references is extremely limited, but these sources are among the most useful for freelancers, especially when they're acquiring general background on a chosen topic.

About People

The *Biography and Genealogy Master Index* will send you to the right source about notable persons from all over the world, living or dead. For comprehensive and readable essays on contemporary personalities, consult *Current Biography.*

Biography Index contains facts about experts in various occupations. It contains biographies of such people as Mahatma Gandhi, General Norman Swartzkopf, and Kevin Costner, and indexes to such activities as skiing, skating, song writing, truck driving, politics, religion, crime, and journalism.

Who's Who in America outlines famous living persons' achievements. Other similar sources include *Who Was Who, Dictionary of American Biography, Who's Who in the West* (and all other regions), *Who Knows—and What, Who's Who of American Women, World Who's Who in Science,* and the British *Who's Who.*

The *Encyclopedia of Associations* tells how to contact the organizations that people belong to because of their interest in various hobbies, sports, and professions. The following sample of those listed shows that associations reflect some of the major issues of our society and therefore offer rich topics for writers: California Wilderness Survival League (932 members); Section on Gay and Lesbian Legal issues (100 law teachers); Center for Coastal Studies (1600 members); National Dance-Exercise Instructors' Training Association (27,000 members); and Surrogates by Choice, a group organized to support surrogate parenting as an alternative to childlessness (100 members).

About Public Affairs

Public Affairs Information Service Bulletin, known as PAIS (also available by computer), indexes by subject current books, pamphlets, magazine articles, and government documents in the field of economics and public affairs. It covers material published in English from all over the world and includes such subjects as crack, AIDS, advertising, abortion, busing of school children, city planning, housing, job hunting, and the Mafia.

Facts on File publishes a weekly world news summary called the *Facts on File News Digest,* along with a twice monthly cumulative index to the subjects, people, organizations, countries, and U.S. companies covered in its articles. For the latest developments on any issue or the actions of any newsworthy person or organization, the *News Index* is a good place to begin your search.

The New York Times Index, in addition to an index to its entire contents, contains summaries of news stories and articles on social and political issues. If your subject is local or regional, ask the librarian about indexes for newspapers published near you.

Monthly Catalog of U.S. Government Publications and the *Congressional Quarterly Weekly Reports* are important guides to the great number of books, periodicals, and pamphlets published by the U.S. Government, the largest publisher in the world. All of these documents can be quoted without permission.

Statistical Abstract provides statistics on what Americans do or buy or use, such as how many families own television sets, two cars, vacation homes, VCRs, what percentage of the work force now consists of women, how diets have changed in the last decade, and on and on. Another good source for statistical information is *American Demographics.*

About Books on Any Topic

Books in Print is a multivolume index published annually. It lists by author, title, and subject most of the books still in print in the United States. *Subject Guide to Books in Print* is a more manageable two-volume companion to use when you want to know what books are now available on a particular topic, regardless of author and title. No library will contain all these books, but a reference librarian can tell you how to borrow those you need from the interlibrary loan system.

These brief recommendations of useful research tools do not include descriptions of such obvious and well-known works as the *Information Please Almanac, World Alamanc,* or *The Guinness Book of World Records.* There are other omissions, too; a complete list would be a small library in itself.

SPECIALIZED IN-DEPTH RESEARCH SOURCES

Sheehy's Guide to Reference Books, often called the reference bible, is an invaluable source for in-depth research in a special area. You may be familiar with several general encyclopedias, but many people are surprised to discover such specialized ones as the *Encyclopedia of Pop, Rock, and Soul, The Encyclopedia of Furniture, Scarne's Encyclopedia of Games, An Encyclopedia of Fairies, Encyclopedia of Mystery and Detection,* or many others on an astonishing variety of subjects. For example, suppose you want to write a definitive article on suicide among war orphans. *Sheehy's Guide to Reference Books* would send you to *Bibliography on Suicide and Suicide Prevention* by Norman L. Farberow. This tireless bibliographer has done an impressive amount of research for you. In one fourteen-year period alone, he lists 2,542 titles, some of which might help you with war orphans' special problems.

Subject Collections: A Guide to Special Book Collections in Libraries or the *American Library Directory* tell you where special collections are housed. They also give you an idea of the amazing variety of subjects about which people have collected documents and memorabilia: sewing machines, ships, baseball, and such persons as famed architect Frank Lloyd Wright or songwriter Johnny Mercer, for a small sample.

TAKING NOTES

Taking notes while conducting research is an individual matter, but two suggestions may help. Use index cards instead of sheets of paper and confine the notes you put on each card to one aspect of your subject. At the top of the card write a key word to indicate the nature of the note, then take the trouble to write down the source, author, page number, and date of publication if the source is a magazine. Even though you may not always use all of this information, it is surprising how often you will need it or an editor will ask for it.

When you copy word for word from a source, be sure to use quotation marks to distinguish this material from other selections you merely paraphrased. Otherwise, in transposing this material to your manuscript, you may have forgotten what you must quote word for word and what you can summarize or simplify, without quotation marks.

Footnotes are rarely used in popular magazines. Instead, the source of a quotation or paraphrase is included in your text with the borrowed material. Here is an example:

"One of the underestimated tasks in nonfiction writing is to impose narrative shape on an unwieldy mass of material," says former Yale professor William Zinsser in *Writing to Learn.*

Clearly, notetaking is as individual as your thumbprint. Over time, you will find your own style for speed and efficiency. But for locating the most fruitful sources, their overwhelming volume and complexity brings us back to the first recommendation: get to know a reference librarian. The good ones are priests of their profession; you are merely a disciple.

SUMMARY

1. A reference librarian can be of help in finding sources unknown to you and in identifying the proper headings that lead the way to specific information. Otherwise, consult the *Library of Congress Subject Headings.*
2. Before trying to perform computer research, ask a reference librarian to demonstrate the procedure for you.
3. Remember that most database material goes back no farther than 1970,

so professionals use both computer and paper research to cover the most important sources.

4. For information on news events and issues, consult *The New York Times Index, Public Affairs Information Service Bulletin,* and *Facts on File Index.*

5. For biographical material, see *Biographical Dictionaries Master Index, Current Biography, Biography Index,* and *Subject Guide to Books in Print.*

FROM PRINCIPLES TO PRACTICE

1. Suppose you decide to write an article on cave exploring. You know people who enjoy the sport, but you've never tried it yourself. Test your ability to do preliminary research on this subject by answering the following questions:

   a. How could you find out if there is an association of cave explorers?

   b. If there is one, what information would you request in a letter or call to its headquarters?

   c. While you are waiting for this information, how would you use your library facilities for building a general background of knowledge about the sport? List specific sources that should be consulted.

   d. How could you find out if there are any famous cave explorers who should be mentioned in the article?

2. For your instructor, prepare a list of the sources you're using to research your assigned article.

3. Read one of the Appendix articles assigned by your instructor, and describe specifically the research techniques employed by its author.

CHAPTER

9

FINDING FACTS
BY INTERVIEWING

Library research is important, but to give your writing a heartbeat you have to dip into a human reservoir of data. With the background you've gained from books and databases, you are ready for the next phase of research: asking probing questions and listening to the fascinating, funny, strange, and sometimes shocking things people say.

Most interviews are conducted either to seek information from experts or to explore the quirks and passions of some unusual person for a profile. For a serious, informative article you will survey as many authorities in a special field as time and expense permit. For a profile you will probably talk at length with your subject (and more briefly with his or her friends and associates) to reveal what makes this person unique.

The following lead from an article about a famous boxer will give you an idea of the alert observation and extensive interviewing that are the staples of research for professional writers. "A Fighter, Not a Hater" was written by novelist Budd Schulberg and published in *Parade*. Note the plentiful visual details and the number of people, in addition to the central character, that Schulberg interviewed.

Evander Holyfield, heavyweight champion of the world, cut an arresting and theatrical figure at the high-tech gym in Atlanta, his red Coca-Cola trunk shirt and black-and-red exercise pants tight on his ripplingly muscled body. His chest an inverted triangle rising from a ballet-dancer's waist to the broad shoulders of a weight-lifter, he looked lithe as a tiger. After watching his unprecedented and grueling all-day workouts at Gold's Gym, after several long talks with Evander, after talking with his manager, his mother, his body-building team, his relatives, and finally, his cook, I came away with the clear impression that this dynamic but self-contained young man was probably the most unusual title-holder I'd ever known.

Interviewing is an art all magazine journalists study and practice. With experience, you, too, will learn to observe as keenly as you listen. You'll learn to look behind the masks that all people wear to find the essence of the human beings hiding there. You'll look at the possessions your subjects have surrounded themselves with. What do they signify, these books and cars and clothes and pictures on the wall? And what if there are no books or pictures? What does that imply? You'll watch the flickering changes in facial expressions and listen to the nuances of tone of voice. You'll learn to study body language like a sculptor. Does it contradict what the subject is saying? What does it tell about the person's anger, anxiety, ambition, truthfulness? Such scrutiny can reveal significant secrets that will give your articles depth.

The interviewer listens attentively. A successful interview is like an exciting conversation with the subject doing most of the talking. Working for the moment when one question transforms the ping-pong question-and-answer rhythm into a sustained volley, an experienced writer controls the interview with blazing interest. Sparks fly from two minds engaged in a topic both find absorbing. Talk speeds along, the interviewer eager to learn what the subject knows, asking here and there for clarification, sometimes playing the skeptic, but mostly listening with mind ajar.

PREPARING FOR THE INTERVIEW

Beginners are usually stunned to discover how carefully professionals research their subjects and how much thought they put into phrasing their questions. The aggressive Italian journalist Oriana Fallaci, who has interviewed political leaders all over the world, says: "I prepare myself for these interviews as a boxer prepares himself for the ring. I read a lot; I study; I try to be rested. And I should say I am usually nervous inside, though you would never realize it watching me. . . ."

Failure to do her homework once embarrassed a young reporter when she asked Katherine Hepburn to name the sexiest man she had ever known. Kate haughtily replied, "That, my dear, is a question you should not have had to ask."

Never go to an interview without having an angle or tentative thesis in mind. If you let the subject know in advance what you plan to explore, it will keep both questions and answers focused. The angle may be changed as the conversation proceeds or even as you write, but you need at least a tentative list of questions centered around the point you want to make.

Never rely on your ability to ad-lib questions during the interview. Write them down, wording each with care. Stale questions engender stale answers while unusual questions elicit answers that surprise. Avoid questions that can be answered with yes or no. For instance, instead of asking a woman scientist if she has a new project under way (to which she may merely say no), ask her to tell you what she hopes to accomplish professionally in the next twelve months.

Like any good conversation, the interview should begin with a question or remark about some subject of mutual interest (one of the things you should look for while doing your homework). What you say in the first few minutes is crucial because the subject will be sizing you up, deciding whether you are intelligent, sincere, warm, hostile, deeply interested, or indifferent. In short, this person will be deciding whether you can be trusted.

Psychological and communications research has shown that the more alike people are in intelligence, values, and cultural and economic status, the greater the trust and therefore the more information shared.

A modern metaphor confirms that theory. When two people are truly communicating, they are said to be on the same wavelength. Narrow the gaps that stand between you. Dress as formally or informally as you think your subject will, think about the level of language usage you might expect, and be prepared to match it if you can. If you know that the person is suspicious of journalists, think about how you can be disarming. In *Creative Interviewing,* Ken Metzler tells about a reporter who was interviewing a doctor known to be hostile to the press. The newsman cleared the air at once by saying, "Doctor, I won't blame you for the sins of the medical profession if you won't blame me for the sins of the newspaper profession."

Think of ways to get good anecdotes—short illustrative stories that can pick up the tempo of a sluggish article. Suppose, for example, you are writing about a circus clown. Try asking some of his associates to tell you their favorite stories about him. And look for experiences or situations in his life that will elicit anecdotes if you ask him the right questions. Sometimes you may especially want a story told in the subject's own words rather than secondhand from a family member or associate. In that case, you can simply ask, for example, about the time he was almost killed by one of the circus's lions.

Before an interview, spend some time analyzing your feelings about the person you plan to write about. Hostility is contagious, so if you don't admire or respect this person, take care that your hostility doesn't seep into your questions. An interview does not obligate your approval. Even if you're writing an investigative piece on a politician, you usually want to begin with courtesy before later playing hardball. A nonthreatening attitude opens up the conversation, so phrase your questions accordingly. Weed out the words that reflect your bias.

Be aware that awe is almost as hazardous as hostility. Practice thinking of the person, no matter how famous or distinguished, as a human being who feels the same emotions you do. Hero worship could hinder the comfortable atmosphere you'll be striving for.

ASKING FOR AN INTERVIEW

When you call to ask for the interview, identify yourself, say that you're writing an article for *Travel & Life* (or whatever your target is) and explain what kind of piece you have in mind. If you've received an editor's encouraging response to a query letter, say so. A person who is knowledgeable about magazine publishing may ask if you have a contract to write the article. As a beginner you probably don't, so you must tell the truth. But you can describe the research you've conducted and tell exactly how you plan to proceed. Finally, state that you have an excellent chance of placing the article, if not with *Travel*, then with a similar magazine. Stress the benefit to this person of having the article published.

In short, asking for an interview can demand some selling on your part. You may be acutely aware of your inexperience, but admitting that you're a beginner may give you an advantage. People will want to help you, and they may be more relaxed and open with you than with an experienced journalist. A student was once so persuasive in a long-distance call to a New York businessman she wanted to interview that he took a plane to Atlanta the next day to be available. Granted, this man was unusually eager to have an article published about him and his ventures, but willing cooperation is not so rare as you might think. Americans love to be interviewed. Most people are flattered that you want to tell their story. And remember that an interview usually benefits both the interviewer and the interviewee.

A common problem with interviewing well-known professionals is that some will agree to talk with you provided you let them check the manuscript before publication. Without knowing the pitfalls, you may readily agree to this restriction. But when they see the completed article, they may censor what you've said, especially the passages that show their human foibles. They may change their quotes to read like a business letter, or they may change the way the article is put together.

The solution is to insist that the magazine article is essentially your creation, and your reputation depends on its honesty and style. Therefore, it is in your interest to make it informative, entertaining, and above all accurate. If they say no approval, no interview, then you must make your choice on the spot. Concede and take the risk, or thank them courteously and go elsewhere. But first, counter with the proposal to read all quotations to them over the phone to be sure you haven't changed their intent. Or, right after you've mailed your manuscript to the publisher, you might offer to furnish a copy for their records, not for their approval or editing.

When interviewing technical people or scientists strictly for information rather than for a personality profile, your attitude should be different. Seek their collaboration and checking. In fact, many magazines will want the scientist's signature on the manuscript or a release sheet guaranteeing the accuracy of your information.

Call to schedule the interview at least a week in advance and try to have it where your subject will be comfortable, uninterrupted, and in familiar surroundings. If the purpose of the interview is to get information from an authority, the most suitable place will probably be the person's office. If you're interviewing for a profile, the home is ideal. In either case, because surroundings tell you a great deal about a person, be there a few minutes early to absorb the general atmosphere of the setting.

THE DEBATE OVER TAPE RECORDERS

When you schedule the interview, ask permission to use a tape recorder if that is your preference. Believing that it will ensure accuracy, some people insist on its use, but others object, knowing they would be inhibited.

Experiment with using a tape recorder, with taking notes, and with using both procedures until you find what works best for you. The tape recorder is ideal for capturing the lively speech patterns of a person who speaks with wit and style. It's also excellent for recording controversial or technical material for legal protection.

But the method has some disadvantages. Tape recorders don't always work, and it's tedious to transcribe even an hour of steady talk. Most beginning writers think the mark of a professional is a tape recorder, but a surprising number of established writers prefer to take notes or to rely on carefully trained memories. They want to establish a relaxed atmosphere in which two friends talk about a subject in which both are intensely interested. No tape recorder and very little notetaking. Common sense is called for, however. Too much reliance on memory makes some respondents nervous. They prefer the security of the tape recorder to the spontaneity of a friendly chat.

The best solution may be to use both methods, taking notes while you record. But if you decide to rely solely on notes and memory, the key is to go immediately from the interview to a quiet place and write down your impressions, the facts you learned, and especially the quotes you want to use. Even an hour's wait may cost the clarity and flavor you're after.

How accurate must quotes be? Can you change a single word of a quotation? Some authorities say no, but practicality urges hedging here. Unless you use a tape recorder, you can seldom get every word. You must always quote meticulously the sense of what your subjects say in words as close to their own as possible. When the late Ava Gardner said to an interviewer, "You do drink—right, baby?" it would have been a distortion of her personality to have written "Do you drink, sir?"

Still, some editing is essential. You must choose which sentences to use from the hundreds of statements made, deleting the subject's wordiness and sometimes cleaning up the grammar. People seldom speak in perfectly structured sentences, and sometimes the ungrammatical or idiomatic can add flavor. Indeed, conversation is a kind of shorthand aided by many nonverbal signals such as gestures, facial expression, and tone of voice. Nevertheless, your job is to report without distortion the *intent* of the speaker. You want to tell the truth, but obviously you cannot tell it all. Readers count on you to distill great masses of material, passing on to them only the pearls.

ASKING GOOD QUESTIONS

Don't ask flashy questions just to be impressive. Ask only because you are genuinely curious. Although you want to avoid the obvious, sometimes a simple uncensored question is better than a pretentious or technical one. For example, a group of reporters were clustered around some astronauts recently returned from one of the moon landings, bombarding them with technical questions. The one that everyone there was dying to ask but didn't dare was posed by a child brought along for the historic occasion: "Were you scared?"

Because what is asked during interviews depends on your topic, your angle, and the persons involved, only broad suggestions can be given for what to say. Nevertheless, three questions should be posed frequently no matter what the occasion: Why? How? and For example? Interviewing actress-director Jodie Foster for a profile, *Time* reporters tried to find out why she is so different from the usual Hollywood star. Their questions focused on discovering how her past explains her present. They asked about the important influences in her life, how she spends a typical day, how she would like to be remembered, what she values most in life. They wanted to know if she is dissatisfied with her accomplishments and what she hopes to achieve. They wanted to know about the crises in her life and her disillusionments, also how she is trying to solve her problems and correct her weaknesses.

Ask factual questions: Who, what, where, and when. Ask how many, how often, how much? Don't ask the college football coach if he enjoys working with young men. Ask him how many students he has coached in his career, how many of them have become famous or very successful, either in sports or other fields, how many write to him occasionally, and how many have become his friends. Seek to convert the general answer into a concrete revelation. Frequently ask your subject to elaborate, to say it in simpler words. Never hesitate to say you're not sure what he means. If *you* don't understand, your readers won't either.

Look for contradictions, irony. If the man you're interviewing talks non-stop, make a note of it if he criticizes his wife for talking too much. An Atlanta politician denies being ambitious, swears that he seeks no higher position, but a large painting of an eagle dominates his office and he wears a golden eagle in his lapel. Ask questions that allude to such seeming inconsistencies (why he is attracted to such a regal bird) and check his body language during the response.

The British journalist David Frost was searching for irony during a televised interview with General Schwarzkopf during the Gulf War. He asked the general to explain how he could be in the killing business and yet describe himself as a Christian. The general's answer acknowledged the irony but his explanation was smooth, unapologetic, and one of the highlights of the show. He discussed at length how devoutly he believed that the cause for which the United States fought, the liberation of Kuwait, was right and that the war, though violent, would save lives in the long run. He was convinced that Saddham Hussein had to be stopped to prevent further aggression.

When interviewing authorities, experts, and celebrities, it's imperative to think of original questions. Ruthlessly shun those that too readily occur to you, for they have probably been asked hundreds of times before. Surprise a famous actress with a question about a little-known phase of her life and you will be much more likely to get a fresh story with memorable quotes.

MANAGING THE INTERVIEW

As the interview begins, it's as important for you to feel at ease as it is for your respondent. Tension, like hostility, is contagious. So for a few moments follow your plan to talk about something you know this person is interested in—a hobby, a child or grandchild, a recent honor or publication. But move swiftly to the topic you agreed to discuss, thus indicating that you value time. Describe again the particular area or interest you want to explore so that there's an understanding of your basic plan for the article. A painter, for example, would need to know whether you intend to discuss a recent exhibit or if you seek his opinion on the arts in general.

Even though you have carefully planned the first question of an interview, be flexible. During the first moments of small talk, you will feel each other out, seeking affinities. If you sense now that the question you have planned would be a less effective opener than another one, follow your instincts. Your list of tentative questions is a guide and a prop, but you can discard it and play the interview by ear if the subject strikes a more promising note.

You will also need to be flexible if the answers to your prepared questions are not what you expected. In those instances, you must be able to change directions. For an interview with a woman airline pilot, a student once made a list of questions based on her research. They anticipated that the woman had had painful experiences in a primarily masculine field and was resentful about discrimination. To her secret dismay, the student found that the pilot enjoyed good relationships with her colleagues and felt that she had been very well treated. Too inexperienced to handle this unexpected turn, the student left the interview in confusion. Later she realized she had tried to force the answers she wanted to hear rather than listening to what the woman wanted to say. Fortunately, the student asked for a follow-up session where, with different anticipations, she was able to unleash a torrent of talk from the flyer and came out with a better article than her original plan would have produced. It had the bonus of surprise.

Make your subjects feel that you are talking with them to learn something others need or want to know. If their contributions to their field have been criticized, give them a chance to respond. Instead of sounding critical, say something like "Your opponents claim that. . . . What would you like to say in your defense?"

When respondents refuse to answer a question, you can say so in your story. If they try to evade a question by "bridging" (easing from a sensitive subject to a comfortable one), ask the question again in a different way, perhaps later in the interview. Be aware of what has not been said. Politicians are especially skillful at taking control of an interview and steering the conversation away from topics they want to avoid.

During the interview you need to get striking quotes, illuminating anecdotes, and all the information an interested reader will want. If all goes well, the subject will be doing most of the talking so that getting quotes will be no problem. But unless you plan to follow a straight question-and-answer format in the *Playboy* interview manner, only a small part of the finished manuscript will consist of direct quotes. The trick is to listen for ideas memorably expressed. When they are, you will want to record every word.

Listen for astonishing statements and quote them verbatim.

Don't hesitate to ask your subject to wait a moment while you catch up with your notetaking or insert a new tape. It's exhilarating to prompt exciting, fluent talk, but if the conversation rushes on at too fast a pace, you may miss some excellent material.

What should you do if you're hanging hungrily on every word and your subject suddenly says, "This is off the record, of course." First ask if you can use the facts or the gist of what has been said without attribution. If the answer is no, under almost all circumstances you should accede. Off the record means confidential, and if you report anything told to you in confidence, you may lose a good source and your own self-respect. On very rare occasions, however, you may decide that your readers have a right to know this "secret" information. In that case, many professional journalists would decide to print it if the matter vitally concerned the public welfare. Even so, they might first try to get the same information from another source.

Before closing an interview, ask your subjects if you have failed to mention something they would like to talk about. Sometimes this fills in some gaps and sometimes it begins an entirely new interview.

Schedule another session if you need more time to talk. The subjects will be flattered that you care enough to do whatever is necessary to get the whole story.

As you leave after the final interview, thank the respondent cordially and say that you will call if you need to clarify some important point or to verify quotations.

How much material from an interview must be included in the finished article? You are not obligated to report everything. Many of the quotes should be paraphrased, condensed, and summarized. For variety in sentence structure and rhythm, the interview article should blend different types of statements, yours and the respondent's.

On this subject William Zinsser, noted magazine writer, says: "Try to achieve a balance between what the subject is saying in *his* words and what you are writing in *your* words to explain and connect. If you quote a person for three or four consecutive paragraphs, it becomes monotonous. Quotations are livelier when you break them up, making periodic appearances in your role as guide. You are still the writer—don't relinquish control. But make your appearances useful; don't just insert one of those dreary sentences which shout to the reader that your sole purpose is to break up a string of quotations ('He stopped and tapped his pipe on a nearby ashtry and I noticed that his fingers were quite long')."

So much takes place during an interview that you will constantly be making choices: what to include and what to discard; what to quote and what to paraphrase or summarize. Your task is to convert what may have been a disjointed, oral romp into a coherent written portrait.

SATURATION AND PARTICIPATION RESEARCH

Saturation research combines interviews with intense observation and sometimes participation. If your topic lends itself to this kind of research, it will give your article a sense of immediacy, vitality, and authority you can acquire in no other way. Instead of being a remote, secondhand report, your article will be an intimate story. Instead of a black-and-white snapshot it will be a full-color movie.

If you're writing about a person, plan to immerse yourself in the subject's life, perhaps for days or weeks. If you're writing about an activity you may take part in it, becoming as deeply absorbed as possible. The object is to convey the realism and emotional involvement of fiction when reporting fact.

To get an idea of the vivid kind of writing produced by such exposure to the subject, review "Stalking the Wild Orthographers" in Chapter 2. Because the article is about a spelling bee that lasted only a few hours, the author probably spent less than a day onsite. But the point is that he was there in the tavern as the event unfolded, observing and mentally recording every detail of the wild competition, taking notes and listening to the participants and spectators. Just as important, he was absorbing the noisy atmosphere of the place. He may also have gone there many times before or after the contest to get a feel for the tavern's mood and color. By the time he was ready to write, he was literally saturated with the sights, sounds, and smells of the place. He had noted and enjoyed the irony of the situation and had chosen its metaphor: war. And when he began writing, he naturally turned to narrative to reproduce the suspense, conflict, and humor that surrounded the contestants who were oblivious to everything but the fierce competition of the spelling bee. The article reads like a short story with fully developed scenes and dialogue. The difference is that this event actually happened.

Saturation reporting has evolved from the belief of many nonfiction writers that traditional journalistic techniques are too restrictive and that they yield stereotyped, shallow writing. Some claim that the old ways never came close to revealing truth, for the truth is lost in a catalog of facts. A writer should get it all down. Its chief proponent Tom Wolfe has said in *The New Journalism:* "The true moral duty of a writer is to collect details the way philatelists collect stamps—with a passion." A writer should crawl into the eye sockets of his subject, Wolfe insists, until he knows how that person looks, thinks, reacts to people, cries, laughs, and faces crises. "Saturation Reporting, as I think of it, can be one of the most exhilarating trips, as they say, in the world. Often you feel as if you've put your whole central nervous system on red alert and turned it into a receiving set with your head panning the molten tableau like a radar disk."

THE HAZARDS OF SATURATION RESEARCH

Saturation reporting helps to produce writing that sears itself into the consciousness. It also has drawbacks. It takes huge blocks of time to gather the data, it creates long articles that occupy a lot of space in magazines, and its credibility has been weakened by some writers whose "facts" turned out to be fiction. It's doubly difficult to maintain objectivity while conducting saturation research because the method often leads to close relationships between writers and their subjects.

Partly because of these objections, most freelancers today use a modified form of saturation research (as the author of the spelling bee article did). Few can afford the luxury of spending weeks or months observing a person or an activity, and not every editor is willing to print or pay for the long articles that result from such immersion. Some of the exceptions are *The New Yorker, Playboy,* and *Vanity Fair.* Nevertheless, modified saturation research and its close cousin, participatory research, can be potent techniques for any writer.

THE STRENGTH OF PARTICIPATION

The participatory method was used to good advantage when *Time* magazine sent correspondent Edwin Reingold on a day-long cooking assignment for a cover story on the McDonald's hamburger empire. After working behind the counter at a McDonald's in Illinois, Reingold sent his editors the following report of his experience. If you take the time to analyze this unpretentious little piece, you will find that although its topic seems trivial, even dull, it contains most of the ingredients of superb writing: suspenseful narrative; appropriate similes and other figures of speech; precise nouns and verbs that show rather than tell; economy of detail in depicting lifelike characters; rich detail in evoking setting; variety of sentence length, structure, and rhythm; realistic dialogue; and an understated, ironic conclusion. These ingredients are made possible by participatory research.

The sun rises like a giant cheeseburger over Naperville's golden arches as the early crew slogs on with its 5 A.M. ritual of scrubbing, vacuuming and window washing. At 7 A.M. customers start wandering in and by 11 A.M. all 20 cooks and countergirls are busy turning out burgers, fries, shakes, fish sandwiches and apple pies for the fast-thickening lunchtime crowd.

Putting on my apron and my jaunty red paper cap that falsely identifies me as the manager, I watch in admiration as 16-year-old Grillman Dick Caspermeyer fries his Quarter-Pounders. He lays them on the grill, flips, swivels, scrapes and dispenses them with the speed and grace of a natural athlete. Little do I realize that I will soon fail miserably at imitating him.

At 12:30 P.M., just as the lunch crowd begins to subside, Manager Ralph Follin slaps a stack of quarter-pound beef patties into my hand and leads me to a sizzling, lightly greased grill. "You're on," he says. I flop them crudely, unevenly on the grill and find a salt shaker thrust into my hand. "Salt," he commands. I salt. "Now hit the timer," and I reach up and push the timer button. This is easy, I think, and start to relax. "Scrape your grill," he orders sharply, and I start rubbing it with the scraper. "No, get the edge into it," Follin corrects. I look over the grill and see two dozen customers staring at me—accusingly, it seems. "Hey, your light is out!" Follin shouts.

I lunge for the spatula and flip the burgers over, splashing grease all over my apron. "When you lift them, don't be afraid to get your fingers on them—they aren't hot," he lies. I turn to face a bewildering array of buns, cheese slices, onion pieces, ketchup, mustard and unidentified sauces. Dick Caspermeyer comes over and shows me how to apply them. I scrape down my grill again, better this time. Soon it is 1 P.M. and there are no new orders for Quarter-Pounders. I place my spatula and scraper aside, hang up my hat and apron. "Not bad," Follin says—"for a reporter."

Try to imagine what this selection would have been like if the author had not actually participated in the frenzied activity behind the counter of a McDonald's during lunchtime rush hour.

Saturation and participatory research enables you to do what all thorough research should do. From a mountain of material of varying quality, it allows you to select the very best. It requires that you collect data with the dedication of a scientist, using all five senses "on red alert." Then when you boil down the brew and extract the essence, what is left is meaty, rich, and savory.

SUMMARY

1. To conduct a successful interview, prepare for it in advance by researching the person and subject matter thoroughly and composing a list of fresh, incisive questions.
2. Have in mind a thesis for the article and explain the purpose of the interview when you call for an appointment.
3. If you know it may be difficult to get an appointment, stress the value of the interview to the respondent.
4. Try during the interview to get anecdotes and memorable quotes that will give the article suspense and surprise.
5. Tape-record interviews with articulate people whose speech patterns are interesting, but take notes instead if the subject is uncomfortable with a recorder.
6. Pay attention to body language—yours as well as the respondent's.
7. For an in-depth article, collect as much data as possible by saturation research or a modified form of it.

FROM PRINCIPLES TO PRACTICE

1. Review "Stalking the Wild Orthographers" in Chapter 2. Be prepared to discuss the article as an example of one produced by saturation research. What would the article lack if it had been based only on reading and interviews?
2. Submit for your instructor's approval a list of the tentative questions you plan to ask when you interview an authority or a personality for your article.
3. Describe the saturation or participatory research you plan to conduct.
4. Interview a classmate and then have her interview you. Write a summary of what you learned about effective and ineffective questions. Did the interviewer make you feel comfortable? How well did she listen?
5. How could you conduct saturation research for an article about the overemphasis on sports in high schools and colleges? List specifically the kind of information you would seek, the observations you should be prepared to make, and the experiences that might interest you.

CHAPTER

10

THE FIRST
DRAFT

Writing the first draft of an article is an intensely personal and private endeavor. Although this chapter can give you hints and suggestions, no one can tell you exactly how to do it. And no one but you should see the rough results. Fewer beginners would fear writing if they could get over the feeling that a testy teacher is peering over their shoulders to see if they are writing according to The Rules. No wonder they're terrified. Experts like to be watched while they perform. But amateurs need the privacy of a quiet, faraway corner for their first stumbling efforts. You'll face a blank sheet of paper or an empty computer screen with less dread, therefore, if you remember that your first draft is indeed private. It doesn't have to be correct, much less artful or brilliant, for no one will see it but you.

The purpose of the first draft is to provide a base to build on as you rev up for the real work that is to come. No matter how crude it seems, it is a beginning—a core that can be cut, enlarged, altered, rearranged, improved, and finally polished to become a creation of integrity and utility, even perhaps of grace and beauty.

Beginning will be less painful if your research has made you an expert on your subject with ten times more information than you can use. In fact, if thorough research produces little solid information, you should choose another subject, for padding is the parasite of good writing. Fruitful, exhaustive research enables you to prune the trivial, the unimportant, and the dull so that only the most compelling material remains.

WHAT DO YOU REALLY WANT TO SAY?

Writing the first draft is simply a matter of putting on a computer screen or paper what you are bursting to say. The stronger the urge to tell someone about your topic the better. Writing it should be no more difficult than telling your best friend about it. You need only make your point, in whatever words tumble out. At this stage do not fret about grammar, spelling, punctuation, sentence structure, or any other worrisome or frightening details. You have a conviction. Tell about it simply and enthusiastically.

For some writers, this emotional spillover of strongly felt beliefs or important facts produces a surprisingly good rough draft. Robust writing can erupt from their first uncensored outpouring. But for beginners, such spontaneous combustion is rare. For you, it may be better to proceed more methodically.

The following tips are given with caution and with the knowledge that the creative process resists straitjackets. Nevertheless, the suggestions are worth your consideration. You can ignore those that don't work for you.

Before beginning your rough draft, think once again about your audience and the purpose of your article. Are you writing to persuade, to entertain, to amuse, or to inform? If you're sure the readers will be keenly interested in getting needed information from the article, the natural mode of writing will be exposition, a clear and logical presentation of the facts. Entertaining digressions or embellishments may not be appropriate; in fact, the reader may be annoyed by such distractions. How-to articles, for example, often consist only of a clear set of instructions given in chronological order. No stylistic frills. No amusing anecdotes. If, on the other hand, your purpose is to entertain, examine your notes for opportunities to use narrative and thus to insert anecdotes.

Most popular magazine articles have a dual purpose, to inform and entertain. Consequently, the map of your journey must often be scenic as well as practical, and you will then use all three modes of writing: exposition, description, and narration. Beware, though, of letting yourself get into the story unless there is a reason to do so. If you are an authority on your subject or a participant in the adventure you write about, do not hesitate to let your light modestly shine. Otherwise, use *I* sparingly. Readers are usually interested in your subject, not in you.

Some writers, especially when preparing for an essay, begin by brainstorming. They write down, in random order, every word that occurs to them when they think of their subject. The psychological process of association sometimes exposes connections between your ideas and reveals images that might not have occurred to you. Such discoveries can be very useful in igniting the fires of creativity.

DON'T LET OUTLINES INTIMIDATE YOU

You may not want to hear this, but an outline makes writing easier, and it's easier to prepare one than you might think. In fact, your research has already produced one for you. Here's how you can uncover it. After writing your thesis on a card and keeping it before you, begin sorting out your research notes just as you would separate the suits in a card game, putting notes on different aspects of the subject in separate stacks. Labeling each stack with a descriptive word or two, or even with a complete sentence, will produce a tentative outline. The stacks of cards merely represent separate sections of a yet-to-be-written article, sections which can finally be arranged in the most attractive and logical order.

As you can see, an outline does not have to consist of Roman numerals with subheadings of A, B, and C. In fact, for a short article, a written outline is not absolutely necessary. But some sort of guide, written or mental, is essential to avoid writing that is disjointed and difficult to read. Remember, though, that your outline is a loose guide, not an armed guard. It can always be revised if a detour is more inviting than the main road. The rough draft based on a tentative outline is a kind of discovery, and, above all, it is yours. Write it to please yourself. An unruly runaway can be disciplined later.

If you still resist preparing an outline—and most students do—consider this: most professionals write from some sort of guide. And even if they don't, the most careful ones outline their work upon completion to be sure that it is logically rather than haphazardly organized.

Let's examine a short article by a professional for signs that the author wrote from an outline. In other words, we will see if the piece reads easily and smoothly, with no bumps and jumps and bewildering loose ends. If the author had an organizational plan in mind or on paper, it may not be noticeable, but for the reader's comprehension and pleasure, it must have been there.

The article is from *Sports Illustrated*.

Hazards at the Northernmost U.S. Golf Course
Arnold Schechter

Even under ideal conditions, golf is a demanding game. So imagine what it's like to play on a course where the fairways move, the greens resemble sand traps, and the hazards have claws or antlers.

Welcome to the northernmost golf course in the U.S.: Alaska's Fairbanks Golf and Country Club, a mere 165-mile chip shot from the Arctic Circle. At first glance, the Fairbanks course seems positively tame: a flat nine-hole 3,000-yard layout lined with spruce and cottonwood trees and uninterrupted by bunkers or water. But under the shallow topsoil lurks a thick layer of permafrost, a frozen subsoil that softens or hardens with changes in temperature, causing the topsoil to heave, ripple, and gape.

This terra *un*firma creates the most treacherous fairways imaginable. A player can hit a shot down the middle, only to see his ball bounce 90 degrees off line, straight for the rough. Or a fairway section may suddenly collapse; just such a mishap once dropped the club tractor and its startled driver into a hole 12 feet deep and 20 feet long.

The permafrost also makes it difficult to cultivate grass for the greens. So the greens here, as in other grass-poor areas of the world, consist of sand mixed with motor oil. Highly lofted balls end up buried in this gritty compound, which requires players to rake a flat path to the hole before every putt. According to club manager Eddie Dean, the course could have real greens if the club were willing to put in a very expensive irrigation system. But no one has pushed for it.

Then there are the roving hazards—the massive wild animals that roam the area freely and show golfers no respect. One Chicago visitor watched in dismay as a bear became entangled with his golf bag and dragged it off into the forest, bouncing it off trees like a drunken caddie as it went. And Dean will never forget making a blind shot that conked a mother moose. The injured party chased Dean to a nearby radio station and trampled his abandoned set of clubs before returning to her calf.

But despite the wildlife, most of which remains aloof, and the uncertainties of playing on top of permafrost, an outing on this course is normally a delight. During the season, which runs from May through September, temperatures are usually in the 60s or above, rain is infrequent, and the peaceful forest bordering the club is a bright, vibrant green.

A visitor can rent clubs and a pull cart for $4.25 a day and squeeze in as many holes as he likes for $5.50. These fees are even more of a bargain than they may seem because a Fairbanks summer day can have almost 22 hours of light. And no matter what your score is—whether you break the nine-hole course record of 28 or challenge the worst-round record of 115, set by a tipsy barmaid who had consumed her own concoctions—the club will award you its Greens' Badge of Courage, a certificate testifying that you survived a round on the northernmost golf course in the U.S.

The author, Arnold Schechter, leads us between the sections of his article as smoothly and seamlessly as a perfect Sam Snead drive. He glides from idea to idea toward a specific point or destination that is hinted at in the first paragraph, leading the reader along without a single jarring distraction or leap of thought.

Schechter makes the point that despite its many unusual and sometimes dangerous hazards, this northernmost golf course in the U.S. is a delightful place to play. In paragraph after paragraph, he piles up the evidence (consisting of entertaining and surprising details) to prove his thesis.

The organizational pattern of the article is established in the first paragraph: 1) the fairways move, 2) the greens look like sand traps, and 3) wild animals roam the course. And, just as the reader anticipates, the succeeding paragraphs develop these sections in exactly that order. The author concludes, then, by describing the delights of the course that compensate for the challenges of its startling hazards.

AN OUTLINE IS LIKE A BLUEPRINT FOR A HOUSE

A carefully planned outline, even a very informal one, gives an article a logical structure. Structure is simply the way the parts of the article are arranged to form a unified, coherent whole. If structure seems a vague concept to you, think of a house. There is a reason for the arrangement of its various parts: the basement doesn't belong on the second floor. The front door doesn't belong in the basement. All the windows don't appear on the same side. The placement of its parts is both practical and pleasing.

When you consider the structure of an article, you should be striving for the most effective sequence for the communication of your ideas. By the time you are several paragraphs into the article, you should have stated, or at least hinted at, your point and certain other facts (usually the famous five W's: who, what, where, when, and why). Otherwise, readers will feel some frustration that you are not feeding them the clues they need to follow your train of thought. In other words, you can't build the first or second floors until you have created a basement or foundation. You will continue to give your readers information throughout the article, but they must be in on the basics fairly near the beginning.

There are other ways of constructing articles; we will discuss them in the chapter on revising and rewriting. The point here is that most articles, like houses, proceed from foundation to roof (from thesis to conclusion) more or less in chronological order or in order of importance. Occasionally, however, a creative architect will design an octagonal house. You, too, can experiment. All that matters is getting and keeping the readers' attention, making them feel that they are in sure hands, and never giving them a moment of bewilderment or confusion due to sudden leaps of thought or detours.

No matter the ultimate plan of the house, every article must have a *beginning* containing in some form the thesis, a *middle* presenting the proof of the thesis with evidence and examples, and a *conclusion* tying it all together. When writing your first draft try not to get more complicated than that. But use the checklist at the end of this chapter to keep you on track.

At some point you may experience a "block." If so, it is usually better to forge ahead, settling for whatever words and ideas occur rather than putting the work aside, hoping for inspiration later. When you falter, simply stop and ask yourself: What am I trying to say? Force yourself to answer as simply and clearly as possible and you may be surprised at the eloquence of your plain words.

Remember that there is no one correct way to write a magazine article, no perfect pattern, no foolproof formula. For now it is enough for you to begin—your way.

SUMMARY

1. A rough draft should be written without any thought of a critical censor. It should be as private as a love letter and written quickly, with no thought of grammar, spelling, or punctuation, and if possible, without stopping until you have made the main points you had in mind.
2. Having an abundance of information about the subject will ease the writing of the first draft.
3. If the article is long, it is helpful to write out the thesis and a rough sentence outline as a guide.

FROM PRINCIPLES TO PRACTICE

1. Write a simple sentence outline of an article in the Appendix assigned by your instructor. If it has an unusual pattern, analyze how the transitions have succeeded or failed in giving the article coherence.
2. Following this chapter's suggestions, write out a tentative outline for the article you have researched, and then compose a rough draft. Apply the following checklist to what you have written:

- Have you said what you wanted to say, or does some of it seem incomplete?
- Does the draft proceed in logical order, or are there some confusing leaps in thought?
- Did you follow your original thesis and outline, or did you alter both as you proceeded?
- Have you included enough supporting evidence?
- Do you need more examples?
- For greater interest, could you convert any part of the exposition to narrative?

CHAPTER

11

LEADS AND CONCLUSIONS

Most people, even those who love words, shuffle along in daily life, numbed by the drone and blur of so many media messages that their attention is immune to all but an unexpected bang. In magazine articles, the bang must come from an unusually attractive or compelling lead.

A GOOD BEGINNING IS VITAL

Now that your first draft has been written and you're ready to think about improving it, turn your attention to the most important paragraphs, indeed the few most important words, in the entire article: the first ones. The opening paragraph is crucial because readers will test, or taste, the article by reading the first few lines. Consequently, the initial bite must be rich and savory.

Considering the lead's importance, how long should it be? Since there are no absolutes regarding length, some leads consist of only one dramatic sentence: a startling statement, an insightful quotation, or a disturbing question, for example. But if the article is long and complex, it may take nine or ten paragraphs to explain its main concept and to seduce the reader into continuing. An even longer lead may read like the beginning of a short story, with dialogue, characters, and action.

With that much flexibility, obviously some leads will accomplish more than others. For example, some may simply sidle up to you and beguile you with one titillating sentence that seems to have nothing to do with the subject of the article. It's merely enticing you to read on. If the subject of the article is of vital importance, the lead might bluntly state the thesis and include a transition into the body of the article itself. And still others will create a scene that sets the tone and mood of the article, thus hinting at the thesis rather than stating it.

But don't let these varieties of shapes and forms confuse you. Just remember that you have many alternatives and that there is no rigid formula for the right way. Whatever its length or content, the lead's function is always the same:

to attract attention, give some idea of what the article is about, and convince readers that the rest of the article merits their attention.

How, then, can you write an irresistible lead? The best way is to think about the needs and desires of magazine readers and to construct your lead accordingly. Goaded by the fear of missing out on something in this fast-changing society, readers are looking for knowledge, diversion, excitement, laughter, adventure, new ideas. They covet variety and surprise.

So how do magazine writers give readers what they want?

- ❑ Inform them about a new development in medicine, money management, politics, and so forth.

- ❑ Shock them with a bizarre story.

- ❑ Delight them with beautiful language.

- ❑ Surprise them and make them laugh at the absurd.

- ❑ Invite them to participate in an unusual situation.

- ❑ Appeal to their preoccupation with famous people.

- ❑ Entertain them with an adventure story.

- ❑ Seize their curiosity by dropping a strange clue about what is to come further in the article.

Examine this list carefully and then look for the techniques that accomplish these goals in the leads that follow.

EXAMPLES OF EFFECTIVE LEADS

Because of readers' intense curiosity about the private lives of public people, a great many articles today are profiles of celebrities. It is important, therefore, to learn how to write this kind of piece whether you're researching the local postmaster, a supreme court justice, or a rock star. The first lead presented here appeared in *People* magazine upon the publication of a very famous person's autobiography: Kirk Douglas. In movie-like realism, it shows Douglas behind the wheel of his careening BMW as he tears around Hollywood on an ordinary day in his life. Part of the lead's appeal comes from the familiar details: the dimpled chin, the tight jaws, the bloodshot eyes. But the real hook is the last sentence which implies that the article will tell you who Kirk Douglas really is.

Buckle up. Grab the dashboard. There's a 71-year-old wild man at the wheel. Javelin jaw slammed forward, shark lips yanked back at the corners, Kirk Douglas is gunning his BMW through the mansioned serenity of Beverly Hills in a stuttering succession of jerks, jolts, lurches, swerves and exuberant vavarooooooms. No, he isn't drunk. He's on the way to his morning workout and just doing what comes naturally: splurging energy, killing gnats with sledgehammers, living in the present intense. "He's a volcano," says a friend. "You almost expect to see smoke pour out of that crater in his chin." Intensity has scored his cheeks with stress lines, exploded tiny blood vessels in his eyes, packed his chest with a pacemaker. But beginning his eighth decade, Douglas still drives himself as hard as he drives his car. "I've always lived to the limit," he says as the BMW rocks to a halt in front of a star-struck parking attendant. "Lived for the next job, the next adventure. I've never looked back. But now it's time to face who I really am—and that's why I wrote the book."

The next lead appeals to the reader who savors irony, a form of surprise arising from a sense of contradiction. Written by a student, Sarah Mixon, it describes a situation in which our expectations of church members are shattered. The article, "Death Detested," is about a group of young, idealistic lawyers in Atlanta who are working for very poor pay, trying to save the lives of people condemned to die in the electric chair. The lead consists of a long, unusual quote.

"The worst experience, but not that atypical," said Stephen A. Bright, director of a committee that works to stop state executions and improve prison conditions, "was when I went up to St. Philip's Cathedral to talk to a class up there and I noticed when I came that one of the guys had a law book, which surprised me a little, but I didn't think too much about it. So they asked me what I had to say and I described what I do . . . about the racial discrimination, arbitrariness, and poor lawyering, and just the lack of fairness and those sorts of things.

"And when I finished, this fellow said, 'Do you have a sister?' And I said, 'Yeah, I have two sisters.' At that point he opened his law book to this case that involved a very long and drawn out grotesque description of how a guy who was under death sentence had just abused this woman terribly before he killed her. Cut her up, sexually abused her, literally poured hot wax in the wounds, salt. . . . It is one of the most gross descriptions of the horrible degradation of a human being. . . . He would read it and stop every so often and look at me and say, 'This . . . is . . . *your* . . . sister.'" Bright imitated the man by pointing his index finger to emphasize every word. "And then he'd read a little bit more about, you know, cutting off her nipples, and then he'd look up at me and say, 'This . . . is . . . *your* . . . sister.' And then he'd go on like that. . . .

"And you know, it was just an odd way to treat somebody that you invite to the church. I felt like the guy, after he got through reading it to me, was going to throw the book at me. I mean, he was just personalizing it so much. I've learned that that's to be expected. It's rough. In fact, I think I've told the people at St. Philip's, well, I think there's only one thing worse than being thrown to the lions, and that's being thrown to the Christians when I have to talk about the death penalty.

"The hatred was just so clear."

It would be difficult to find a more shocking lead than the following one tucked unobtrusively into the Food section of *In Health* magazine. Its shock is deliberately accentuated by the opening description of the dull, ordinary surroundings and the chatter of women at a Mary Kay cosmetics party. Wondering why the author is going on at such length about a cosmetic party, the reader is led on by curiosity. The author, Katherine Griffin, stretches out the scene until the last possible second before lowering the hammer. The only clue to what's ahead is whispered in the title, "Good Earth."

Lyndell Travis folds up her tray of Mary Kay cosmetics and sighs. Her friends Onece Johnson and Vanessa Kirkin aren't buying any of the soaps and toiletries she's brought to Onece's house this cool Mississippi evening. In fact, they're showing far more interest in the snack being passed around.

"Hmm," Johnson says, looking up toward the ceiling as she nibbles a toast-colored nugget. "I've tasted some similar to this before. It has kind of a gritty taste."

Travis helps herself to a bite. "I don't like it," she declares, her native Mississippi drawl molasses-thick. "It's not sweet at all."

"Maybe it's not the best," Johnson says diplomatically. "But it'll pass."

The snack the women are sharing is not bridge mix, canapes, or crackers. It's nothing fried or fat, but something natural and unprocessed. It's dirt—in this case a fine-grained clay dug the day before from a roadbank just up the road from here, some 50 miles north of Jackson in the central part of the state.

Eating earth might seem odd, aberrant, or hazardous by 20th century American standards. But researchers who have studied it say the practice is normal and, for the most part, harmless. In their view, earth-eating is a cultural tradition that in some cases even promotes health.

Curiosity is the carrot that lures the reader along in the following short lead by student Beth Harbin. She wisely withholds the explanation of the miscellaneous list of facts until the very last word.

The largest ones weigh over eight tons—that's about four Lincolns with a couple of Hondas thrown in. At one time they lived on every continent except Australia. They've been hunted by primitives and sophisticates, used as executioners by Romans, as industrial workers by Indians, as war machines by Hannibal, and as entertainers by Americans. They are the world's largest land animals—elephants.

Sometimes, the shortest leads are the biggest flirts. Here is one, with just two sentences, from an article by James Shreeve that also relies on the allure of curiosity. Note the amusing contrast between the words "thieves" and "love." The article, entitled "Machiavellian Monkeys," was published in *Discover* where, unfortunately, the title dispels some of the mystery of the lead. Nevertheless, the informal tone convinces us that the article will be entertaining.

This is a story about frauds, cheats, liars, faithless lovers, incorrigible con artists, and downright thieves. You're gonna love 'em.

Still another effective lead-writing technique is to bring the readers into the action, especially if the article is about something that might directly affect them. The business executive who reads *Fortune* magazine would be likely to identify with "Why Japan Keeps on Winning" by Carla Rapaport. The author looks the reader square in the eye and says:

Look at your watch. If it's lunchtime in Tokyo, chances are good that a couple of dozen Japanese executives are meeting over cold fish, pickles, and rice. Too bad you weren't invited. The table talk could well affect your company—and cost you business. The corporate heft around the table is the Japanese equivalent of IBM, General Electric, American Express, and Citicorp combined. Americans would call it collusion; to the Japanese it's a keiretsu, or business alliance.

Almost all of Japan's familiar blue-chip companies belong to some kind of keiretsu (pronounced "kay-rhet-sue"), and several give the leading groups their names. Among them: Mitsubishi, Sumitomo, and Mitsui. Keiretsu are critical to the country's special brand of capitalism, the reason Japan keeps dominating world markets. Forget lean manufacturing and quality circles. What makes the difference is a system that pulls together government, industry, capital, and the best information on high technology worldwide to create a machine that grinds competitors into powder. Says Jim Martin, head of Rockwell International's Asia Technology Liaison Office in Tokyo: "I don't know which system is better—Japan's or ours. But I know which one is winning."

Humor: Everybody loves it. And so a humorous lead is almost guaranteed to succeed. Besides its entertainment value, we marvel at the irony inherent in good humor, which is especially evident in the example that follows. Humorist Larry King, author of *Best Little Whorehouse in Texas,* is so skillful in handling tone that we can read no more than a few lines before we have lapsed, mentally, into a genuine Texas drawl. Even the title, "Hurtin' Good," is a sample of the fun to come.

Don't talk any gooey Valentine stuff to me, please. My women have a way of quitting around Christmastime. When the Valentine season rolls around I'm still sobbing, threshing sleepless in my lonely bed and swearing off romantic entanglements forever.

And you know what? It's absolutely wonderful.

There never in all history was a romance worth a farthing that didn't end badly. And I'm not even counting those that ended in marriage.

Give me a blonde/brunette/redhead—truth is, she can be anything but bald—who has thrown me over, preferably for an obviously inferior replacement, then deliver me to a bar stool near a jukebox equipped with plain old three-chord hurtin' country songs, and I will have such wretched fun I should pay a luxury tax.

So there you have a whole menu of delectables to dangle above the heads of your readers in tantalizing leads: you can inform, entertain, shock, delight, challenge, surprise, and kindle curiosity or laughter. You can begin with an anecdote, a scene, a startling quote, a question, a portrait of a famous or infamous person. Writing an impressive lead involves the ability to recognize drama and irony in your material and to put them in the place of greatest importance.

THE DIFFERENCE BETWEEN STOPPING AND ENDING

Too many writers neglect conclusions, taking for granted that they will evolve naturally. Sometimes they do. But their quality should not be left to chance because the conclusion solidifies the final impression of the article. It unifies the whole piece by echoing an idea or image presented earlier. It lingers in the reader's mind partly because it is last, but partly because a good one emphasizes the most important point of the article. A poor one, or none at all, is like omitting the period at the end of a sentence.

Students often have trouble writing satisfying conclusions. They recognize the difference between stopping and ending. But how to end? Every reader knows how disconcerting it is to arrive at the bottom of a page and reach for the continuing page only to find that none exists. The writer has merely stopped. There is no sense of completion, of having steered the boat back to shore. The reader is left floating in midstream.

A decisive conclusion, on the other hand, leaves no doubt in the reader's mind that the article has ended.

There are several ways to conclude effectively and several effects to shun, but one rule prevails: End quickly. The writer who signals that she is about to close but instead carries on for six more paragraphs is like the guest who says goodbye and then stands, idly chatting, at the front door with her coat on for another thirty minutes. An old rule of show business applies to good writing as well: Build a scene to a climax and then close the curtain fast.

Not knowing when to quit dampens the conclusion of an otherwise superb article by Jim Wooten. Writing on the political career of Governor George Wallace of Alabama, Wooten concludes that in Wallace's crippled and lonely state, it is hard to hate him any more. The brief paragraph that shows Wallace alone in his big house is a good place for the article to end. But unfortunately, two more sentences are tacked on, apparently in the fear that the reader might not have gotten the point and to echo something Wallace has said earlier in the article:

So now he lives alone in their spacious bedroom in the big white mansion on Perry Street, lives there now with his telephone, his remote-control television set, a little bell for signaling servants, and the fever shapes of the life he has lived—and he waits there alone for his term to end.

He was right. Every man does have his price, but few have paid so dearly as George Wallace.

The last paragraph could easily have been omitted, but if not the whole paragraph, then certainly the preachiness of the last nine words.

Another principle to observe in writing good conclusions is never to end with a condescending summary or a chatty remark to the reader such as "Good luck!" A respected national news magazine occasionally makes a similar mistake by ending with a sarcastic admonition to the person whom the article is about. Here's an example in an article on the notorious corporate raider and CEO of Trans World Arlines, Carl Icahn:

In the '80s, none of that (disagreements between nations on landing privileges for airlines) would have mattered. If Carl Icahn needed millions for a raid, he called up Michael Milken, and that was the end of it. Today, TWA's financing—and perhaps its future—depends on negotiations between the United States Department of State and Britain's Foreign Office. Welcome to the '90s, Carl.

An excellent example of a decisive conclusion, one that is obviously the end of the article, appeared in *TriQuarterly*. In the body of the piece, author Paul West described his struggle to survive a devastating stroke. Although he had suffered this tragedy as a comparatively young writer when he was otherwise in good health, it took years of Herculean efforts to learn how to overcome his limitations. The title, "Portrait of the Artist as a Lion on Stilts," gives a preview of what it is like to be a crippled artist. The play on words in the conclusion's final sentence is like a benediction.

Politicans talk of the art of the possible. Doctors talk of the quality of life. I think about what my body achieved against the odds and what supports the rest of what I do: the art of the passable, and the high quality of that compared with the alternative. I keep managing to come to the end of another book, another essay (as now), and I marvel at the plenary gratitude the human spirit can feel after the Furies have had it and it has managed to slink away, back into the operating theater of words.

Sometimes a new twist can give a conclusion an unexpected punch. For example, Larry King ends the "Hurtin' Good" article thus:

Thank goodness I have risen above all that love, romance, mush, poetry, roses and hurtin-good stuff. I don't have to worry about it anymore.

I'm married. Valentine's Day don't mean squat to me.

You can write a good conclusion by using any of the following techniques:

❑ Summarize.

❑ Epitomize.

❑ Echo an image introduced in the lead or elsewhere in the article.

❑ Restate the thesis in striking words.

❑ Use a quotation or an anecdote that does any of the above.

❑ Slow the rhythm of the final sentence, often by ending with several strong, one-syllable words or with phrasing that requires a series of commas to create pauses.

Bear in mind the close relationship between the lead and the conclusion. If the relationship is obvious, readers will have the satisfying feeling of completion. They will have come full circle, and they will remember what you have said.

A decisive ending gives you the last word.

SUMMARY

1. An article's lead is crucial because it must be attractive enough or raise an issue significant enough to persuade the reader to read the entire article.
2. A good lead arouses the readers' curiosity, surprises or astonishes them with irony, involves them in the subject, and shocks, delights, and entertains them with the deft use of language and imagination.
3. Professional writers often provide a strong link or echo between the lead and the conclusion.
4. An effective conclusion summarizes, epitomizes, or stresses the article's main point.

FROM PRINCIPLES TO PRACTICE

1. From one of your own magazines, choose one or two exceptionally bright or otherwise effective leads to analyze and read in class. Discuss the qualities that led to your selection. Was the quality of the writing important to you or did you consider content only?

2. Did you react negatively to any of the leads in this chapter? If so, why?

3. Are you put off or turned on by the use of the first person in a lead? Explain your answer.

4. Do you agree that a conclusion should be short?

CHAPTER

12

ILLUSTRATING
WITH ANECDOTES

An anecdote is a short, detailed account of a single episode or event. Conversation is salted with such stories that have no function other than to amuse or amaze, but in magazine articles anecdotes are true stories used to give an example of some point the author wants to make. Containing the dialogue and actions of people, they infuse an article with vitality. An anecdote is a juicy slice of life inserted between layers of exposition. And because it shows rather than tells, it is highly persuasive. An anecdote enables a reader to visualize, even to feel, an abstract quality or idea: a politician's pride, a shy child's loneliness. It can help a reader recognize the folly of certain business policies or understand a complex scientific principle. It makes a generalization specific and therefore memorable.

To think of an anecdote simply as a joke is a misconception. It may be funny, but it may also be serious, even tragic. Regardless of its tone or content, an anecdote is simply a very short story, a seamless digression, that smoothly illustrates a point. It must appear to be an inherent part of the article, not an attachment. It must be wedged into the exposition with unobtrusive transitions that avoid shouting to the reader "And now I am going to tell you an anecdote that will illustrate this general statement."

The introductory transition usually consists of some variation of "once upon a time," four magical words that have been irresistible to audiences for centuries. Thus, an anecdote usually begins with some kind of reference to the time the event occurred:

❑ One day last. . . .

❑ I remember when. . . .

❑ There was the day last year when. . . .

❑ Once. . . .

❑ For instance, we once. . . .

❑ A few months ago. . . .

❑ . . . . such as the time when. . . .

❑ She recalled the time. . . .

Since the anecdote is an account of a past event, it is usually told in the past tense, but the present tense may be used to give the impression of immediacy. In either case, at the end of the anecdote, another transition must bridge the gap between the story's narrative and the exposition that follows. Sometimes the transition will be an explanation of the connection between the story and the thesis, but if the anecdote appears late in the article, its relevance may be too obvious to require interpretation.

There is often a strong connection between the imagery or theme of an article's major anecdote and the way the article ends, perhaps because writers use illustrations and conclusions to accent important ideas. As you read analytically, look for that connection or echo, and try to use this device occasionally in your own writing.

While all good anecdotes are suspenseful, the best ones have an element of irony or surprise. Leading the reader to expect a pebble, the writer hands out a plum instead.

THE ANECDOTE ILLUSTRATES A POINT

An example of this type of anecdote follows. It is shorter and less detailed than most, but it succeeds in emphasizing the author's point in an article describing research on the habits of monkeys. Scientists are finding that these primates are sophisticated schemers and deceivers. In a piece for *Discover,* James Shreeve tells about one female who was surprisingly adept at deception in sexual situations. By way of background, he reminds us that a male monkey or chimp fights to win dominance over the females in his group and then keeps a keen eye on his harem to prevent any cheating.

In one particularly provocative instance a female hamadryas baboon slowly shuffled toward a large rock, appearing to forage, all the time keeping an eye on the most dominant male in the group. After 20 minutes she ended up with her head and shoulders visible to the big, watchful male, but with her hands happily engaged in the illicit activity of grooming a favorite subordinate male, who was hidden from view behind the rock.

Anecdotes have an allure that lingers in the mind, so they often occupy an article's places of honor: the lead or the conclusion. The following example is the lead from an article in *Mademoiselle* by poet and novelist James Dickey. There is no one sentence here that you could underline and label "thesis," but this anecdote *shows* the thesis in its narrative, poetic language far more effectively than an outright statement of the point. Note how painstakingly Dickey sets the scene and the suspense before he brings on the action of the anecdote.

A couple of years ago in North Georgia, sitting two hundred feet above a dammed river, on pine straw with my feet at a very real edge, my wife and I were looking down onto a section of the Tallulah River where a story of mine called *Deliverance* was being filmed. Both our sons were below us, far out of the range of our voices, my oldest boy working on the shooting crew, my youngest, thirteen, just visiting. The state-run dam was closed, which meant that the great rocky fall-offs had no water to fall off them. But they had my boys.

We lay at the edge, hoping our mortal children would not do anything foolish, but also intensely interested in what they *would* do, down there beyond us. The filming was taking place on both sides of the river, and, at the edge of a ninety-foot downriver drop, there was a primitive rig where you could walk across the river holding a rope. There was also a place where you had to jump over a kind of trickling gap, presumably still holding the rope. Or not holding the rope. My embryonic movie-making son kept going back and forth, carrying spools of film, make-up kits, impossible messages to Burt Reynolds and God knows what else. Below my son for ninety feet—I kept going up and down the rock-cruelties with field glasses—was nothing but a set of out-croppings designed by the universe eons ago to demonstrate the utter indifference of wild nature to the pain-bearing bodies of human beings; I was shook by the rage of their stillness. Any rock in anybody's descent was certain to be death—or mutilation-dealing. My wife and I said, almost the same second, "I hope Kevin doesn't try it."

But then of course he did. The suffering, hawk-perching parents could do nothing to prevent it: could do nothing, in fact, but watch like strange pinestraw people the adventures of a belovèd creature with the sheer murderousness of gravity in collaboration with the serious cruelty of random stone.

Our child edged out, one foot staying in front of him, along the rope. He came to the gap in the crossing-stones.

He jumped for the place his brother had mastered, and slipped. Helpless in the higher-up, the field glasses hung fire in our hands, but he had not gone over. He swayed half in and half out of life, and pulled himself back into it. There he was, still in the shaking field glasses, four-eyed from the cliff-top and looking good. Then something broke out in him, down there. He started to dance, or do *something:* something with a lot of energy and motion. But it was not done for us: his mother and father, there at the other edge. It was a silent dance of pure delight: he was dancing with the void, and loving what had just about happened to him, and had not. We, creatures in the rarefied air of bushes at the brink, in the leaves of plants that leaned out over the vanished roar of dammed, gone water, knew that his excitement was not a show for Parent's Day, nor was it for the film crew or even for his brother. The adrenaline had hit like a Heaven-through-the-guts, and he rejoiced in the abyss, dancing back in a gangling, curious, beginning-athlete's way to safety, to his brother, to the crew, and eventually to us, who had no word to say, but only deep images, deep energies based on his.

ANECDOTES SHOW RATHER THAN TELL

The addition of a few good anecdotes can resurrect almost any kind of article. But personality profiles need a particularly heavy injection of narrative if they are to come to life. You can rhapsodize or satirize page after page, *telling* the reader that this person is courageous, scheming, rude, honest, charming, and so on. But until you *show* the person in action, the reader will be unable to see behind the public facade that is always there. Anecdotes give new meaning to the old saying that actions speak louder than words.

Such is the case with the following anecdote plucked from a *New Yorker* portrait of Governor Mario Cuomo by Ken Auletta. The writer introduces the anecdote by telling what Cuomo is like. Then he shows him in court as a young lawyer.

Cuomo was smart, resourceful, and verbally fluent; he was also persistent. And . . . "he could be witheringly harsh and petulant," as Justice Ughetta learned. One day when Cuomo was making an oral argument before Ughetta and the four other Appellate Division judges, Ughetta leaned over to whisper something to another judge. Cuomo stopped talking and dropped his arms to his sides. Justice Ughetta looked up and said, "You may proceed with your argument, counsel."

"I won't proceed with my argument until I get the undivided attention of this court," Cuomo said.

Furious, Ughetta glared at Cuomo and told him to continue. He did, and Ughetta quickly stood up, turned his chair around, and sat with his back to Cuomo. Another judge motioned to Cuomo to proceed with his agrument, but he said, "I will proceed when I have the full attention of the court." Justice Ughetta spun around in his chair and said, "Have you no respect for the bench?"

"Have you no respect for my client and the law?" Cuomo said.

After novelist Pat Conroy returned from living abroad some years ago, he wrote an article for the *Atlanta Journal-Constitution* magazine about his experiences in Paris, describing the intolerance of the French for foreigners, especially Americans, who failed to speak flawless French. In the following selection Conroy expounds with glee on the characteristics of the French, as he saw them, before gliding into the narrative. He uses the anecdote for illustration and entertainment.

Parisians and polar icecaps have a lot in common except that polar icecaps are warmer to strangers. . . . The French relish the xenophobic sport of stereotyping and love to offer an infinite variety of theories on the nature of Americans. To them, we, as a people, are shallow, criminally naive, reactionary, decadent, over-the-hill, uncultured, uneducable, and friendly to a fault. To Parisians, all Americans are Texans, grinning cowboys. France is the only country in the world where friendliness is one of the seven deadly sins. I am deeply inoculated with the serum of American cheerfulness, and I had to make a serious effort to become melancholy and funereal in front of that small doughty band of Parisians who called me "frere." To look Parisian, I walked around with my face tragically set as though I had just received a telegram announcing my mother's death. It was an admirable disguise, but my mouth betrayed me. Whenever Parisians heard my execrable attempts at French, they would cover their ears with their hands and moan over the violation and butchery of their sweet tongue. My concierge, with her great black Caesarean slice of a face, grew increasingly indignant at my lack of facility in French. Her dark eyes, circled with bruised rings, would glower as she heard my voice skipping inexpertly through the dense arpeggios of her language. Finally when her hostility had become a palpable, living thing at the Hotel Balcon, I took her aside and, in a carefully memorized speech, confessed

to her I was mentally retarded and had been sent to Paris on a special
program of rehabilitation. With heartbreaking cries of "Oh pardon, mon-
sieur, pardon, pardon," she clutched me in a wrestler's grip to her breast.
From that day forward, I received an extra croissant at breakfast, a mater-
nal pat on the head, and she regarded each pitiful advance I made in the
French language as miraculous and proof of a living God. Not only was I
retarded, she would explain proudly to her friends, pointing an index
finger to her temple, but I was also writing a book on the agonies of retar-
dation on a grant from the American government.

The following anecdote appeared in an *Esquire* article by Joe Kane entitled "Officer Hicks, Gay Cop." The title itself must have attracted many readers because few have ever known a gay policeman. Obviously this man, a
winner of the National Heroism Award, is unusual. "But J.D. Hicks," Kane
says, "is more than just a good cop. He's a good homosexual cop, and therein
lies a distinction far more subtle than anything you might find in Joseph
Wambaugh."

Kane wants the reader to watch Officer Hicks in action to see just how
unusual he is, how courageous and tough, yet how compassionate. Note that
he uses the present tense to create a feeling that the event is unfolding now.

Tonight, shortly after 9:00, comes an assault-with-a-deadly weapon
call from the Sunnydale projects, probably the most hard-core area in
San Francisco. By the time Car 61 arrives, four other squad cars are there
and a grumbling crowd of some seventy-five blacks and Samoans has
gathered. A cold night fog has rolled in, and in the misty, abstract glare of
a single streetlight an old Chevy Impalla sits with its windows caved in
and two little kids crying in the backseat.

Nearby, two frenzied women scream and hurl curses at each other.
It takes two cops on each to restrain them. As is often the case, the degree
of violence has little relation to what precipitated it—this time one of the
women had lightly rear-ended the other's car. But within minutes the
whole desperate frustration of life in the projects had bubbled up, and
one had gone after the other with a tire iron.

With the arrival of yet another police car, the crowd grows more
agitated. Several people hold barely concealed rocks and bottles. A few
cops are visibly nervous; the crowd begins to make noise, and I heard
one of them yell, "Sissy!"

I look to see how J.D. Hicks reacts. And as I do, Hicks is striding out of the glare, guiding one of the women gently toward Car 61, talking to her in careful, even tones, even as she is shrieking, "MOTHER-FUCKINGUGLYBLACKBITCH," with tears cascading down her cheeks. Here is Hicks opening the back door of Car 61, saying, "We'll get this straightened out and get you home just as soon as we can, ma'am," gently helping her in, a slight grin never leaving his face; and then she sits, just silently sobbing in the backseat, as Car 61 glides out of the projects and down Third Street safely toward home.

"Why Mow? The Case Against Lawns," written by Michael Pollan and published in *The New York Times Magazine*, must have given its readers a new realization of the pressure all Americans suffer to maintain a perfectly manicured lawn. This article challenges that pressure, with one of its persuasive devices being the following anecdote:

My father, you see, was a lawn dissident. . . . he could not see much point in cranking up the Toro more than once a month or so. The grass on our quarter-acre plot towered over the crew-cut lawns on either side of us and soon disturbed the peace of the entire neighborhood.

We got the message. . . . Our next-door neighbor, a mild engineer who was my father's last remaining friend in the development, was charged with the unpleasant task of conveying the sense of the community to my father. It was early on a summer evening that he came to deliver his message. I don't remember it all . . . but I can imagine him taking a highball glass from my mother, squeaking out what he had been told to say about the threat to property values, and then waiting for my father—who next to him was a bear—to respond.

My father's reply could not have been more eloquent. Without a word he strode out to the garage and cranked up the rusty old Toro for the first time since fall; it's a miracle the thing started. He pushed it out to the curb and then started back across the lawn to the house, but not in a straight line: he swerved right, then left, then right again. He had cut an S in the high grass. Then he made an M, and finally a P. These are his initials, and as soon as he finished writing them he wheeled the lawn mower back to the garage, never to start it up again.

FULLY DEVELOPED SCENES READ LIKE FICTION

The final selection presented here comes from the much admired writer of magazine articles and books, William Zinsser. Because of its length, it is not, strictly, an anecdote. Instead, it is a scene from a long *New Yorker* piece consisting of a series of scenes that show what happened during an unusual journey. This scene-by-scene construction is a form all beginning writers need to master. Because it is so much like fiction, no other form in magazine writing is so compelling, so real, so emotional. Consequently, many of today's best nonfiction writers construct their articles by splicing together a series of long scenes that have elaborately described settings, action, and dialogue. By using as little exposition as possible, they deliberately write their nonfiction to read like fiction. Such narrative, therefore, is the spine of the article rather than a small appendage. Nevertheless, it illustrates a point just as an anecdote does.

In this case, Zinsser tells a story about going to Venice with a French horn player who, despite his love of jazz, had a lifelong ambition to play and record Gregorian chants in St. Mark's cathedral because of its remarkable acoustics. The article begins with the musician, Willie Ruff, explaining his obsession: The great innovative composers of the sixteenth and seventeenth centuries, he said, were inspired by this church whose sound "gave richness and clarity to what they wrote." Ruff wanted to hear what that sound was like, and Zinsser, a music lover himself, got permission to go with him to write about the sound and the experience. He uses the first person throughout the article and consequently reveals much about his own impressions as a participant in the pilgrimage. The major focus, however, is on Willie Ruff and his mission.

Because he is writing for *The New Yorker,* Zinsser proceeds at a leisurely pace, giving in rich, luxuriant detail the atmosphere of Venice and their adventures there. In addition to playing in St. Mark's at night when the cathedral would be empty, Ruff also wanted to record some Gregorian chants in a few other Venetian churches for a comparison of their sounds to St. Mark's. The following account tells what happened at one of them.

For his first test he (Ruff) had selected a church called San Rocco, on the other side of the Grand Canal—a church that he had heard was quite deserted. We walked to his hotel to get his horn and then made our way through a maze of alleys and over a bridge to San Rocco, Ruff moving with the agility of a native son.

At the church, his research turned out to be correct. Only two or three people were in the nave, and they were finishing their prayers and would soon be gone. Ruff said he would wait until the church was empty—he didn't want to disturb or offend anyone. Meanwhile, he got out his "Liber Usualis" and opened it to a hymn called the Pange Lingua, which he said was one of the oldest and most beautiful melodies in the book. Finally, the last worshipper left. San Rocco was absolutely still.

Ruff lifted his French horn to his mouth and blew what was at the most a sixteenth note. It was stopped by an old sacristan who came running at remarkable speed, shouting, *"Vietato! Vietato!"* and crossing and uncrossing his arms in the motion of a baseball umpire signifying that a runner is safe. He stood in front of Ruff: a small man, barely five feet tall, choking with outrage. *"Chiesa! Chiesa!"* he shouted, meaning that we were in a church.

"This is church music," Ruff said. He couldn't believe what was happening. The old man had struck like a summer squall. Ruff showed him his "Liber Usualis," a black book that looks like a Bible and has the solemn weight of Roman Catholic authority. He flicked through the pages, stopping to point out the Gloria and various other chants that are still used in the liturgy today. The sacristan was in no mood for ecclesiastical proofs. This was a *chiesa,* and there was to be no music.

Ruff made one more start at protesting his good intentions, but in midsentence the humor of his situation hit him. . . . Ruff hardly made it to the door, and when he was out on the steps of San Rocco he doubled up. "That's got to be the shortest note anybody ever played," he said. "I had just finished my inhale and was about to blow out when I saw this flash coming at me out of the corner of my eye—at the velocity of Jesse Owens." Ruff couldn't stop laughing. He said it was the fastest putdown of his career.

One of the decisions you must make in beginning or revising an article concerns the mode of prose that will best communicate your thesis: (1) pure exposition, (2) a combination of exposition and narrative (anecdotes), or (3) a combination of exposition, extended narrative, and description which produces a scene-by-scene structure. All three have advantages and disadvantages. Number 3 is highly readable, even dramatic. But it is not suitable for all topics, it requires voluminous saturation research, it takes longer to write, and it usually produces very long articles. It is also the least direct method of communicating, for it lets readers draw their own conclusions, just as they do in real life, about the implications of what people say and do. Sometimes the readers' interpretations may be different than what the writer intended. In contrast, pure exposition is the most direct, though not always the most interesting, medium for making a point. Using that form, the author looks the reader straight in the eye, states the facts, and explains exactly what the facts mean.

All things considered, the combination of fact-giving (exposition) and storytelling (anecdotes) utilizes the advantages of each and is a popular form for magazine articles today.

SUMMARY

Vivid anecdotes are crucial to effective magazine articles. You should therefore learn their characteristics, functions, and requirements.

1. Anecdotes are brief, factual stories that illustrate some aspect of an article's thesis. To make them up would ultimately erode the writer's, and the magazine's, credibility.
2. Sometimes functioning as the lead or the conclusion, an anecdote may appear in any position in an article.
3. Except when the article opens with a story lead, an anecdote should be preceded and followed by unobtrusive transitions.
4. Anecdotes will enable you to put people in articles even when writing primarily about things or concepts.
5. Anecdotes engage the reader's emotions and thus make more memorable the ideas and qualities they illustrate.
6 When used to demonstrate principles, theories, and arguments, anecdotes can persuade and clarify.
7. Anecdotes bring the blur of generalities into sharp, distinct focus.

FROM PRINCIPLES TO PRACTICE

1. In one of your favorite magazines, find an anecdote that appears in the middle of the article. Underline its introduction and the follow-up transition that links it to the main body of the article. Read the anecdote and its transition to your class.
2. In the article on Officer Hicks, change the verbs from present to past tense to see how the effect of the story changes. Would there be a problem with continuing the narration in the present tense indefinitely?
3. Would the anecdote about Governor Cuomo have been more effective and more concise if his quotations had been paraphrased? What do the direct quotations and their element of repetition accomplish?
4. Would the selection on lawn mowing have been more effective if the author had included some direct quotations?

CHAPTER

13

STYLE AND
TONE

At this stage in the writing process, your rough drafts should somehow contain everything you wanted to say in your article. You have written a good lead, included some anecdotes and dramatic quotes, made your point, and woven it all together with some good transitions. You're fairly satisfied with the *content* of your article. But one of the most important steps lies ahead. It's time to polish: to work on style and tone.

CAN YOUR STYLE BE IMPROVED?

When applied to language, *style* can be used as a general synonym for excellence. But it is usually applied to a specific writer's characteristic and individual way of expressing ideas or telling stories. It is as peculiar to its author as a fingerprint.

If style is so intimate an expression of mind and personality, can it be learned? In one sense, no. By the time you become interested in it, your style has already been "learned." It has grown with you as your values, taste, and personality have developed. Still, you can learn to apply some writing techniques, especially those used in fiction and poetry, that will gradually expand your style to give it greater range and flexibility.

In an excellent technical book on this subject, *Stylists on Style: A Handbook with Selections for Analysis,* author Louis Milic says, "Style might be described as that aspect of a piece of writing that we *perceive* but do not observe, what we respond to in writing without being aware of it." For some readers that is undoubtedly true; for others, style is an artistic element of language that yields an intellectual pleasure all its own. But for every reader, an effective style casts sunlight on facts that otherwise might remain cloudy.

The following selection by the esteemed writer, Vladimir Nabokov, exemplifies style at its best. It appeared in *The Atlantic* in 1943 when Nabokov was a student at Harvard. In these two paragraphs he reminisces about his childhood governess with the improbable name of Mademoiselle O, a large well-fed lady who looked like her name.

This "O" oddly enough is by no means the abbreviation of something beginning with an "O." It is not the initial of Oliver or Oudinet, but actually the thing itself: a round and naked name which seems about to collapse without a full stop to support it; a loose wheel of a name rolling downhill, hesitating, wobbling; a toothless yawn; a melon; an egg; a lake. . . .

A large woman, a very stout woman as round as her name, Mademoiselle rolled into our existence as I was about to be eight. There she is. I see her so plainly: her abundant dark hair which is covertly graying, the three wrinkles on her austere forehead, her beetling brows, the steely eyes behind a black-rimmed pince-nez, that vestigial mustache, that blotchy complexion which in moments of wrath assumes a purple flush in the region of the third and amplest chin, so regally spread over the frilled mountain of her blouse. And now she sits down or rather she tackles the job of sitting down, the jelly of her jowl quaking, her prodigious posterior, with the three buttons on the side, lowering itself warily; then at the last she surrenders her bulk to God and to the wicker armchair, which, out of sheer fright, bursts into a salvo of crackling.

From analyzing this selection we can begin to see some of the elements that contribute to a pleasing style.

First, consider Nabokov's word choice. He pours out a flood of visual details. Through them we see with crystal clarity Mademoiselle's buxom figure and thick dark hair, her wrinkles, buttons, and chins, her eyes and glasses, the color of her skin, the ruffled blouse, the way she sinks into the armchair—and we hear the crackling of the wicker chair.

Next, his figurative language. In a series of metaphors, he compares the O to a yawn, a melon, an egg, a lake, and a wheel rolling and wobbling downhill. Then, extending the metaphor, he says Mademoiselle O rolled into their lives. Without saying that her bosom is huge, he compares it to a mountain. And finally he introduces some military imagery to suggest danger and even violence when she seats her "prodigious posterior": "surrenders," "fright," "bursts," and "salvo."

There's onomatopoeia in "crackling," a zeugma in "surrendering her bulk to God and the armchair," and personification in attributing fright to the chair. (See the glossary at the end of this chapter if these terms are unfamiliar.)

Nabokov gives his prose a subtle beat with alliteration: beetling brows, jelly of her jowl, prodigious posterior. And the many present participles give the selection the pulse of parallelism and the action of strong verbs: beginning, rolling, hesitating, wobbling, graying, sitting, quaking, lowering, crackling.

Finally, note the variety of sentence structure and length: most sentences are fairly long but one is short as a blink, and all of them are complex in structure. Different. No monotony.

This is writing to be read for inspiration just before you have to write something that must be excellent. Nabokov's talent may be intimidating, but close study of his techniques will teach you a great deal and remind you of the many stylistic tools at your command. From this brief selection you can learn to use specific details rather than vague abstractions, to vary your sentence length and structure, and to substitute strong, active verbs for weak ones (such as the verb *to be*). But don't try to change your writing to sound like Nabokov. Instead, simply borrow his techniques. You want your prose to sound like your own. It should be alive with your uniqueness. And don't be afraid to use your imagination. As Alfred North Whitehead once said in an article for *Harper's,* "Imagination is not to be divorced from the facts; it is a way of illuminating the facts."

A good way to understand style is to see it change when the same idea is expressed by different writers for different audiences of different centuries. The style of Shakespeare's *Macbeth,* for example, differs sharply from the "translation" that follows, in which the poet's ideas are expressed in the prose of modern American street slang. First, the somber, tragic dignity of Macbeth's soliloquy:

> To-morrow, and to-morrow, and to-morrow,
> Creeps in this petty pace from day to day,
> To the last syllable of recorded time;
>
> And all our yesterdays have lighted fools
> The way to dusty death. Our, out, brief candle!
> Life's but a walking shadow; a poor player,
> That struts and frets his hour upon the stage,
> And then is heard no more; it is a tale
> Told by an idiot, full of sound and fury,
> Signifying nothing.

And here is *Eternity* magazine's prose version, with its angry, despairing slang lurching along in a staccato rhythm:

Dig it. Life is a bummer. The days keep truckin' on and on, and they're all downers—from now until that cosmic fade-out that's on the way. Yesterday's big hassle led all those dudes nowhere, man, the grave. So you might as well trash it all. Life is nothing but a rip-off; like a bad show with faded superstars freaking out all over. Let it fade from sight in a cloud of hash. It's like a rap told by a straight, full of hot air and empty words but into nothing.

Both versions abound in metaphor (life's a shadow and a bummer) and in personification (life struts and frets his hour; the days keep truckin' on). But Shakespeare's version is far richer in alliteration (tale told, petty pace, poor player) and in repetition (to-morrow and to-morrow and to-morrow) which makes his passage much more rhythmical than the modern prose version. The most obvious stylistic difference, however, appears in the diction. Shakespeare uses remarkably simple language and familiar imagery, yet his references to the theater and to life as a dark procession toward death have a dignity that is lacking in the modern version. The latter is told in street slang with the imagery of drugs and bums and trash and freaks. It is an uglier picture of life without meaning, and therefore its tone is angrier. It snarls. In contrast, Shakespeare's lines are the noble language of a king who has lost all hope. They convey not anger or the whimper of self-pity but a profound, reflective sadness—a sigh that comes from the soul.

WHAT TO LOOK FOR IN STUDYING STYLE

The following list contains the major elements to be examined in studying style:

1. Level of usage. Is the language formal, informal, or colloquial? Is it appropriate for the subject matter?
2. Sentence length and structure. Is there ample variety of each? Is the word order conventional or unconventional? Is there a noticeable amount of subordination of the less important ideas or facts?
3. Words. Are most words simple and familiar or unusual and long? Are most concrete or abstract, general or specific? What about unusual combinations of words?
4. Parts of speech. Does the writer rely on adjectives, for example, or do concrete visual nouns and verbs predominate?

5. Figurative language. For greater clarity and emphasis, does the writer employ metaphor, simile, personification, or symbol?
6. Rhythm. What is the source of rhythm: alliteration, word repetition, or parallelism?

With these elements in mind, examine a passage of your own recent writing, noting especially the freshness of your word choices, the shapes of your sentences and paragraphs, and their characteristic rhythm. Do you exaggerate or understate, use long words or short plain ones, prefer figurative language or no-nonsense facts? Are you wordy or concise? Are your sentences terse and staccato or flowing? Does your prose move with athletic verbs or stand still with forms of the verb *to be?* Is it fat with adjectives or lean with nouns that paint pictures?

After you've analyzed your own style, compare it with the style of the writers you most admire, especially the passages that have had a marked effect on you, examining how they elicit a positive response.

HOW TO EMPHASIZE IMPORTANT POINTS

In general, a pleasing style results from originality of word choice and word combinations, from language that seems fresh and sometimes surprising. But according to Milic, ". . . the most significant results depend on placing the proper emphasis on the significant parts of the message."

For example, experienced writers place the most important words at the end of a sentence or a paragraph. Why? Because the empty white space following the period causes that word or idea to linger in the mind.

You can often make use of unusual word order to gain emphasis. For example, Bernard Cooper describes a flock of blackbirds thus: "Endless they were, like winged pieces of letters, like a moving sign in Times Square." Note that he also includes two similes. One warning, however, about unusual or inverted word order: It can seem contrived, so use it sparingly.

Emphasis can also be achieved by a technique called violation of expectation. This simply means that now and then you should surprise your reader. If a word you've chosen seems too predictable, substitute an unexpected one. Joan Didion follows this principle when she describes a rich man as "a haunted millionaire out of the West, trailing a legend of desperation and power and white sneakers." And here's Joseph Epstein examining envy in a personal essay: "Awards and prizes are no longer the efficient swizzle sticks for stirring envy that they once were."

Still another way to emphasize a thought is occasionally to make a sudden change in the length of your sentences. A three-word sentence following one of fifty words gets fresh attention with its unexpected punch.

TONE REVEALS YOUR ATTITUDE

Tone is a reflection in words of your attitude toward your material. The tone of a passage in print is equivalent to tone of voice in speech. Perhaps because of this, many writers think they should try to hide their emotions and write with a neutral attitude or tone. But in magazine writing, the opposite course is much preferred. Imagine how boring a conversation would be if you limited yourself to the deadpan tone of a robot.

Because tone is one of the most subtle elements of writing, casual readers may be unaware of its effect on them. Nevertheless, it is a persuasive device that magnifies the impact of the article and enhances the pleasure of an alert reader.

Tone results from the words you choose: their connotations, their combinations with adjacent words, and their total context. Tone, or voice, can be scornful, sad, sentimental, caustic, reverent, disdainful, outraged, admiring, jubilant, or amused. It is seldom neutral.

If you're asked to describe the tone of an article, look for clues in the details included and in the vocabulary of the passage. When words with favorable connotations dominate and the details or images are pleasant, the tone is probably positive, whereas critical words and unpleasant details will signal a negative tone. Sometimes writers will refrain from calling someone a tasteless phony, but they will dwell on the toupee he wears and his cheap "diamond" rings. Sometimes a certain tone results when there's an obvious disparity between lofty language and trivial subject matter or when there's a disparity between adjacent details. For example, journalist Tom Fitzpatrick was obviously sarcastic when he described an "exclusive" political rally to which "only 3,000 invitations were sent out." Likewise, when Terry Southern rendered with rigorous formality the history of a baton twirling institute and then suddenly referred to one of the students as "a real cutie pie," we know he is laughing at the folly of this form of narcissism.

The tone of the following selection from a *Lutheran Standard* article about medical photography reflects the awe and excitement of author Vivian Moss as she describes her first glimpse of new film footage of a human fetus inside its mother.

There it was: an unearthly vision, floating before me—a 40-day fetus, its huge heart, as big as its head, beating away. Nothing in my years of medical films had prepared me for this hair-raising experience. And then another view: a 10-week fetus with its much more human form. He seemed to be pulling his arms up to evade the light. No mother, and certainly not his, had ever beheld this delicate inner-space capsule, its umbilical cord pulsing.

I was astounded when I saw that tiny hand—the whole baby was only a few inches long—in the same position as the one Michelangelo painted in "The Creation of Life" in the Sistine Chapel.

The author's awe and wonder are especially evident in her comparison of the unborn child to Michelangelo's great work of art with all it brings to mind of the sacred and the holy and the creation of life itself. This spiritual feeling that almost leaves the writer breathless is also supported with the words "unearthly vision" and with the article's title, "The Miracle Months." If this writer's attitude and description of the fetus had been purely clinical, the language would have been entirely different. The reverence would have been missing.

A contrasting tone is evident in the next selection by Pat Conroy. He is writing about the insular, exclusive attitude of old, aristocratic residents of Charleston, South Carolina, and its manifestation in their "best" churches.

Society prays without excess beneath three extraordinarily graceful spires that rise chastely above the Charleston skyline: St. Michael's, St. Phillip's, and Grace Episcopal. I name them in the exact order of their social preferability. . . . God himself would have trouble getting a pew in St. Michael's. Even if he could prove longevity and a solid ancestry of good stock, he would need a Charleston connection or two, and it would help if he belonged to the St. Cecilia Society or the Yacht Club. Perhaps he would need a miracle. . . .

But in his quest for a pew, God would also discover that there is something inherently tragic about someone trying to be accepted by Charleston society. It is a milieu in which the mere effort makes you socially suspect. It may be easier to become a manatee or a wolverine than a Charlestonian, and you would look far less ridiculous in the process. In the code of the tribe, heritage is the supreme administrator of who belongs, who is marginal, and who should remain in that sad and whimpering species called common humanity.

The satiric tone here reflects Conroy's wry amusement at the absurdity of the Charlestonians' snobbishness and exclusiveness. But contrary to some satire, which can be bitter and angry, the critical tone in this article is softened by its tinge of sadness.

In the following selection, the sadness the author feels about his subject is much more pronounced. Richard Selzer is writing about the tragedy of AIDS in Haiti, and the title itself sets the somber tone of the article: "A Mask on the Face of Death." In this concluding paragraph, note how he describes the dazzling color of church murals to contrast with the dark atmosphere that pervades the country, and the absence of jogging to show how the people have been altered by the epidemic.

This evening I leave Haiti. For two weeks I have fastened myself to this lovely fragile land like an ear pressed to the ground. It is a country to break a traveler's heart. It occurs to me that I have not seen a single jogger. Such a public expenditure of energy while everywhere else strength is ebbing—it would be obscene. In my final hours, I go to the Cathédral of Sainte Trinité, the inner walls of which are covered with murals by Haiti's most renowned artists. Here are all the familiar Bible stories depicted in naîveté and piety, and all in such an exuberance of color as to tax the capacity of the retina to receive it, as though all the vitality of Haiti had been turned to paint and brushed upon these walls. How to explain its efflorescence at a time when all else is lassitude and inertia? Perhaps one day the plague will be rendered in poetry, music, painting, but not now. Not now.

Tone, or voice, is sometimes difficult to identify, but it is a powerful weapon of persuasion if you want the reader to agree with your point of view. And that's what most writers want.

Although this chapter has examined certain literary devices as elements of communicating with greater force, they are not bows and ruffles that should be basted on for decorative effect. Style, as mere ornament, seems contrived. It is better to be plain and natural than to be fancy and pretentious. The suggestions made in this chapter give you some options, but use them only when they seem natural.

SUMMARY

1. Style must be in harmony with content, and with the article's purpose and audience.
2. The best way, and perhaps the only way, to acquire a distinctive style is by reading and analyzing superlative writing. When this is done with care, you will begin to absorb into your language patterns some effective techniques that will improve your writing.
3. Since style is a matter of emphasizing the most important parts of your subject—your facts or your feelings—remember that the most faithful servants of emphasis are surprise and variety. Too much surprise will exhaust readers, thus making them immune to it. But too much familiarity will bore them.
4. Though readers may be unaware of an article's tone, remember that they are nevertheless affected by it. Tone is contagious. Therefore, take care to choose words that accurately convey your feelings about the subject at hand.
5. Finally, because laziness in word choice, staleness, and monotony are the enemies of style, a writer must occasionally let words cut unexpected capers. "He must strive to remain unpredictable," Milic says. "If there is a secret of good writing, perhaps that is it."

GLOSSARY OF RHETORICAL TERMS

alliteration: The occurrence of words more or less in sequence having the same beginning sound. ("Astronomy shed little light on my place among the planets."—Bernard Cooper)

allusion: Reference to a well-known book, person, place, or event. An allusion is an economical way to enrich the impact of your writing with emotional and intellectual echoes from another work or event. ("The photographs shocked the nation into realizing that something was rotten in Vietnam."—John G. Morris)

anticlimax: A descent from a comparatively lofty vocabulary or tone to one noticeably less exalted. If the descent is sudden, the effect is often comic. ("I began opening my mailbox in anticipation of finding that envelope from the John D. and Catherine T. MacArthur Foundation informing me that I had won a fellowship and might now, baby, let the good times roll."—Joseph Epstein)

connotation: The implications or suggestions evoked by a word. Connotations may be highly individual, stemming from associations based on pleasant or unpleasant experiences in a person's life; or universal—that is, culturally conditioned. (Compare, for example, the difference in effect of *law enforcement officer* and *cop*.)

denotation: The literal meaning of a word, exclusive of the writer or speaker's attitudes or feelings.

hyperbole: Exaggeration as a means of achieving emphasis, humor, and sometimes irony. ("Anna Wintour is beautiful. She makes men stare, and she makes every normal woman want to run shrieking to the phone to dial the Liposuction Hotline. She probably intimidates inanimate objects; linen wouldn't dare wrinkle in her presence."—Judith Newman)

imagery: In its most common use, imagery suggests visual detail or pictures, though it may also refer to words denoting other sensory experiences.

irony: A discrepancy between what is said and what is meant; incongruity, or the opposite of what one expects. ("'I'm not an advocate of the plastic, every-piece-of-hair-in-place look,' explains Wintour, who looks like it might require a wind tunnel to ruffle her own coif."—Judith Newman)

metaphor: A comparison of two unlike objects without using the word "like." ("The Sabbath was folded back with its pristine linens into drawers for another week."—Albert Goldbarth) ("When Rahm flew, he sat down in the middle of art and strapped himself in. He spun it all around him."—Annie Dillard)

onomatopoeia: The use of words whose sounds seem to express or reinforce their meanings: *hiss, bang,* or *bow-wow,* for example.

oxymoron: Two apparently contradictory terms that express a startling paradox. ("The plane seemed to hold its head back stiff in concentration at the music's slow, painful beauty."—Annie Dillard)

parallelism: Writing in which similar or related ideas are expressed in similar grammatical structure, thus achieving balance, rhythm, emphasis. ("It is strangely comforting to surrender an unadorned, eminently imperfect body to the ministrations of another human being: someone who will rotate the stiffened joints, knead the balky muscles, unknot the drum-tight nerves, and coax the sluggish skin into alertness."—Michelle Green)

periodic sentence: A suspenseful sentence, usually long, in which the main idea is not completed until the very end. ("Every four or eight years a large band of men, mostly without previous experience of government, mostly young, all dangerously euphoric because of recent and often accidental political success, all billed as geniuses by the Washington press corps and believing their own notices, all persuaded that they were meant by the stars to reinvent the wheel, are given great ostensible, and even actual, power on the White House staff."—John Kenneth Galbraith)

personification: A figure of speech in which inanimate objects or abstract ideas are endowed with human qualities. ("*Vogue* has been forced to limber up and trot. It's younger. It's looser. It moves with fluidity and grace."—Judith Newman)

pun: Word play involving the use of a word with two different meanings or the use of a word that is pronounced similarly to another with a different meaning. ("He's a science writer who can make the language of numbers as easy as pi."—*Time*)

simile: An expressed comparison between two unlike objects, usually involving the use of *like* or *as*. ("The first cannon to be fired at the Battle of Gettysburg was like a capital letter to mark the beginning of a ferocious sentence."—Arthur C. Danto)

zeugma: A construction in which one word stands in the same grammatical relationship to two other words, one of them literal and the other figurative. ("All my attempts to obtain a crew cut ended in an extremely short haircut that, mocking the power of prayer and pomade, would not stand up."—Joseph Epstein)

FROM PRINCIPLES TO PRACTICE

1. Carefully analyze the style of an assigned article in the Appendix.
2. What is the article's thesis and where is it stated?
3. List the examples of alliteration, metaphor, simile, onomatopoeia, repetition, and personification that you find.
4. Do these devices add to or detract from the article? Defend your opinion with evidence from the article or with evidence of a contrasting approach from another article. If you are critical of the style, how could the author have developed and proved the thesis more effectively?
5. Find examples of the author's use of varied sentence length and structure.
6. Look for some sentences that seem especially rhythmical. What is the source of their rhythm?
7. Find some examples of the use of alliteration, of rhyme.
8. Do you see any details the writer includes that seem to be irrelevant but actually help create a special effect? Explain.
9. Look for examples of an unexpected word instead of a cliché.

CHAPTER

14

REWRITING
FOR QUALITY

Before beginning a discussion about the need for revising your early drafts, let's review a list of ten qualities that are evident in the very best magazine articles. If your rough draft has a high proportion of these elements, you may not need to rewrite, but most people are not so fortunate.

1. A significant point made about a significant topic.
2. A high proportion of narrative.
3. Striking quotations.
4. Visual details.
5. Irony.
6. Similes and metaphors to help explain abstractions or difficult concepts.
7. Contrast.
8. Humor.
9. The intimacy of a warm and personal conversation.
10. A pleasing or graceful style of writing.

Admittedly, not all articles need to display even half of these qualities. Indeed, some, such as humor, would be inappropriate for certain topics. But if you are now reading more analytically than you formerly were, you are no doubt noting the presence of these qualities in published articles, even the technical ones. The point, then, is to use this list as a reminder of techniques that are available when you want your writing to resemble the excellence of a great painting rather than a cartoon.

One of the most difficult lessons to learn in becoming a writer is that rewriting is even more important than writing. In fact, beginners tend to think they've finished when in reality they've just begun. The hard truth is that first drafts cry out for systematic revision. And this is as true for the seasoned writer as it is for you. To review your work with ruthless objectivity, you must examine it with new eyes, from a new perspective.

One way is to lay it aside and try to forget it. The colder your work becomes, the cooler your judgment. To judge it as a critical editor would, print it or type it. You can then read it with more objectivity. You may be too tolerant of whatever is written in your familiar handwriting. To see it from the most critical vantage point of all, read it as if it were the work of a competitor. Or try to see it through the lens of an intelligent but uninformed reader, someone who knows nothing about your subject. You may be shocked at the changes that need to be made. But if your first drafts were composed on a word processor, this obedient machine makes rewriting much easier.

Systematic revision requires that you examine your article from four different perspectives. The process is like viewing a distant scene through a zoom lens. First, you see the panorama, the scene or article as a whole. Then, to examine the paragraphs, you narrow the focus to move in closer, where the details are more distinct. From there you zoom in still closer to the next smallest unit, the sentences. And finally you focus on the smallest element of all, the words. In this way, no part of the manuscript will be overlooked.

EXAMINING THE WHOLE MANUSCRIPT

Overall Structure

In checking the manuscript as a whole, the supreme concern is organization: effective placement of the large blocks of material that make up the article. Are they arranged logically so that you succeeded in saying what you intended? Did you place the various sections in the most interesting order? Do any unnecessary sections cry out to be cut? If you have proceeded chronologically, consider beginning in the middle instead, where the greater suspense and meatier content might make a stronger beginning. Or, if the article contains a good anecdote, pull it out and use it as the lead.

If you have written in the first person, decide whether that point of view strengthens the drama of the article or detracts from its objectivity. If you have dealt with ideas or things, consider putting the focus on people instead, by showing how the issues affect them. Look for more opportunities to show rather than tell, to translate exposition to lively narrative.

Clarity and Coherence

When you are satisfied that the overall structure of your article is right for your purpose and audience, test the manuscript's clarity and coherence. Will the article make sense to a reader who can read only your words and not your mind? Did you arrange your sentences and paragraphs in closely linked sequences, or did you retain essential transitions in your head? The latter error is one of the most difficult to detect in your own work. Enlist the help of a friend to test-read the article for clarity or for gaps in logic that must be bridged with transitions. Your aim is to give the article a coherent, liquid flow.

Unity

While examining the coherence of the article, check its unity. Be sure that every sentence and every paragraph is directly related to the point you are making. You may have included material that, though interesting, relates to another topic, and thus gives your article a split personality. Such a shift in thought will confuse your readers, causing them to wonder if the printer made a mistake. A reader is like a hunting dog who sniffs happily along after a good strong scent but who, if the scent evaporates, quickly becomes bored and goes home.

Your article must have a distinct destination: to prove a single, specific point or thesis. The sequence of ideas must be so logical, so obviously linked to each other, that the reader feels certain of where you are headed. Bewilderment results when an article has no discernible destination.

A unifying image that threads through the entire article will tighten the unity of the piece and give it depth. Remember, for example, the military imagery in "Stalking the Wild Orthographers" in Chapter 2.

PARAGRAPHS

The next step is to move in closer and examine the paragraphs. Check each one for a clearly worded topic sentence followed by supporting evidence and examples. This suggestion may sound like a return to freshman English, but even professional writers sometimes follow a false scent.

Check, also, the shape of your paragraphs for variety. When you see a printed page, your eye usually falls first on the short paragraphs of quoted material, a sign that most readers would rather join a conversation or read dialogue than slog through a long paragraph of uninterrupted droning. The additional white space created by shorter paragraphs and quotation marks looks less formidable, more inviting.

SENTENCES

When you are pleased with the coherence and variety of your paragraphs, check the sentences for the same qualities. Each should echo or relate to the idea in the preceding statement. Your sentences should constantly glance back over their shoulders, so to speak, to form an unbroken chain of thought. At the same time, they should vary in structure, in rhythm, in length.

You may be prone to composing blocks of monotonous sentences that begin with the subject. Vary them by putting something else first: a prepositional phrase, a participial phrase, a subordinate clause, an absolute construction, a modifier. In case you've forgotten these technical terms, study the following sentences. They show five different ways of beginning the same short sentence. Notice that varying the structure also varies the sense and emphasis.

She became disconsolate in the spring and longed for the return of winter. (subject)

In the spring she became disconsolate and. . . . (prepositional phrase)

Becoming disconsolate in the spring, she. . . . (participial phrase)

When she became disconsolate, she. . . . (subordinate clause)

Disconsolate, she longed for winter. . . . (adjective modifier)

Perfectly respectable in magazine writing, an occasional sentence fragment is often more emphatic than a complete statement. For example:

She came striding in like a gym teacher, cheeks ruddy, eyes dancing, tightening the knot on her babushka and pumping hands all around. Katherine Hepburn. Very much in person.

A final suggestion: End your sentences on a decisive note. Use an important word in this place of honor.

WORDS

Words are the last and smallest unit to scrutinize, but in choosing them you should summon all your judgment, imagination, and creativity. You will be seeking the exact word for the effect you want. In writing as in poker, close doesn't count.

Almost all words are useful, but some have higher octane than others. Strangely, the shorter the word, the more horsepower it has. If you're doubtful about that principle, think of all the four-letter words that we use when we're feeling powerful emotions: love, hate, damn, and many others that come to mind. Then think about the foggy language of business and institutions, language that has lost its humanity among the seven-syllable words that crowd out communication. The words are impersonal, abstract, and pretentious. If you want to write with eloquence, use short words that speak from the heart.

It's hard to come up with handy substitutes, but try to avoid institutional words. On that subject a former student once said, "I'll never forget your railing against using words with Latinate endings such as *-ity, -tion, -ization, -ment, -ize,* and so forth. Now that I'm an editor I see how awful they really are. In a sentence they're like chunks of marble."

Write primarily with visual nouns and verbs—especially verbs. Watch Annie Dillard as she uses fifteen verbs to *show* the acrobatics of a skilled stunt pilot:

The plane moved every way a line can move, and it controlled three dimensions, so the line carved massive and subtle slits in the air like sculptures. The plane looped the loop, seeming to arch its back like a gymnast; it stalled, dropped, and spun out of its climbing; it spiraled and knifed west on one side's wings and back east on another; it turned cartwheels, which must be physically impossible; it played with its own line like a cat with yarn.

It's almost always necessary to revise by shrinking. "His personal desire" is stronger when "personal" is erased because the idea of "personal" is built in to "his." Needless words sap the energy of writing and put the reader to sleep. Words that preen and show off should also be cut down to size. For example, "protuberance" lacks the honest force of "lump" just as "serendipity" is a fancy form of "luck." Euphemisms, another windy fault, hide the truth. "His son almost passed" tries to rationalize "he failed." "Mr. Jones terminated her employment" means "Linda was fired."

You must be willing to trim your prose before you build it back up with more telling detail, more visual and figurative language, more narrative. Paradoxically, the more you trim, the stronger the prose. Then, after the pruning, the flower can bloom. For example, read the following dull, lifeless paragraph, and then turn back to pages 93–94 and read again the short piece on McDonald's. That comparison will show you how riotously the following prose could be made to flourish with visual details, quotes, and humor.

I arrived at the fast-food restaurant early in the morning to see what it would be like to work there. The crew was cleaning up, getting ready for the customers who would come in for lunch.

I watched one of the cooks as he fried the hamburgers. Then the manager let me try my hand, but I was very slow and awkward. There were many ingredients that had to be used.

When I prepared to leave after lunch, the manager told me I had done all right.

To read this listless prose is to yearn for a huge shot of vitamins, or a miracle, to bring it alive. While there's nothing wrong with its common words, they're limp, predictable, and general. The McDonald's article in Chapter 9 blazes with the color and action of a movie. It has a specific setting, a cast of real people, lively dialogue, and suspense. You can learn a great deal about word choice, and about writing in general, by comparing these two pieces. Above all, you'll see that it's smart to use words that make your reader see, hear, taste, smell, and feel. Then the two of you will be sharing an experience. Brevity is a virtue, but to create reality with words takes time, space, and details. Significant details.

When you're adding details, you may run into another kind of problem: prose that gushes, is overwritten, or tries too hard to be clever. It's better to be plain than too fancy unless you have the baroque talent of a Tom Wolfe or a Pat Conroy (and even they have been criticized for their flamboyant prose).

Here's an example of "colorful writing" gone wild. In fact, it won a prize in a bad-writing contest.

Like an expensive sports car, fine-tuned and well-built, Portia was sleek, shapely and gorgeous, her red jumpsuit moulding her body, which was as warm as the seatcovers in July, her hair as dark as new tires, her eyes flashing like bright hubcaps, and her lips dewy as the beads of fresh

rain on the hood; she was a woman driven—fueled by a single acceler-
ant—and she needed a man, a man who wouldn't shift from his views, a
man to steer her along the right road: a man like Alf Romeo.

Sometimes there's a fine line between writing that is clever and writing
that is corny, and sometimes the line is as wide as a ten-lane highway. Be sure
you're not on the corny side of the road.

Read your manuscript at least once in pursuit of clichés. They're an elusive prey, because they are so much a part of us that we use them unconsciously. But with concentration they can be tracked down and cut. Read your
work aloud and listen for predictable phrases. For example, after "white as" it's
easy to predict "snow." Another way to handle the cliché is to turn a liability
into an asset by giving a cliché an arresting twist. *Time,* for instance, referred to
magic in one of its articles as "a trade of tricks" instead of "tricks of the trade."

Finally, take a lingering look at your words to see that their connotations
cast the right shadows. Very few words are synonymous or interchangeable:
waddle can't be exchanged for *walk; smirk* is no substitute for *smile.*

Words must dress for the occasion; they are no more interchangeable
than blue jeans and tuxedos.

AVOIDING SEXIST LANGUAGE

The main problems in avoiding sexist language are the use of *he* to refer
to both sexes and inaccurate assumptions about gender and roles. To use *he* in
reference to every generic term such as *writer* or *juggler* or *doctor* is to imply
that all are male. The best way to let your language reflect the truth—that a
woman can be a scientist and a man can be a nurse—is simply to make those
occupational terms plural and use *they* as the pronoun to refer to them. For
example: Instead of saying "A scientist may have problems with his marriage if
he spends too much time in the laboratory," say "Scientists may have problems
if *they.* . . ."

If you're writing about an athlete and it isn't feasible to use *athletes* in
every reference, try to use *person* or the athlete's name.

Authoress or *housewife* are no longer acceptable; say *author* and *home-
maker* instead. But *actress* and *waitress* are still in use.

Avoid describing a woman in terms you would not use in describing a
man. For example, if it would be inappropriate to say "a handsome, seductive
man," then don't say "a beautiful, sexy woman" (or worse, "girl").

Never say "Almost *everyone* has problems with *their* income tax." This agreement error is unfortunately becoming more and more common because it's easier to say *their* than the awkward *his or her*. But it's incorrect to use the plural pronoun *their* to refer to its singular antecedent *everyone*. The solution is to recast the sentence to read: "Almost all people have problems with their income tax."

MECHANICS: SPELLING, PUNCTUATION, USAGE

Student writers are often impatient with the mechanical details of writing, especially spelling. They love to communicate but hate to spell. One of the most important steps in polishing a manuscript is to double check its mechanics, for correct spelling and punctuation are vital to communication. Every error, especially in spelling, is a distraction for the reader. No matter how brilliant your ideas or how smooth your prose, a misspelled word will stop the reader's concentration on your carefully built argument. The reader's mind will register the error instead, and confidence in you will sink. The next thought may be that you didn't care enough to check, and the thought after that may be the fear that you also neglected to check your facts. After these distractions, the reader returns to the typed message of your manuscript, but with a feeling of unease.

Punctuation errors present another kind of distraction. They can cause readers to misread a sentence so that they have to back up and try again to see what short-circuited their comprehension. Commas, semicolons, and periods are like traffic signals. Given the wrong signal, a driver may plunge into oncoming traffic instead of yielding or stopping. Similarly, a comma placed where a period should be will send the reader crashing into a separate thought. This time the reader is distracted *and* confused.

Spelling and punctuation errors transmit messages, too. They communicate, just as all symbols do, but their messages are distinctly negative. They certainly offer no supporting evidence for your thesis.

It's not as difficult to convince beginning writers of the importance of good grammatical usage. They know that double negatives and incorrect verb forms are disastrous to communication. The trouble is that, like the person with poor table manners, the violator is too often unaware of the error.

The only solution is to study a good handbook until you know the rules and principles of good usage and to take the trouble to check with an authority in case of doubt. Recommended reference books for such matters are Strunk and White's *The Elements of Style* and a recent edition of any one of a number of standard college English handbooks.

During the years of your writing apprenticeship, you may have to operate at first on a slim budget of knowledge and skills. Under those circumstances you cannot afford mechanical errors.

SUMMARY

1. To revise and rewrite an article critically, you must see it anew. Let as much time as possible lapse between drafts.
2. Revise systematically, examining and improving overall structure, paragraphs, sentences, and words—in that order.
3. Rewrite bland passages by elaborating with concrete details but prune every unessential passage, sentence, and word.
4. Strive for variety in the structure of paragraphs and sentences and for surprise in word choice.
5. Rewrite with reverence for the subtle but crucial differences in the meanings of synonyms. Choose words with fanatical concern for what they imply as well as what they say.
6. Check carefully for errors in spelling, punctuation, and usage, for they interrupt communication.

FROM PRINCIPLES TO PRACTICE

Apply the principles of revision discussed in this chapter to the article you have chosen to write. Pay special attention to its lead and conclusion.

Throughout the article, have you included enough detail to put life into the piece but not so much as to bore the reader? This dilemma is one of the most difficult that all writers face. It is one of the reasons that all writers need a good editor.

CHAPTER

15

THE CASE HISTORY
OF A MAGAZINE ARTICLE

"All my life I've backed into the things I've done. I never set out to do any of them. They just happened."

Stuart Culpepper, freelance writer, actor, and critic, was talking about the sudden surge his writing career had taken following the publication of his magazine article, "Fear and Loathing on the Streets of Atlanta." Appearing in *Atlanta Magazine,* the article was an example of stumbling into success by chance rather than choice. Culpepper had intended to write about the kinds of people who own guns today and why they are buying them. The article he actually wrote was on an entirely different subject, and the treatment he gave it was, for him, an experiment. The result was a surprise to everyone concerned with the article: Culpepper was gratified that his gamble with a new style had created the effect he wanted, and his editors were amazed that "he could write like that."

While working on the original article idea, Culpepper had gone to a local firing range to check out the kinds of people who might be sharpening their aim. An excellent shot himself, he was practicing with a pistol when he began a casual conversation about marksmanship with a young policeman who was watching him. That chance encounter changed everything, perhaps even Culpepper's life.

Years before that incident, however, Culpepper had backed into another experience that had a long-range effect on him. When he was still in his teens, he was sworn in as a deputy sheriff in a small Alabama town, before he was old enough to be licensed to carry a gun. During the days of civil rights violence, courageous law enforcement officers were sometimes hard to find in the South, and the sheriff's department welcomed this plucky kid who wanted to be a cop. But their enthusiasm cooled when they discovered that Culpepper often sympathized with the blacks.

Later, he became a police and civil rights reporter. One day when he was covering a particularly tense story, something happened that almost ended his life and did end his career as a reporter. Three whites, one of them the son of a high-ranking police officer, turned on him and savagely beat him with clubs and handcuffs.

When Culpepper was released after months of hospitalization, he moved to Atlanta for a complete change of scene and career, and for several years earned his living as an actor, director, and writer. His life had settled into a satisfactory but unexciting routine until the day he met the policeman at the firing range and changed his mind on the subject of his next article.

Because his own career in law enforcement and police reporting had ended in trauma, his attitude toward the police was typical of Atlantans: mostly outrage at the police for allowing violence to get out of hand. People were robbed, mugged, and burglarized every day, and the police seemed helpless to prevent it.

But that day at the firing range, as he talked with the young cop, some old memories were revived and Culpepper noticed the strain the man was under, how difficult it was for him to have a relaxed conversation, how separate he seemed from other people—all, apparently, because he was a policeman. Culpepper became more and more aware of the mental cost of being in law enforcement in a city where the police are the bad guys.

In spite of his painful memories of law enforcement officers, he liked the man and wanted to know him better. He wondered what his life was like, on the job and at home. It occurred to Culpepper that during the outcry over Atlanta's crime, no one had taken the time to get the lone police officer's side, as opposed to rhetoric from chief and commissioner and mayor. At that moment, Culpepper knew he had found a fresh subject for a magazine article.

Accordingly, he began to work on winning the young policeman's confidence and earning his friendship. He made slow but tangible progress until the officer discovered he was a writer.

"That almost ruined it," Culpepper said. "For him, an interview with a reporter meant bad publicity. He shied away, becoming more aloof than ever."

The inside story might never have been written if Culpepper hadn't decided to spend a night cruising with another policeman. Answering a burglar alarm at a business address, the police officer asked Culpepper to serve as a back-up for him while he crawled through a small hole in the wall to enter the building. The officer trapped the burglar inside and was restraining him when Culpepper intercepted an accomplice and held him at gunpoint until he could be handcuffed. The incident changed everything. Culpepper's willingness to lay his own life on the line had won the respect, not only of the young officer he had hoped to cultivate, but of many other members of the force.

For two months Culpepper worked full time on the story. Many days he spent up to seventeen or eighteen hours with his main subject or with other policemen who now seemed eager to tell him their problems. He was finally allowed to meet the officer's wife and son, and he could then observe and talk about the effects of job stress on family life. Culpepper carried a cooler of beer in his car every day so that he could not only work with the men but also unwind with them off duty. In short, he was conducting saturation research.

As his relationship with the officer deepened, Culpepper became more and more involved with the paradox of police problems. But one thing bothered him. In talking about the story with friends, taking pains to conceal the identity of the central figure, he noticed that they never seemed to care about his man as he did. They remained hostile or cynical toward the police in general.

Why don't they care about this cop as a human being? Culpepper asked himself.

The answer eluded him until he began to write the article. He wrote a conventional lead stating his conviction that in Atlanta, where it is extremely stressful to be in law enforcement, the police are conscientiously trying to do a good job despite being overworked and underpaid. In succeeding paragraphs, he explained the complexities of police politics in Atlanta and discussed low salaries, low morale, and the high expectations of the taxpayers.

It didn't work. What he was writing was cold and distant and intellectual. Explaining the problem was good sociology but poor communication. The academic analysis failed to show the fear and humiliation of the men who day after day had to endure verbal and physical abuse for trying to uphold the law.

"I finally saw that the old soap-box technique was not going to do what I wanted to do with the story," Culpepper said. "The reason I loved the main character, Ted Cotton, was that I knew him so intimately . . . knew what he was feeling when he had to enter an empty house at night with a weapon whose ammunition made it more like a cap pistol than a gun. Somehow I had to discover how to put those things on paper. Fortunately my theater experience helped. It taught me how important suspense is. It also taught me that to portray a character convincingly you have to crawl into his head until you think his thoughts. That's what I began to do with Ted Cotton. After I had gone on a call with him, I'd ask him to go over the whole scene step by step, telling me what he was thinking and feeling at each instant, and describing the mental debate with himself as he made decisions that could save his life if they were right, or snuff it out if they were wrong.

"As I began to know other men in the police department, I saw that they wanted to develop a strong bond with me—that they wanted to tell me all the things that were on their minds because they were convinced now that I would tell their story fairly. I often took hot dogs or steaks or booze to their homes for dinner so we could continue to rap. Talking with their families was like group-encounter sessions.

"I learned that race was not the issue with them, though many critics claimed it was," Culpepper said. "For them, there was no black and white. For them it was *us* in blue. I saw white officers being tender and solicitous to blacks in trouble—and the same compassion toward whites shown by black officers.

"For my story it was indispensable to become involved in the men's family lives as well as their lives on the job. That way you share other people's pain and shame and suffering and degradation."

Culpepper learned, though, that such intense involvement with the main characters of an investigative article generates an enormous amount of data. He used a tape recorder placed on the seat of the police car when he was cruising with an officer, but he said it was a "horror" to go home and have eight hours of tape to transcribe. The bulk of material was bewildering when it was time to convert all these seemingly miscellaneous facts to meaningful prose. Still, the tape recorder was valuable.

The hours of recorded conversations furnished the new form he ultimately used for the article. It showed him that the interior monologues, the descriptions Ted Cotton gave of what he was thinking and feeling in dangerous situations, were emotionally powerful. They revealed the core of Ted Cotton.

Gradually Culpepper learned to let Cotton tell his story from his own point of view, including his intimate thoughts. When he read to his friends the opening scene written in the new style, they begged him to continue. "What happened?" they demanded. They, too, had begun to care about Ted Cotton.

Culpepper has been asked how much of the recorded material he used in the article and how much censorship he exercised. "I had to be very selective," he said, "simply because of space limitations in the magazine I hoped to sell the article to—although once the editor saw the manuscript and began to read it, he never complained about its length. He did push me to finish on deadline, however, and I'm dissatisfied with the hurried ending. I stopped *showing* and returned to preaching. If I had had more time I would have closed with another scene showing Ted Cotton cruising the streets again. But there was so much I wanted to say on the crime problem in Atlanta, and the editors went along with that. There are many things about the article I'm not happy with. But I spent too much time on research and that left too little for the writing. If I ever revise the article, the word 'mucilaginous' in the first sentence will go. It's in my vocabulary; I use it frequently. But few other people do, I've found. I censored some of the obscenities, but everything else is accurate. I also may have made the characters sound too perfect. The wife, for instance, is too saintly. But I portray Ted as a hero because to me that's what he is. It wouldn't have been honest to present him in any other way. He's an idealist. He really loves to catch burglars and he wants to protect the very people who pay him too little."

When Culpepper is asked about the most satisfying result of the article, he says, "Ted Cotton cried when he read it. And when his wife (who had left him because of problems brought on by the frustrations of his job) read it, she understood for the first time what her husband has to endure."

In the story, Culpepper weaves material about police problems into the narrative by using a stream-of-consciousness technique. For example, as Ted Cotton rushes to answer a burglar call, his thoughts carry the narration along and show the frustration and fear he must deal with. One of his problems is that he dare not exceed the speed limit by more than five miles an hour because there is no insurance on his police car: "Even a *minor* accident involving another vehicle could cancel Christmas for his wife and kid this year, he broods . . ." Throughout the article the point of view is usually that of the main character. Potent verbs indicate that he is thinking, making decisions, reacting: he figures, decides, broods, fears, knows, curses.

The language of his thoughts reflects his speech patterns: "Am I gonna be late?" And part of it is a sort of mental shorthand. He thinks in fragments of sentences. Sometimes a single word telescopes a complete thought. Sometimes he gives himself orders as though he is observing himself: "Get out of the light, fast!" Sometimes he uses the first person and refers to himself as "me."

Occasionally the author enters the narration and describes what is happening to Ted Cotton. But more often he enters Ted's mind and reports the fear and the questions that arise when Ted hears a strange noise: "Movement? A board creaking? Whispering? Weight shifting?"

One of the story's best scenes is the angry dialogue that scorches the air during Choir Practice, "a time for all the good little boys and girls in blue" to gripe and drink away their frustrations. Reading more like a play than an article, the scene unfolds in a stream of almost uninterrupted dialogue that allows the men themselves to describe their problems. The climax comes when a black sergeant speaks straight to the author in blunt but eloquent words, almost weeping over these men's struggles to maintain their manhood and pride in spite of corrupt politics and poor leadership.

At the end of the Choir Practice scene, for twelve eloquent paragraphs Culpepper steps out of his cinematic role of showing characters in action. Instead, he speaks directly to the reader about the policeman's coping with a high degree of stress and low morale. In these expository paragraphs he summarizes the police officer's ironic dilemma, including some conflicts he has already "shown," perhaps, but adding some statistics that could not have been included in the narrative.

For most full-time freelancers, this article would have been an unaffordable luxury; it would have required too much time for the fee it earned. But for Culpepper, partly because of his past, the article became an obsession he could not abandon, and he had other sources of income that gave him leisure. Above all, the time, expense, and effort were fully justified because the article attracted so much attention that it strengthened his resolve to do more writing of this kind in the future.

Fear and Loathing on the Streets of Atlanta
Stuart Culpepper

The steaming, sauna-wet August night is mucilaginous—thick enough to make any movement at all an act of defiance against nature. Less than a year out of the Police Academy, 24-year-old Patrolman Ted Cotton cruises alone up and down a northwest Atlanta neighborhood looking for a peeping tom who's been reported by two different callers half a block apart.

He figures the perv is either gone by now or knows a cop is on the street and won't show himself again until Ted's driven out of the neighborhood. One more time around the block, Ted decides, and then he'll move on and give the creep a chance to crawl out from under his rock.

As he turns the corner, his call numbers erupt in a crackle through the radio for a Signal Six. Acknowledging the call, Ted reverses directions in someone's driveway and turns toward the designated address several miles away, mentally mapping the fastest possible short cuts.

The "six" means a burglar in a house, and it's one of Ted's favorite calls. He's had a personal vendetta against burglars since the night he found himself helpless, trying to explain to an impoverished and tearful 70-year-old black woman why somebody would break in her house while she was in church and steal her little black-and-white TV and her 1954 Philco radio.

To Ted, burglars are "scum," along with child molesters and rapists.

He pushes the City's white Chevrolet Impala about five miles an hour over the speed limit, using the blue lights to clear a path. No siren. As much as he wants this burglar, he won't allow himself to unleash the Chevy's horsepower because there is no insurance on his police car. If he has an accident, he is liable for damages to the cruiser as well as the property of anyone else involved—regardless of the nature of the emergency.

Even a *minor* accident involving another vehicle could cancel Christmas for his wife and kid this year, he broods as he maneuvers through the erratic Friday night traffic, controlling his urge to get to the burglar faster. He radios the dispatcher for more information.

"Do you have anything further on the call?"

"Negative."

"A call back number?"

"Negative."

Now he fears it could be a bad call—a possible false alarm. He also knows that if Kelley, his partner, is anywhere nearby in his own prowl car, he will hurry to back him up. Kelley will possibly drive faster than Ted since both know that *nobody* on the streets will help them except another "blue suit."

As time seems to stop, Ted presses toward the location, each minute passing like an hour. His mind races over the problem. He knows that from the time headquarters got the phone call to the time Ted got it from the dispatcher, a *minimum* of two minutes passed. Since it will take him five or more minutes to get to the address, at least seven minutes will have elapsed since the call was initiated. No telling how long it took the caller to make the original contact with the police after something happened.

If there *is* a burglar, he'll probably be gone by the time Ted gets there. Unless it's the scum's first time and he's either real stupid or real greedy. Or unless, for some ominous reason, he's not worried about getting caught.

Ted continues to mentally gnaw at the problem. In seven or ten minutes he could be too late to help.

Should I drive faster? No! I'm not bustin' my ass, pushin' it, even for a burglar! But am I right? Am I gonna be too late? Is somebody in trouble? Like that 97-year-old woman who was raped and suffocated by that punk burglar a few weeks ago? Have I worked this address before? I don't *think* so. What's the street like? Run down. Nobody cares. They're just barely hangin' on there. It's all gonna be condemned.

Have I busted anybody who lives on that street? I don't think so. Not at their *home*, anyway. I know *two* houses on that street, but I haven't seen those people in a long time. Last time, they were all drunked up and throwin' furniture at each other from one yard to the other. Nobody got hurt, but they tore hell out of their stuff. I *could* have locked 'em up, but I was able to talk 'em down. Besides, they were exhausted from heaving all that furniture at each other. I guess I'm okay with *them*. Damn! Possible setup? How long'll it take Kelley to get over here and back me up?

There it is! About a block ahead, on the left. Kill all the lights. Dark! Jesus! The whole damned street's dark. No street lights. If somebody wants to blow me up, they picked a righteous spot. Cut the motor off and coast to the curb a couple of houses away. *Big* tree out front. Couldn't see an albino elephant under it. Better hit the street fast, get to the tree and reconnoiter.

With the car at the curb, Ted grabs the keys, gulps a breath of hot, stagnant air and bails out, leaving the car door open. He scrambles through knee-high weeds, flashlight in his left hand and .38 Smith and Wesson revolver in his right.

It's dark enough to hide an *army* of bad guys in the shadows, but the open areas are illuminated by a moon full enough to make him a sweat-glistening, sitting-duck target between the car and the tree, the tree and the house.

Get out of the light, fast!

He reaches the tree in several stumbling strides. Checking the darkness immediately around him with his light, he leans his back against the trunk, controlling his breathing, forcing it slow and easy.

Motionless, Ted strains to burn a path of sight into the darkness surrounding the house. He dimly sees steps going up to an old, narrow porch. No lights glow in the surrounding houses. The magnolia tree blocks the moonlight from the front of the house, its blossoms probably the only flowers to ever live here.

Black as a tomb. Still as death itself. Even the mosquitoes are sitting it out. It's 1:47 a.m. in a high crime zone, and Ted is on his own—for the taxpayers—in the dark night. No traffic—people *or* cars.

Does everybody else know something he doesn't?

Peachtree and Boulevard and Stewart Avenue and Campbellton

Road and Piedmont and Auburn Avenues are bumper-to-bumper right now. Here, nothing but stillness. Dead air. Darkness. Maybe death himself.

Listen, dammit! Listen! Use the ears. Is there sound anywhere? Anyone in there talking? Crying? Moving? Nothing.

Use the nose. Smoke? Burning? Cigarettes? Cigar? Nothing.

No sound. No smell. No spit in the mouth either. Nothing to swallow. Hard to even *open* his mouth. Eyes burning from trying to pry secrets from the night.

Between his shoulder blades, the muscles bunch tightly as though grabbed in a vise. His pistol and flashlight are clenched hard enough to crush them were they less solid.

Relax, dammit! Relax! Gotta make the porch now. Go!

Ted's leonine speeds reveals little more than a blur as he hits the steps, springing from the second of four to the porch. He presses his back to the wall beside the dark doorway. Eyes riveted on it. *Defying* it to open!

The flashlight quickly sweeps the porch to his left, away from the door. Clear there, unless someone's just out of sight behind the corner. He sweeps the light back to the right across the door to the other side of the porch. Again, seemingly clear.

He wants to check around each corner over the edges of the porch, but to do that he must cross in front of two windows, where he'd be a hulking silhouette—an easy hit for a shotgun.

Silently cursing the mayoral policy which won't allow him the same firepower his adversaries have, he flashes his light back to the door. On the knob. Around the jamb. Closed tight. He flicks off the light. No sign of light around the jamb. Or from the windows.

Listen again. Movement? A board creaking? Whispering? Weight shifting? Smell. Cigarettes? Cigars? Joints?

Still nothing.

Ted points his .38 at the door, his back still flattened against the wall. Holding his breath, he reaches out with his right foot and kicks lightly against the bottom of the door. Taps it several times.

Nothing but the hollow sound of hard shoe leather against old wood echoes through the night.

He works spittle into his mouth which has been too dry to form words. Summon up the breath support! Can't sound scared. It won't work.

"Anybody in there?"

Five seconds of silence crawl through the fetid, lonely night.

Again, he sweeps the light to the left and right corners. Nothing. Back to the door. The knob. Moving? No. Are the cracks between the door and the jamb the same size they were? Yes.

He kicks more firmly with his foot. The effort jostles a plunging rivulet of sweat from his left eyebrow down into the corner of the eye below. Startled, he blinks and squints rapidly, frantic to clear it. His eye stings. He can't see! He rubs it quickly with the top of the wrist of his flashlight hand, gun still ready, daring the door to spring open.

"Anybody home? This is the police. Did someone here call the police? Open the door!"

Five more seconds of the silent, unholy night pass.

Ted scans the light to the left and right corners yet again. Clear. The tension attacks his neck and shoulder muscles with renewed vigor. The vise tightens. Sweat dances a goddamned minuet across his face.

S--t! It's a s--t call! Nothing here! Maybe. Maybe they got the address wrong. Maybe it's supposed to be one of the houses on either side of this one. But they're dark and quiet also. No, this is it. This is what they said.

Wait a minute! There *is* something!

Something shifted weight in there. *More* than that: a small . . . thump. Inside? Yes! A moan? Somebody moaning? Snoring? Again! No, dammit, somebody's hurtin'. Or playin' a sick joke.

Where is Kelley? Where the hell's my sergeant? At least *he's* got shotguns! Where're the street lights? Dear God, I'm *sorry* about those street lights I busted when I was a kid. It all comes back on you, don't it?!

Okay. That sound justifies goin' in. Now what happens when I go through that door? I'm a plu-perfect, silhouetted clay pigeon in that open doorway from inside the house as I go through. A double-barrel could shred me like lettuce! It's gotta be dark as a Peachtree Sweat Hog's soul in there. Ohhh, Christ, I'm tired. Where is everybody? *Any*body?

He decides to hold where he is for another few moments to give his partner or the sergeant a chance to show.

But dammit, somebody in there may need help! Maybe so, but these puny .38 caliber bullets are no match for the shotgun or magnum that could be pointed at me from inside.

An eternity passes in the three more minutes it takes Kelley to arrive from another call several miles away. He parks silently behind Ted's car and makes the same trip to the magnolia tree. With a couple of mutters and a few gestures, each knows what the other will do. Quietly, they check both sides and the rear of the house. Still nothing. Kelley takes the back door and Ted, the front.

Once more, Ted identifies himself as a police officer and hears no response. Standing aside, he reaches out and tries the door. It's not locked—opening easily, even quietly.

He leans slightly toward the opening and checks the front room with his light, peeking around the edge of the frame. Seeing no one, he sidles into the room, again throwing his back against the wall. Feeling a light switch with his shoulder, he flips it on, but nothing happens. The flashlight reveals the broken bulb overhead.

Except for piles of litter and a stomach-churning stench, the room is empty. The house seems to have been abandoned.

Ted and Kelley cover each other and quickly clear the few rooms. All the lightbulbs have been broken or removed. The gas and water still work. The toilet is backed up and overflowing with excrement and urine.

But what the hell made that awful sound?

Almost missing it in their hurry to get away from the retching smell, Ted and Kelley stumble across the body of a pregnant dog in the dark refuse of the house. Her stomach has been ripped open, the gashes deep and jagged. From her limp warmth and still-oozing blood, it's obvious Ted heard her dying. But there is blood only in this one back room with an open window. A lot of it, missed the first time they peered into the darkness. A genuine mystery.

Did someone hear the dog's agony and call the police?

Had there been an ambush that quailed at the last minute and changed its mind?

Was someone still in the house when Ted arrived?

What if it had been a *person* lying there all that time?

The sergeant and the shotguns finally arrive, the houses next door are checked and found empty, reports are filled out, and the men are quickly back on the streets, each going in separate directions, headed for his next call.

Before the Morning Watch is over at 6:30 a.m., Ted will answer some 14 calls: several "drunk and disorderly's"; one "chicken bone" family fight, one man semi-scalped in the yard of his girl friend by his common-law wife hefting a sling blade; one real burglary; several false alarms; and a mini-gang fight between two car loads of teen-agers who briefly, but thoroughly, terrorized the neighborhood in which they happened to stop to fight. He also will back up Kelley on another call that sounds like "trouble" before it's discovered to be a false alarm.

Further, he will check the license plates of four cars being driven "too carefully" or too fast, arrest a drunk driver and ticket a speeder.

At 6:50 a.m. the birds are scrambling to be early, and the heat is rising with the sun to mix with that of the night which had never cooled. Bone-tired and muscle-bruised from being kicked in the left thigh by the woman he was trying to keep from being beaten up by her husband in the family fight, Ted begins the 20-mile drive home, across town and out of the city limits to a small, pleasant house in a quiet neighborhood which he can barely afford.

Responsible for a wife and small son, he works an extra 40 hours a week to supplement the salary the City pays him. The hours are worse on days when he has to go to court. Worse yet, waiting for his cases to be called up in court.

Bedraggled and stinking of his own sweat, he replays the duty shift from start to finish as he drives, rethinking decisions made, actions taken or not taken. With less than a year on the force and still quite young, he's too raw not to kick himself for the debilitating effects of his own fear. He was *scared* in every situation he encountered, and he blames himself, forgetting—if he even fully understands—that every other lone centurion in the field last night was also scared.

They were scared that each incident might turn into more than it seemed or that in a split-second of misjudgment, they might exacerbate an already hairy situation and find themselves in the position of fighting for their lives—or the life of some taxpayer.

Ted is haunted by the nagging memory of that pathetic, disemboweled bitch dragging her unborn pups around and around that room.

Oh God, what if that had been a pregnant *woman* in there. I'd have heard *her* going, and for the lack of a shotgun—for damned politics!—I didn't get in in time to help her. Maybe there'd have been no *time* to save her, just like with the mama-dog, but at least she wouldn't have died *alone*. Someone who cared would have been with her. He pushes back the memory with a loud, raging stream of profanities that floods up from his very bowels and groin.

His anger and frustration unresolved, he finally swerves his 1972 Ford Maverick into his driveway and limps, scowling, to the front door. He has to be at his extra job in less than seven hours, and he needs a shower, food and sleep.

He throws open the front door and stalks down the hallway to his bedroom, unconsciously ignoring his young son waiting near the door to surprise him. At this moment, he doesn't even smell the bacon frying in the kitchen.

"Good morning, Dad."

Ted doesn't notice or hear his grinning son, standing to the side with a glass of cold orange juice as a "welcome home" present. Young Teddy Jr. has been at the front windows, watching for his father for 15 minutes, but Ted knows none of this as he slams the bedroom door and begins peeling off his bullet-proof vest and uniform.

In his shorts, as he opens the bedroom door to ask his wife for a shot of whiskey in a glass of milk, he hears a timorous voice from the kitchen:

"Mommy?"

"Yes, punkin?"

"Here's Daddy's juice back. He's not home yet."

"I know, Teddy. Don't worry, he'll get here."

Tears blur Ted's sight as his shoulders slump and he reels back into the bedroom, softly shutting the door. He sits on the edge of the bed, unsuccessfully struggling to hold back the wetness streaming down his cheeks. Finally, he throws water in his face in the bathroom, slips on a fresh pair of pants and hurries into the kitchen with a big smile for his lonely little family.

He reaches down, scoops up his son and carries him over to his wife, where he hugs them both—long and hard.

Proper "good mornings" are exchanged. No questions are asked about "the job." Soon everything's all right. In the steaming shower a few minutes later, Ted vows aloud to himself and to God that he will never again walk in the front door of his home an angry cop. The "real world"—

the "mean streets"—have to be shut out *on the way home.* By the time he hits the front door, he must be a father and a husband.

Even as he makes the vow, he knows he can't keep it, but he'll try harder, for sure.

Already his son thinks if he forgets himself and is "real bad, Daddy'll put me in jail." Neither Ted nor his wife has told the youngster that. They've tried to reassure him it's not so, but he knows that's what his father does "at work," and Teddy's "always worried" it will happen to him, too.

He snuggles against his father in the big bed, even though he's not sleepy, pretending he wants to take a nap. Teddy lies there as still and quiet as he can, trying to absorb what he can of his father, even though Daddy's already asleep.

At least, Daddy's home.

After clearing away the breakfast things, Ted's wife, Linda, slips into the bedroom to see her husband and son. Teddy gingerly gets up and asks to go outside to play. Linda sits on the floor beside the bed, her chin and arms on the edge. She watches her husband's breathing, giggling at his light snores, and she finally relaxes.

At least for now, Linda doesn't have to worry about the phone ringing in the middle of the night or another police officer coming to the door and asking her if she'd like to sit down. She knows Ted had a bad night and wonders when it will come out: whatever it was that happened.

She has a lot of housework to do before Ted gets up to go to his extra job, but for now she just sits and watches his "life." Everything needs to be clean and neat and perfect when he gets up because Ted will walk out that door later tonight—and he may never see any of it again.

Monday night he's off, she remembers. It would be so nice to go to some little, quiet, inexpensive restaurant. Go early, take Teddy, just the three of them. At the same time, she doubts he'll do it since he's so paranoid around groups of people. And he always has to sit with his back to the wall, facing the door. She smiles, watching his stern face softening in sleep. And I always have to tug at his shirt to keep his gun covered and out of sight, she thinks. Well, maybe we could take Teddy to a movie, but Ted'll want to see a cop movie, and then he'll get angry with how phony the movie cops are, and it'll put him in a bad mood.

Maybe we can just be home together. And watch a cop show on TV.

Linda giggles over the thought, breathes a solemn kiss at her snorning, exhausted man and slips out of the room to check on Teddy, clean the house and work on the front yard.

At 3 p.m. Ted rises, showers, shaves, drinks several fast cups of coffee and a glass of V-8 juice, bolts down two boiled eggs (all the while, listening to Waylon and Willie on Linda's portable record player) and leaves for his *extra* job. Linda has cleaned the house, boiled the eggs, set up the coffee, ensconced young Teddy with a neighbor and gone off to her own part-time job while he slept.

He feels good, if still a little tired, after six hours of sleep. The "extra job"—one in which he is useful because of his "cop skills"—goes well. By 9:15 p.m., he's back home—still in civilian clothes—for a light, quick dinner with his family.

The damned clock is inexorable, though, and conversation dwindles as it nears time to don The Uniform. Soon Teddy is put to bed, and both Linda and Ted are silent as he dresses.

It's almost as though he's a werewolf or something, Linda thinks, watching her lean, muscular husband concentrate to shift roles from "loving husband and father" to the visage of a "walking blue target." God, he's so handsome, she sighs to herself. And so vulnerable out there alone in the streets.

He digs out his service revolver and backup gun from where they had been hidden from Teddy's rampant curiosity. With a quick kiss (but no "good-byes"), he's out the door, headed for a 10:30 p.m. station roll-call—and the dark streets and alleys of Atlanta.

Still mentally focused on making the transformation from sensitive, nice-guy civilian to hardened, single-minded keeper of the peace, Ted steers purposefully across town to his precinct, without music on his car radio.

Peel away the softness. Pare it all down to "cop." Accept the fact that from now until I take off the blue suit and badge, I'm a moving target, and nobody on the street gives a s--t that I have a wife and kid at home or if I'm the nicest guy in the world. There is at least ten per cent of the citizenry out here that could give a s--t less if I'm wasted in the street. The other 90 per cent will forget the day after. Gotta face that mentality. Also gotta accept responsibility for now for the lives of my taxpayers out here. They're important to me. Not important enough for me to die for them, though. Well, a child, maybe, or another officer, sure—but not for some doped-up 23-year-old "waterhead."

I'll go in after a burglar again because of my "vendetta," but it's a joke 'cause after I catch him, he'll get seven [years], serve two, and the creep'll be out in eight months, doin' it all over again.

But good God Almighty, Rosannah! For the moment I've got him, it's dynamite. I'm alive! At least I've stopped him for a short while. *Tomorrow,* I'll worry about the court lettin' him go so he can come back! But for now—*tonight*—damn! I want a burglar!

He doesn't get one, though.

Ted works his shift without much variety from the preceding night. Hot. Alone. Scared. He gets two burglar calls, but both "perpetrators" are gone before he can arrive. A wave of false alarms occupies him most of the evening. A missing-person call on his beat tonight is a sad one with little hope of a happy ending. And he's called every vile name a drunken driver can muster because of Ted's warning to stay put in the parking lot of a shopping center rather than getting out in the traffic and getting killed or arrested.

At 6:30 a.m. the shift is over once again, but this morning is different. No court today. For many of the men and women on this shift it is often necessary to decompress before going home—to wash out the dirt and sweat and fear and blood and anger with a bout of serious "down an' dirty" drinking.

Choir Practice: an off-duty cop euphemism made famous in a brilliant novel by ex-cop Joseph Wambaugh and then tarnished in a silly, sleazy movie. Choir Practice: a time for all the good little boys and girls in blue—the "Choir Boys"—to maunder to a secluded spot and *drink away* the pressures and frustrations rather than taking it out on the family or the cat; a time to swap war stories and hold a motley kangaroo court *in absentia* for bad superior officers, departmental policy and the ones that got away the night before.

Daylight. Sunday. The birds and squirrels are nattering over breakfast. The taxpayers are going to work, sleeping late, dressing for early Mass or dreaming of bloody marys and quiche brunches. The "New Centurions" are swigging beer and booze from the trunks of their cars circled up in a clearing in the woods.

Snatching off bullet-proof vests, stripping to tee shirts, leaning on their cars, sprawling on car hoods or the ground, the men move only to schlepp more beer from a trunk. The litany of grievances slowly circulates, round-robin, broken by the deep silence of heavy pulling on bottles and punctuated by the snap-pop of beer cans opening.

"Everybody signed their Teamster cards?" asks a stocky young blond officer. He drains a can of beer in one long draw and stands up to get another from a car trunk.

"Grab a *handful* of 'em," yells a lanky, older black stretched on the ground, his head against a tire.

A desultory chorus of affirmative replies answers the union question.

"It's gonna happen, whether we or anybody else in the department want it," answers a black sergeant. "They're trying to slow it down, but it's happenin'. I don't wanna be a f--kin' Teamster, but what else can you do? After you beg an' plead for so many years to get things straightened out . . ."

"You know that last sickout we had?" interrupts a well-endowed female officer. "It started out as a joke, really. Most of us didn't have but about six hours' notice or there'da been a lot more. The ones who *did* go to work said *they'da* stayed out if they'd had any notice. The amazin' thing about it was the department didn't know what was goin' on. It was two shifts before they found out. That's how out of touch they are with us. They don't have any comprehension of what's happenin' to us or how we feel.

"We got a bunch of *scholars* leadin' us. They can read all the text books and get all the degrees they want, but it won't tell 'em what's happening in the streets."

"That's right!" adds another. "I get out there and stop a car and walk up on him, and I don't know if he's gonna jump out an' kill me or he's gonna pass out an' fall over in his seat or what's gonna happen.

"They got no comprehension of that kind of fear. They can't provide the answers because they got no background. They can't see the problems, and you can't tell 'em what the problems are 'cause they didn't come from the streets. They didn't come up through the ranks. It's like tryin' to explain the theory of relativity to me. I can hear you, but if I don't know the laws of physics, I can't grasp the meaning of what you're sayin'."

"Anybody out there last night *not* feel scared?" chortles the black sergeant.

Hooting and profanity drown out the few serious answers.

"Well, ya see, the captains and lieutenants an' majors know we under stress, but all they think about is how glad they are *they* ain't under it out here," continues the black sergeant.

"Now the Chief . . . s--t! He don't even know to begin with. He's never been any kinda police before. All he knows is the Mayor says shotguns scare the black voters an' we used to hit on too many black voters with the shotguns in stake-outs an' such, so we can't have 'em anymore.

"Well, sheeeit, man, it was true! We *was* knockin' down a bunch of black dudes—*an'* some honkies—but *they* was the ones knockin' down the liquor stores and banks an' stuff.

"When the Mayor's buddy, ol' Reginald Eaves, came along, what he 'sentially said was, 'Brothers an' Sisters, the police department's beating up on you too much. I'll take care of you. Come under my wing.'

"An' the ol' Mayor, he said, 'Ya'll are scarin' the brothers and sisters with shotguns, an' you killin' too many brothers with big bullets. So they took 'em away an' gave us these funny little bullets to put in our guns, an' crime's gettin' worse ever since.

"When the dudes on the street know we're 200 men short to begin with an' they *know* they got more firepower than we got, they just get braver and braver."

"Thank God I've never had to shoot anybody so far," says Ted, who is sprawled on his belly across the hood of a car, occasionally turning sideways to chase his beer with a pint of sour mash bourbon. "But if I ever do have to, I have to live with myself for the rest of my life, and I want it done right. If I have to pull my weapon, it's him or me, and when I draw, it means I may never see my wife and kid again if I don't do it right.

"If that happens, then I want the other sonuvabitch with the gun to go down fast—before he can fire back. I can't afford that.

"Hey, Claude," Ted calls across the circle to a wiry short man with a

Clark Gable mustache, "Watcha gonna do if you're passin' a liquor store an' four perpetrators with shotguns run out right in front of you and you know they just hit the place?"

"S--t an' play dead, man!" Claude grins.

"That's right," Ted grins back, shaking his head. "The Chamber of Commerce thinks we should hop out and draw down on 'em and the Mayor and the Chief think we should politely ask them to put down their shotguns and line up an' wait for another car to come along so we can invite 'em downtown to be booked. If we had shotguns, we could take a chance with 'em, but they're gonna *keep* gettin' away because all we can do is sit still and pray they don't see us while we radio for help."

" 'Course they long gone by then," yawns the black sergeant, "an' then we got a higher unsolved crime rate."

He turns to the reporter drinking with them and says:

"These guys let people get away all the time, but it ain't their fault. They ride alone, an' there are places an' situations where they'd be certifiable crazy to go in by themselves without more gun than they carry. Ain't nothin' they can do! They handcuffed! Ain't nothin' they can do . . ."

"We're damned embarrassed about it sometimes," Kelley drawls from a low tree limb on which he's been lying without movement or sound for the past hour.

"Tell *me* 'bout bein' embarrassed," snorts the sergeant. *"I'm* the only one here allowed to carry a shotgun, an' I'm also of a 'politically sensitive' color."

The sergeant gets up and brushes himself off, tossing an empty beer can into the bushes.

"Littering!" shrieks a patrolman. "Somebody call a cop an' have 'im turned into the Chief. He's hell on litterbugs!"

"So's our 'Frontier Mayor,'" cackles Kelley from his tree perch. "We better wipe up the oil stains from our cars when we leave here."

Ignoring the other men, the sergeant lumbers stiffly over to the writer and says, very quietly, right in his face:

"I'm goin' home now, but I want you to know somethin', an' I'm not afraid to say it. You can even use my name. I don't give a s--t. We are *not* a racially divided or split bunch of police officers. Sure, there's a *hell* of a lot of racism—downtown at headquarters. But it's politics! Not *just* racism! Politics! Kissin' the ass of the people in power. Well, right now, the power down there is black, so that the color of the ass, an' a lot of people on the force don't like it 'cause they came on when it was white asses that had to be kissed, an' now they're confused. But it's all the same game of kissin', and the color's gonna change from time to time, but the s--t never does.

"Right now, we're hurtin' 'cause of the politics. It's gotten worse instead of better, but the men out here on the streets—these guys you been drinkin' with this mornin'—they're good cops. They don't care—an' I don't care—who's black or white. They're over-worked, out-numbered, out-gunned, under-paid, paranoid an' cryin for help.

"Mayor Maynard promises them the moon—if they'll just hang on—but all they get is cold grits, more promises an' that fat smile! The Mayor got himself a fat raise an' a big new house. He got one of the biggest staff of flunkies in the country an' enough bodyguards to capture Roswell. But all my men have got is debts an' extra jobs so they can squeak by.

"*All* these guys out here got extra jobs. Too many extra jobs! I don' even wanna know how many extra hours they're workin'. I'm afraid to know which ones are workin' 40 and 50 extra hours a week, 'cause I ought to cut 'em back. Some of 'em come to work so tired, I'm afraid to let 'em take a car out, but if I don't, then we're just that much shorter on the streets. They're so tired and frustrated, one of these days soon somebody's gonna call a cop an' nobody'll be *able* to come.

"Listen to 'em. You think they're bitchin'? They not bitchin'. They're cryin'. They're *beggin'* for help! Support from the administration *an'* from the public. They don't wanna be Teamsters, an' they don't wanna quit, and they don't wanna move. They wanna be Atlanta police officers.

"There *was* a time—an' these younger guys never saw it—but there *was* a time when I was real *proud* to be an Atlanta police officer. I ain't seen that time in awhile, but it could come back. Even losin' nine, ten men a month like we are now, we still got enough good men to bring this force back. We just gotta have help from the taxpayers and the 'ministration. All it'd really take is the taxpayers' *demandin'* it from the Mayor, an' they'd have a good city again. The Governor—*he's* done some good, sendin' in the troopers. But it's got the Mayor scared. He don't like it, but what can he do?

"You listen to these guys here . . . an' you *better* believe 'em!"

The sergeant slowly walks to his car and drives away, and his men—the city's battered and bruised Choir Boys—continue drinking for a couple more hours.

They are under fire from every corner of the city and trying to hold the thin, crumbling line between chaos and civilization while politicized, ill-equipped and under constant stress.

According to the American Institute of Stress, there is no other occupation in the world as consistently stressful as police work—with the possible exception of air traffic controllers.

Every contact with a civilian is a close encounter of a stressful kind for a police officer. The kinds of stress Ted encounters are not always obvious, and they range from the necessity of instant, split-second, on-the-spot decision-making and the constant fear of being killed or hurt to the sights, sounds, smells, tastes and feel of human misery and cruelty.

A police officer is under stress because of the high expectations placed on him by his superiors as well as the taxpayers. He is expected to be too macho to be afraid. In a single duty shift he is often expected to possess the skills of a doctor, a family counselor, a lawyer, a psychiatric social worker and a big brother, as well as those of a hunter, boxer, wrestler, track-and-field athlete and Kojak.

He is also expected to handle a multitude of weapons issued to him or pointed at him without hurting anyone, while acting with absolute impartiality and no prejudice. Immersed in crime and surrounded by unlimited temptation and opportunity for corruption, he must somehow remain inhumanly, scrupulously honest and saintly.

Adding further to his stress is the often parietal attitude of his superiors in enforcing departmental rules and regulations—ranging from the length of his hair and sideburns to the shine on his shoes and whether or not he accepts free coffee or food from an establishment.

His self-image is mangled in the confusion of the taxpayers' cursing him for monitoring their driving, the courts' overturning his field judgments and the department's nit-picking him about details and policy.

A large part of his job consists of enervating boredom, dulling his mind and lulling his body. Yet, there is always a part of him straining at the leash, knowing that at any moment all hell can break loose around him. Statistically, he knows the odds are slim he will be killed by a perpetrator, but a large part of his stress comes in fighting to keep those odds down.

As a result of stress, the incidence rates of divorce, alcoholism, mental illness, suicide and general alienation from society among police officers are higher than those of most other professions combined.

Lt. Dick Webber, of the Atlanta Police Academy, was particularly harried when contacted in August for information on the school's stress training program, admitting that the City's former stress officer had just resigned "because of stress."

Yet, at a time when major crime in Atlanta is spiraling, the city's police officers are among its lowest paid employees.

Walking time bombs—begging to be defused!

CHAPTER

16

WRITER-EDITOR
RELATIONSHIPS

The phrases *selling yourself* and *making contacts* may first strike your ear with the discord of a cash register bell. Shouldn't they apply to a business person rather than to a writer? you may ask. Yet professionals all agree that writing is a business and that to freelance successfully, you must learn to sell yourself and establish good relationships with editors and other writers.

Mitchell Shields, freelancer and former editor, says friendships with other writers are helpful because friends can intercede for each other with editors. "Writers have to work together," he says. "They are not competitive. For example, Larry Wright interceded for me with *New Times* where he was known and I wasn't. Paul Hemphill interceded for Michelle Green with *The New York Times* where he was known and she wasn't. Most established writers will call or write an editor friend to introduce you, but the first article you submit must be good. After that you're on your own. As your work is published, you can prepare a portfolio for editors who want to see samples of your work. But get to know other writers when you're starting out. You need someone who believes in you."

How can you get to know other writers and editors? By joining one of your community's writers groups, attending writers' conferences (they're listed in *Writer's Market*), or joining a professional society as soon as you publish enough to become eligible. You also might take a course in magazine writing at a college or university near you. Instructors often have valuable contacts within the writing community and are thus in a position to give you introductions or recommendations.

Writers cannot afford to be hermits. They must hone their public relations skills by reaching out to other people in their profession. You have already begun this process by reaching out with your query letter. The next interaction between you and an editor will take place when you mail your completed article.

FIRST IMPRESSIONS ARE CRUCIAL

Part of selling yourself is presenting a manuscript that looks crisp and businesslike. Its appearance will convey an important message about your professionalism. Type or print it in the form illustrated at the end of this chapter, following all instructions given there. Make a copy for reference and for back-up in case the manuscript is lost. For mailing, fasten the pages of the original with a paper clip—never use staples—and place the unfolded manuscript in a heavy manila envelope containing an identical self-addressed, stamped envelope. Enclose a brief letter to the editor (let's call her Ms. Jones), reminding her of your promise to submit the manuscript on speculation by this date. Note any major changes that have become necessary since your last correspondence, thank her for her advice and help if any has been given, and say that you will be anticipating a reaction to the article. Like the query, this letter should be immaculate in form, well written, and cordial.

If Ms. Jones responds by saying she wants to buy the article for a price that is satisfactory to you, she may also enclose a contract stipulating the rights she wants to buy, the fee to be paid, when payment will be made, a kill fee, and the reimbursement for expenses incurred in writing the article. If she does not include a contract, write a letter to her in which you state the terms *you* want (see the sample letters of agreement at the end of this chapter) and ask for her signature. Without a letter of agreement or a contract, you're inviting trouble.

As a novice, you may have wondered if you should have an agent to handle the legal and commercial side of writing. Surprisingly, most magazine writers (except for a famous few who also write books and movie scripts) prefer to do their own selling and contracting because in the exchange of letters and phone calls, they develop working relationships with editors. In this way, they keep up with the editorial needs of a group of magazines, and the various editors recognize them when they call or write to submit ideas—a situation that can lead to more assignments.

HOW MAGAZINES ARE EDITED

Having a general idea of how magazines are edited and produced will help you understand why good relationships with editors are important. Some magazines have surprisingly small offices and staffs; only two or three people edit, write, and design the entire "book." The atmosphere is hectic but informal. An almost frenzied tension pervades such offices just before the final publication deadline, but a more leisurely pace settles in soon after, with time for planning and writing and attention to queries from freelancers, many of whom get to be known by their first names.

Other magazines have impressive buildings, smartly decorated offices, and large staffs who by necessity are more impersonal and businesslike. Policies of different magazines vary as much as their physical plants: rates, time required for editorial decisions, contract specifications, reimbursed expenses, the number of changes made in freelance manuscripts, all are different. A few magazines still pay on publication, but it's advisable to do business only with those that pay on acceptance. Otherwise, you may never be paid. Because editors work months in advance of publication, deadlines for edited copy will be at least two months before the issue is mailed. Seasonal material is considered as far as six to twelve months in advance.

When a manuscript arrives at a magazine's editorial offices, the editor who responded to the query will probably give the article its first reading. This person writes reactions and recommendations on an attached form and sends the manuscript on to the next editor in the chain of command, or sometimes delivers it by hand and discusses it with the colleague. Comments on the reaction sheet are important, but what is said to the other editor, and how it is said, is even more so.

Obviously, then, your relationship with editors can have crucial impact on the promotion of your work. If you have established rapport, if your sales techniques have been dignified but forceful, certain editors may become advocates for your work. Their initial enthusiasm for your article can provide the momentum for favorable reactions by the rest of the staff. Therefore, use every opportunity short of being a pest to keep in touch so that the editorial staff will begin to think of you as an individual.

Of course, neither letter writing nor neatly typed manuscripts can substitute for the best sales device of all: an article of quality. But the dependable reputation you gradually build is also important. Editors hunger for good material; they also value reliability, punctuality, and accuracy. When you have agreed to a deadline for completing an article, meet it without fail. And while you research the article, check and double-check the facts. Some publishers can afford a staff of fact-checkers who verify every piece of information in an article, but many have to rely on the writer's accuracy. Show editors that you can be trusted, that you are flexible enough to take suggestions and make changes, and they will promote your material with colleagues.

During the article-selection process, a manuscript can easily be sidetracked, so don't expect an immediate answer. Editors are often distracted by the hundreds of details they have to deal with, they often delay making difficult decisions, and occasionally they even lose a manuscript. You have little recourse if your article happens to be lost, but you can avoid catastrophe by always keeping a copy.

If you fail to get a reaction to your work within two or three weeks, write a discreet inquiry to the editor to be sure the manuscript has been received and that it is under consideration. The American Society of Journalists and Authors recommends that freelancers recall a manuscript after three weeks if no decision has been made to buy or reject the work. But beginners who need to be published will probably wait longer. Sometimes a phone call rather than a letter gets prompt action. Whatever step you take, be courteous. You may want to try this market again, so don't antagonize the editor by rudely demanding that your manuscript be returned at once. Remember that editors have to consider many factors in buying an article, and all these decisions take time: Does the article suit the magazine's style and slant? Is it too similar to other articles published recently? Will the article give balance or contrast to a future issue now being planned? Is it the right length for the available space? Are appropriate illustrations available?

Ultimately, how patient you are will depend on how eager you are to sell. In most cases, if the editors are going to buy an article, they will make the decision within two or three weeks. Still, there are exceptions. Editors sometimes procrastinate for six months or a year.

After repeated but unsuccessful inquiries, you may decide to recall your article, especially if it's in danger of becoming dated. If the manuscript is not returned despite your requests, make a fresh copy and send it to another market. Then inform the editor who ignored your inquiries that you are submitting the article elsewhere.

In another situation, suppose an editor writes to you promptly, expressing interest in your article but asking for extensive changes. Do you revise as requested, or do you thank the editor but ask for the return of your article, explaining that you feel strongly about retaining its original flavor and integrity? Again, the answer depends on how eager you are to publish right away and on the extent of the revisions. Never change an article's content so that it no longer expresses your beliefs or attitudes. But you may profit from an editor's experience by revising the *way* you have expressed your ideas. As you grow in experience and prestige, you can demand more from editors: sometimes more pay, more generous expense allowances, a guarantee to buy when extensive revisions are needed, or a kill fee if the revised article is turned down.

WORKING ON SEVERAL ARTICLES AT ONCE

Later on, your writer friends may urge you to increase sales by working on several different articles at one time. If so, they will warn you to keep careful records of works in progress: copies of all letters, manuscripts, tapes of interviews, and notes on phone calls and visits with editors.

In addition to having several articles on different topics in progress at one time, you may want to try another technique professionals use for boosting profits: writing several pieces based on one research project. For example, suppose you want to write an article on the importance of a healthy self-image. After a search in *Writer's Market* for an appropriate magazine, you settle on *Northwest Airlines.* It is 75 percent freelance written, pays on acceptance, pays 100 percent kill fee (which is unusually high), and will consider work by unpublished writers. Published primarily for business travelers, it sounds like a good target.

You research the subject thoroughly, reading everything you can find on self-image, its effect on the person and on others, the contrast between the way people see themselves and the way others regard them, and the problems created by poor self-image. You delve into books on psychology and pore over psychological journals both academic and popular. Then you interview experts in the field—counselors, psychiatrists, psychologists, professors, personnel managers—face to face or by phone. You find that some professionals have elaborate equipment to help people see the image they project to the world: recorders and large television screens with stop devices to freeze certain facial expressions or gestures. Clients can watch themselves as they respond to questions that bring a laugh, talk about an emotional concern, or describe themselves as they think they are seen by others. As you pursue the topic, you discover more and more facets of it to write about. You decide that the *Northwest Airlines* article should be an overview, purely informative. Its thesis should be that people today who are concerned about their image—especially business executives, salesmen, teachers, pastors—can discover how they are perceived and change that image if they want to.

In the course of your research, you hear about an innovative specialist in this field who lives in your city. Because this man helps local people, you plan to submit an article on him to the Sunday magazine section of your local newspaper. You also learn that this "image-maker" is unique in his field because of some of the equipment he uses and the theories he holds. So you decide to write a success story for *Parade,* a national general interest magazine that often features active, interesting, and exciting people. It pays well and you would like to crack this market, but this article must be quite different from the local version.

Your thoughts begin to turn to people who might have special problems with self-image, so you plan at least two more articles: one for *Working Woman* and one for *Ebony.* You learn that seminars are held all over the country for women executives who have self-image problems because of the roles they are pioneering. Then there is *Seventeen,* which caters to the group with the greatest curiosity of all about self-image. And it's an excellent market for free-lance material.

Now you have the possibility of selling six articles instead of one, all based on the same body of research. The challenge is to query these editors in the right order and to be sure that none are competitors. If an article is published in one magazine before you query another, be sure to let the editor know about the first publication unless the approach is so entirely different that you are certain there will be no conflict.

Writing is like any other business. You must constantly sell yourself—your courtesy, your fairness to the editor, your dependability, your integrity. There is no substitute for a good product, but it is also mutually helpful to have friendships with editors and other writers who believe in you.

SUMMARY

To be a successful freelancer you must present yourself as a professional:

1. Make your manuscript look as perfect as possible by neatly printing or typing it in correct manuscript form.
2. Develop cordial relationships with editors by keeping close lines of communication with them, calling or writing when appropriate.
3. Establish a reputation for dependability, accuracy, and excellence.
4. Revise your article at an editor's request only if the revision concerns structure or style, not attitude or convictions.
5. Keep complete records of research, interviews, works in progress, and correspondence.
6. To increase your sales, write several articles for noncompeting magazines on different aspects of the same topic.

FROM PRINCIPLES TO PRACTICE

1. List magazines other than your primary target that might be interested in the article you are writing for this class.
2. Are all of them noncompeting publications? How can you tell?
3. Without doing more research, could you revise your original article after its publication by developing a different aspect of the topic? Would the article be new and different enough to query another market? In this situation, what are the ethical issues? The practical issues?

Doe   2

On each succeeding page, place your last name in the upper left corner and the page number in the upper right corner. Begin typing about an inch and a half from the top of the page.

John Doe   Copyright 1992 by John Doe
2979 American Avenue   About 2,000 words
Small Corners, Iowa 50607
Phone: (xxx) xxx-xxxx

Title of Article
By John Doe

Print or type your article on a good quality plain white bond paper, using standard type that is easy to read. Avoid the digital type of many personal computer printers.

Place a copyright notice in the upper right corner of the first page. Below the copyright notice give the approximate number of words in the article. Type your name, address, and phone number in the upper left corner.

Center the title of the article about three inches from the top of the first page and include your by-line. Doublespace the text except when you occasionally skip four spaces to indicate a major transition in the article. Type on one side of the paper only.

Leave margins of slightly more than an inch, and indent five spaces at the beginning of each paragraph.

Dear Ms. Doe:

I'm delighted that you are intersted in using my article, tentatively entitled _____, in a summer issue of __(name of magazine)__. If the article fulfills your expectations I understand you will buy first North American Publication Rights, that the fee will be _____ to be paid on acceptance, that the kill fee you pay is _____, that I will see a proof of the article after it is edited for publication, and that you will pay for the travel and phone calls I have made while researching the subject. If any unusual expenses arise, I agree to seek your permission before incurring them.

The deadline for delivery is _____ and the article will be_____ words long.

Please indicate your approval of these stipulations by signing this letter below my own signature.

Sincerely yours,

Sue Wright

Sue Wright

Suggested Letter of Agreement

originating with the writer (to be used when publication
does not issue written confirmation of assignment)

EDITOR'S NAME & TITLE   DATE
PUBLICATION
ADDRESS

Dear EDITOR'S NAME:

This will confirm our agreement that I will research and write an article of approximately NUMBER words on the subject of BRIEF DESCRIPTION, in accord with our discussion of DATE.

The deadline for delivery of this article to you is DATE.

It is understood that my fee for this article shall be $ AMOUNT, with one-third payable in advance and the remainder upon acceptance.[1] I will be responsible for up to two revisions.

PUBLICATION shall be entitled to first North American publication fights in the article.[2]

It is further understood that you shall reimburse me for routine expenses incurred in the researching and writing of the article, including long-distance telephone calls, and that extraordinary expenses, should any such be anticipated, will be discussed with you before they are incurred.[3]

It is also agreed that you will submit proofs of the article for my examination, sufficiently in advance of publication to permit correction of errors.

This letter is intended to cover the main points of our agreement. Should any disagreement arise on these or other matters, we agree to rely upon the guidelines set forth in the Code of Ethics and Fair Practices of the American Society of Journalists and Authors. Should any controversy persist, such controversy shall be submitted to arbitration before the American Arbitration Association in accordance with its rules, and judgment confirming the arbitrator's award may be entered in any court of competent jurisdiction.

Please confirm our mutual understanding by signing the copy of this agreement and returning it to me.

Sincerely,

(signed)

WRITER'S NAME

PUBLICATION

by _____
         NAME AND TITLE

Date _____

NOTES

[1] If the publication absolutely refuses to pay the advance, you may want to substitute the following wording: "If this assignment does not work out, a sum of one-third of the agreed-upon fee shall be paid to me."

[2] If discussion included sale of other rights, this clause should specify basic fee for first North American rights, additional fees and express rights each covers, and total amount.

[3] Any other conditions agreed upon, such as inclusion of travel expenses or a maximum dollar amount for which the writer will be compensated, should also be specified.

© 1991

CHAPTER

17

LAW AND
THE WRITER

As a writer you must know what you can and cannot say in print. Freedom of speech is a treasured right, but even in the United States you are not free to print whatever you please. Freedom of expression is limited by libel, privacy, and copyright laws. Without libel laws, people would be helpless to defend themselves from published false statements that could harm their reputations. Without the right to privacy, ordinary citizens could suddenly become the subjects of embarrassing articles describing intimate details about their personal lives. Without copyright laws, a writer's work could be stolen and his income from royalties severely reduced. Since violations are sometimes committed through ignorance or mistake rather than malice, and since they can result in costly lawsuits, you should learn as much as you can about libel, right of privacy, and copyright law.

Unfortunately, the law is not always clear or consistent, and it constantly changes. Some aspects of copyright law are vague. Libel and privacy laws vary from state to state. And, even within a state, jury verdicts on similar cases vary. To understand fully the legal principles involved, study an authoritative book on communications law and consult it frequently: Wayne Overbeck and Rich Pullen's *Major Principles of Media Law*, for example, or Harold Nelson and Dwight Teeter's *Law of Mass Communications,* on which this chapter heavily relies. It is essential that magazine writers understand the laws of libel and right of privacy because, unlike large newspapers, many magazines do not retain legal counsel for on-the-spot consultation. So, when in doubt over a questionable statement in a manuscript, consult an attorney who specializes in communications law, but remember that even the experts have no crystal ball. They cannot always anticipate when someone will sue, nor can they foresee the decisions of judges and juries.

LIBEL DEFINED

Libel is a false published statement that harms a person's reputation or business or exposes him to ridicule. A good name has always been considered a precious possession; in fact, it has a tangible value because a person's ability to earn a living often depends on his reputation. Publications and writers are consequently subject to libel suits if they publish statements that destroy a good name.

For a person to sue for libel, the following conditions must be established:

1. The defamatory statement must have been published.
2. The person defamed must be identifiable in the published article. Even though his name is withheld, physical descriptions, membership in organizations, or alliance with a cause may identify him.
3. Damage to the person's reputation, humiliation, or mental anguish must be evident.
4. Actual malice must be proved (that the editor or writer was negligent in checking the accuracy of a defamatory statement or in publishing a statement knowing it may have been false). Unfortunately, no one knows how much negligence must be proved for a plaintiff to be awarded damages. Judges and juries make this decision based on the testimony in each case.

Defenses Against Libel

If you are sued for libel, you may be able to prove your innocence with one of the following defenses known by the legal terms of truth, privilege, and fair comment:

Truth: Proof that the statements complained of are true. Unfortunately, as Friedlander and Lee say in *Feature Writing for Newspapers & Magazines*, "It's incredibly difficult to prove truth. So, many libel lawyers prefer to fall back on a 'reasonable research' defense, to state that a libel defendant used reasonable research and interview methods and did not know the statement to be false, and had no reason to suspect it was false."

Privilege: Proof that you obtained the material from a privileged source, that is, from records that are open to the public or from the sessions of courts, legislative bodies, or other meetings held to conduct public affairs. The idea is that you can publish a report of anything to which the public has access. Even though vigorous public debate, especially in court, seldom takes place without defamatory accusations being made, you may report them provided you do so, not in malice, but as an honest summary, properly attributed, of proceedings the public has a right to know about.

Fair comment: Proof that the defamatory statement is your fair opinion of the performance of a public figure who occupies a position of power and influence; for example, a government official, scientist, artist, author, actor, musician. Recent decisions by the Supreme Court, however, have narrowed the definition of a public figure, so seek legal counsel if there is any doubt regarding the person you're criticizing. Someone who is ordinarily a private citizen but who is taking vociferous action in a public controversy can also be legally defined as a public figure. You must limit your criticism to the person's public performance, and your judgment must be based on facts.

Opinion and Fact

The law distinguishes between opinion and fact, and between public and private persons. *Opinions* must be fair and based on evidence; they are permissible no matter how derogatory if limited to public figures. On the other hand, published *facts* about both public and private persons must be provably true. For instance, in an article you might be safe in calling the mayor of your city inept (an opinion) but in danger of a lawsuit if you call the mayor a liar (a "fact" you had better be prepared to prove). The philosophy behind this apparent license to defame is that the public has a right to know about the actions of the people who handle public affairs and that the people of a democracy have a right to express dissenting opinions. When evidence proves that an official is corrupt, the public needs to know it and the press is free to give this person the lashing of exposure.

Still, every time you write a sentence that might hurt someone's reputation, stop and ask yourself: Is it provably true? Did I get the information from a source that is open to the public? Have I criticized fairly a public figure—not a private citizen? If you can say "yes" to these questions, you need not fear losing a lawsuit for libel. There is no guarantee, however, that you will not become the defendant in a suit over an apparently harmless article. If you write about a cunning counterfeiter and if an honest printer has the same name and similar physical appearance, you may be in trouble. If you incorrectly identify the individuals in a photograph or if a photograph includes persons unrelated to the main unsavory activity of the picture, you may be guilty of libel. Even a criminal may be libeled: if you write about a forger and say, in error, that this person was convicted of robbery, your statement is libelous.

Know the law, be aware of the pitfalls, and be truthful as well as accurate. Then you may write boldly, secure in the knowledge that courts are reluctant to limit freedom of expression unless it is used maliciously to harm an innocent person.

INVASION OF PRIVACY: FOUR PITFALLS

The right of privacy means the right of private citizens to be left alone to live their lives as they see fit. For citizens it means freedom from harassment by the media or from the publication of pictures and articles about them without their consent. However, a person who deliberately enters public life by running for office—or deliberately seeks the spotlight by becoming a dancer, writer, actor, or artist—yields some rights to privacy, especially in the performance of official duties or artistic endeavors. Even so, the privacy of such individuals' personal lives is protected by law unless their actions affect their conduct of public affairs (such as a severe drinking problem). Anyone can also temporarily lose some privacy rights if involved in a newsworthy event such as an accident, or if the person is witness to a crime.

Invasion of privacy encompasses four legal wrongs to persons. (Institutions and businesses generally have no right to privacy.)

1. *Appropriation:* The use of a person's name or picture for commercial gain (in an advertisement, for example) without permission.
2. *Intrusion:* The use of secret and illegal means to get information about a person—wiretapping, using a hidden camera, breaking into private files.
3. *The publication of private information,* even though truthful, about private citizens: information about their finances, sexual practices, private conversations, or details of personal tragedy.
4. *Publication of false information* about a person even though it may not be defamatory.

Writers need to be legally knowledgeable about privacy rights, but common sense, courtesy, and caution should, in most instances, keep them out of trouble. Honorable journalists don't bug their subjects' bedrooms or allow photographs to be used in advertisements without written consent. Most articles are about newsworthy people, in which case invasion of privacy poses little threat of legal action, or about private persons who have consented to interviews and publication. Newsworthiness and consent are the most effective defenses against invasion-of-privacy suits.

Nevertheless, there are pitfalls, and writers should be aware of them. It is wise, for example, to obtain written permission from all persons appearing in photographs that are to be used as illustrations, to use the photographs only for the purpose for which permission to publish was granted, never to retouch or change photographs, and to keep all permissions up to date. A man who was willing to have his picture used ten years ago might not be so agreeable today; or if he agreed to have the picture used in *Sports Illustrated* he might object to its use in *Penthouse.* It is common practice to publish, without permission, pictures of newsworthy people taken in public places, but it could be dangerous to publish similar pictures if the subjects were private citizens and if the photographs could be embarrassing.

Writers are very much concerned about the publication of private information, for that is often the type of material in greatest demand by editors. Fortunately for the media, judges have been reluctant to restrict the private information that may be published to what people *should* read; instead, they apply the yardstick to what the public wants to read. In other words, if the information is something that would interest a large segment of the public and if the revelations are not too intimate or embarrassing, then probably no liability for invasion of privacy exists. The courts have generally recognized that people like to read about tragic, bizarre incidents and that they like to read about famous people; public figures who must be prepared for a certain amount of unfavorable publicity when they deliberately enter the public arena. The publication of private information can become dangerous, however, when it concerns private individuals who have given no consent to be interviewed or publicized.

Magazine writers must be especially wary of the invasion of privacy by publication of false information. A violation can result from fictionalizing a piece of writing. When a story is embellished with imaginary rather than factual details, a court can classify it as an untrue report. In this book you have been urged to write narratively, to use the techniques of fiction in reporting fact, but you have also been urged to stick to the truth. To make up dialogue, to change the setting of incidents, to exaggerate the inherent drama of the situation you are describing in a "factual" article, such techniques are dishonest. Some courts, according to Don Pember, author of *Mass Media Law*, have said that "minor fictionalization, the creation of dialogue, does not constitute invasion of privacy in an otherwise true story." But you cannot depend on such a decision. The court might decide that by embellishing the story you have placed the subjects in a false light and thereby invaded their privacy. Many courts agree, according to Pember, that a false impression of a person, even though the impression is not unfavorable, is an invasion of privacy.

COPYRIGHT LAW CUTS TWO WAYS

The law of copyright protects literary property from theft. As a writer, it affects you in two different ways, first as a restriction and then as a protection. While you are conducting research, copyright law *limits* the amount of another person's work you can copy and use without written consent. The *proportion* of the work that may be copied, however, is not spelled out by the law. It may be safe to copy a few sentences from a fifteen hundred-word article and a few paragraphs from a three hundred-page book, but even one line from a song or a poem might be declared an infringement. So because there is no specific number of words or lines that would be considered "fair use," the United States Copyright Office gives this advice: "The safest course is always to get permission from the copyright owner before using copyrighted material." Damages in a copyright suit can amount to thousands of dollars.

Once you have written an article, copyright law protects your work from theft by others. You own your article just as you own your car, and no one should use it without your permission. Because of your investment of time and effort, an original article is your literary property to sell or dispose of as you wish.

Facts, events, and ideas cannot be copyrighted, but their presentation or description in words can be. You cannot own words, but you can own the way you arrange them in sentences and paragraphs to explain a concept, describe an event, or analyze a problem. If you transcribe the proceedings of a sensational trial, you cannot copyright the manuscript because it is a record of other people's words and sentences—not your own. You can, however, write and copyright an article *about* the trial, explaining and commenting on the case and quoting some of the testimony. That the article might have no literary, social, or educational value is irrelevant. The individual style and structure of an original composition justifies the copyright, not the quality or value of the work.

The present copyright law, a federal statute, went into effect January 1, 1978, and was revised in 1988. It protects your work from the time of its creation until the time of your death plus fifty years, thus enabling your heirs to benefit from your royalties. It also extends protection for work copyrighted before 1978 to a total of seventy-five years.

You may be surprised to learn that an original article is protected by copyright law until it is published, without even being registered with the Copyright Office. But when an editor agrees to publish your work, you must assert your rights of ownership in negotiating a contract. The editor will usually send you a contract or letter that you should examine carefully. It may specify whether you continue to own the copyright or whether you will sell all your rights to the magazine. To sell all rights is seldom wise. And be especially wary about signing a contract or a check that refers to your article as a "work for hire" because the law says that a writer's employer is considered the author of a work a regular employee produces while being paid a salary. If you're a staff writer for a magazine, for example, your employer would own the copyright of your work unless both parties sign an agreement to the contrary.

As a freelancer, to sign an all-rights contract would also mean that the publisher would be paid for any future use of the article—royalties from domestic and foreign reprints, book rights, or television and movie rights. By all means specify that you wish to sell *first North American rights only,* also called first serial rights or first publication rights. To sell first North American rights means that a magazine (which may have a Canadian edition) can publish your article one time. *You* still own the article and therefore can collect royalties from reprints or other use.

Since most magazine articles have no value beyond their first publication, you may have nothing to lose in signing an all-rights contract. But it's often best to retain as many rights for yourself as possible. Reprints are an excellent source of effortless income, and it's sometimes even possible to sell an article as the basis for a movie or TV program.

If an editor insists on buying all rights, you have three alternatives: yield, ask for more money, or refuse to sell the manuscript to this market. The chairman of the American Society of Journalists and Authors' copyright committee says: "Whichever way you approach it, remember that, unless there is a signed agreement to the contrary, you own the work." But as an additional safeguard, write "Copyright 1992 by John Doe" in the upper right-hand corner of every manuscript that you produce. By attaching the copyright notice, you are announcing that you own the piece.

If you ever sell an article to a magazine that does not copyright its entire contents, after five years your article would fall into the "public domain" (where it becomes everyone's property), unless you request that the editor print a copyright notice on the first page of the article.

Should you always go to the trouble of registering a copyright? Many professionals don't bother, but if you suspect that someone might steal your work, there's a distinct advantage in registering *before* the infringement. *Writer's Market* says, "You must register the work before you can bring an infringement suit to court. You can register the work *after* an infringement has taken place, and *then* take the suit to court, but registering after the fact removes certain rights from you. You can sue for actual damages (the income or other benefits lost as a result of the infringement), but you can't sue for statutory damages and you can't recover attorney's fees unless the work has been registered with the Copyright Office *before* the infringement took place. Registering before the infringement also allows you to make a stronger case when bringing the infringement to court."

The registration procedure is simple. Write for an application form for copyrighting a magazine article. The address: Register of Copyrights, Library of Congress, Washington, D.C. 20559. Return the completed form with two copies of the published article (one copy if unpublished) and a $20 fee.

SUMMARY

Knowledge of the preceding phases of communications law can inform you of your rights and help to keep you out of trouble. The main points to remember about libel, privacy, and copyright law are:

1. The best protection from libel suits is to be scrupulously fair and truthful when dealing with reputations and to criticize only those who have sought the spotlight of public life.
2. Avoid invasion-of-privacy suits by writing about newsworthy people and their public lives, or about private persons who have given consent to be publicized.
3. Any article that you write is yours unless you sign a contract to the contrary. Even so, if you sell your manuscript to an uncopyrighted magazine or newspaper, protect it from theft by asking the editor to print a copyright notice on the first page of the article.
4. Register your copyright after the article is published if you fear an infringement suit.

5. If you plan to resell your article, never sign a sales contract or endorse a check that stipulates "all rights." Likewise, never sign a contract that refers to your article as a "work for hire." In the latter case you would receive no pay at all.
6. Ask permission before using another person's copyrighted work, even small proportions of it. And remember that merely giving credit to the author is no protection against an infringement suit.

FROM PRINCIPLES TO PRACTICE

1. What changes have you noticed in the last few years in the media's concern for public officials' rights to privacy? Cite some examples.
2. What is the usual defense given by journalists for the change?
3. In your opinion is this position justified? Explain.
4. Have you read a magazine article recently that seems to violate a private or public person's right to privacy? If your answer is yes, give the evidence that supports your view.

ARTICLES BY
THREE PROFESSIONAL WRITERS
AND THREE STUDENTS

Professionals

Willie Morris, "Here Lies My Heart," *Esquire,* June, 1990

David Van Biema, "Master of an Unbelievable, Invisible World," *Life,* August, 1990

James Wooten, "Wallace and Me: The End of the Road," *Esquire,* November, 1978

Students

Beverly Levine, "Travel Without Terror"

Nancy E. Davis, "The Fall and Rise of Richard Hill"

Emilyanne Parker, "Officer Survival: The Real Deal"

Willie Morris—former editor of Harper's Magazine *and author of* North Toward Home, Taps, *and* Faulkner's Mississippi—*writes graceful, emotional prose that illustrates every principle of good writing discussed in this book. "Here Lies My Heart," therefore, will constitute an excellent selection on which to practice your skills in critical reading.*

Two characteristics of Morris's style are especially notable: unusual word combinations ("ferocious Confederate tantrums" instead of "southern temper") and striking contrast in sentence length. He is fond of following a 90-word lyrical sentence, for example, with a blunt, three-word statement.

As you read and later analyze the article, try to determine how he shows much more than he tells.

HERE LIES MY HEART

Willie Morris

It is a shrill and misty Manhattan dusk: autumn 1969. A wan sliver of dying sunlight catches the windows of the skyscrapers. I am standing furtively at a street corner. Soon my wife emerges from a door across the way. No—my *ex*-wife. We have been divorced a fortnight, though I have yet to acknowledge the reality. I have been waiting here for her; I know she is the psychiatrist's last client of the afternoon, and that he himself will sooner or later come out, too. I watch as she drifts away into the New York manswarm, receding from me like a pebble in a pond, my college sweetheart. My heart literally palpitates with rage and fear and guilt, all of it so horrendously vainglorious, yet it is the man I have come to see, as if merely knowing what he *looks* like might ease some grievous wrong.

For weeks I have harbored the vengeful incubus that he and he alone has razed my marriage. That even had she been an ax murderess he would have counseled her, as surely they all did in that histrionic and debilitating American era: "Do what you must to be happy. If it feels good, do it." The *presumption* of him: He is my faceless bête noir, incognito as the great city night, and he has unleashed my most ferocious Confederate tantrums. Frequently have I been tempted to compose for him epistles of nearly Herzogian sweep, have even seriously contemplated what I imposed upon cruel-hearted adults in my small-town Mississippi childhood: gift-wrapped fresh cow manure or dead rats or possums deposited on their front porches in the yuletide.

The mist has turned now into a grim, unhurried rain. Everywhere is the anguished bedlam of the Manhattan Sixties, the panhandlers, the junkies, the crowds so dense that people appear to be standing in queues just to walk down the sidewalks, the staccato clamor of the jackhammers, the steam pouring upward from the sewers as if the world underneath were an inferno, the tall, ominous visage of buildings, so of death, others' and my own. What indeed if someone drops a big mahogany table out a top window and it lands right on me? Such then is my midtown paranoia, real now as my darkest nightmares.

Then, suddenly, he emerges

from the same doorway. In stark intuition I know it is he. My heart begins beating fast, and surreptitiously I hasten across the raucous thoroughfare for a closer view. In my anonymous khaki trench coat I could be Gene Hackman tailing the Gallic drug czar down these same streets in *The French Connection.*

I am nearing him now as he pauses at a newsstand in the Gotham ritual of buying the afternoon's *Post,* then *The Village Voice.* I slip into an aperture near a Chock Full O'Nuts and observe him. He is of medium height and wears a gray overcoat. He is young! He looks innocent! He has red hair! This is my final subjugation. I really want him to look like Bernard Malamud. As he walks away I consider moving in on him at the flank, in the manner of Stonewall at Chancellorsville, confronting him nostril to nostril, as Lyndon Johnson did in that day with special antagonists, demanding what arcane knowledge he has appropriated of our joys and sufferings and the things we shared together: the fragrant spring twilights at our university those years ago, the gallant Longhorns whipping the loathsome Aggies, the catfish and beer in the Balcones Hills, the midnight chimes at Oxford, the birth of our child, the old love and promise and hope. Then helplessly I watch as he descends into the steely entrails of the asphalt earth as New Yorkers do, down deep to the rattling IRT, disappearing forever toward whatever cramped Bronx domicile lends him sequester for his cosmic jurisdictions.

All that was more than twenty years ago, another lifetime really, and during my tenure in the East, nearly three marriages in four were ending in divorce. One summer forenoon in the Hamptons, at a lawn party off a blue and sparkling inlet, I gazed across at the celebrants, some fifty couples I more or less knew from the city: With only two or three exceptions, I was drawn in an instant to note, everyone there had been divorced at least once. Among my contemporaries in those days there seemed a profound desperation about abiding relationships. I searched my friends who had dwelled in the crucible of them for answers, but I found that they knew nothing I did not know. So, as with me, since self-righteousness is surely the mightiest mode of survival, the blame fell on the partner. Everyone was too highly keyed, seething with fickle introspection and aggrandizement. Nothing lasted. It all seemed of a piece with the American Sixties.

She and I were very young when we married, and a very long way too from the East. The Almighty has always been southern in that regard: Get on early with the pristine charter of procreation. One of the clichés of the day held that young marriage was singularly desirable; you would "grow up together," the irony being that growing up can also mean growing apart.

Nonetheless, it survived eleven years, across many terrains, American and otherwise, in good times and bad, and the denouement was terrible, and more than one would ever have bargained for, and the trauma of the ultimate break lasted longer than its duration. The anger, bafflement, jealousy, and sting threatened never to go away, and their scar tissue is probably on my heart forever. Yet whose *fault* was it? I ask myself now, hundreds of miles and a whole generation removed. And what did it say about ourselves? And what on earth did it mean? As with many strange and faraway things in one's life, one wonders, did it ever mean anything at all?

She came from a raw and sprawling metropolis on the rise, I from the flatland and canebrakes of deepest Dixie. I remember as yesterday the first time I ever saw her. I was playing in a fraternity intramural football game, and I sighted her on the sidelines talking with some friends, a stunningly beautiful, dark-complexioned brunette, and she was caught for me in a frieze of mirthful laughter, and to this day I could show you the precise spot near the university where we first kissed. The two of us were important on the campus in those languid Eisenhower years. I was editor of the student daily; she was a Phi Beta Kappa and was even elected "Sweetheart of the Univer-sity"; five thousand students sang "The Eyes of Texas" to her in the school gymnasium. On my twenty-first birthday she gave me a book of English verse, and she wrote in it the inscription:

> Grow old with me,
> The best is yet to be,
> The last for which the first is
> made.

We were married in a chapel in her city, not far from where she grew up. My father died while we were on our honeymoon, and I remember the passion and the grief.

Not many American marriages begin in that Home of Lost Causes, that City of Dreaming Spires—Oxford. I had a scholarship, and to this day I cannot believe we were actually there. There were the impenetrable fogs, the chimes at midnight in the High, always too many bells ringing in the rain. Arm in arm we strolled through the gardens and hidden places of the magical town, reveling in its bleak gray treasures. A wing of an old house was ours, surrounded by lush gardens, the Isis twisting upon itself in the emerald distance. The bachelor Yanks were eternally there, all of them a little in love with her.

On a cold and frosty Christmas Eve, the two of us sat at the high mass in the cathedral of King's College, Cambridge. There was a thin skein of snow on the magnificent sweeping quadrangle outside, and the wonderful stained glass and the elaborate flickering candelight and the resounding organ and the grand processional in Henry VIII's vaulted chamber, the little English boys in their red ceremonial robes coming ever so slowly down the aisles with their flags and maces, their voices rising, and this was one of the most beautiful things we would ever see in our lives, and we were happy. And then a term break in Paris, and I am walking up Rue Git-le-Coeur, which abuts the Seine, and with the ineffable sights and sounds I conjure Gershwin, and soon there she is, leaning indolently against the upper balcony of our pension, five months pregnant and in a red dress, looking mischievously down at me as I approach, and her sunny words come down through time: "My distinguished husband."

After that, our heady New York days were suffused with happiness, and then slowly advancing pain. Did the city itself implant the seeds of our growing recklessness? We were Upper West Side people, back when the Upper West Side was an authentic neighborhood, and at nighttime in the Vietnam years came the echoes of sirens and mayhem from Columbia up the way. On the very day she received her Ph.D. in Bryant Park, Bobby Kennedy was shot.

The fields of fame and ambition grew heavy with pitfalls, though I doubt either of us would have acknowledged that then. Imperceptibly at first, our lives became tense and theatrical—all of celebrity's appurtenances. I was editor of a national magazine, she a young scholar, and our lives converged portentously with the great writers, the critics, the publishers, the millionairesses, the Hollywood heroines, the avatars of the moment's culture: dinner at Clare Booth Luce's or Bennett Cerf's or Punch Sulzberger's, literary celebrations, our photographs in the newsweeklies and newspapers. It happened all too swiftly. In our provincial years our friends thought we would last forever because we were so similar, mainly, I suspect, because we liked books, yet almost against our mutual will we were seeming to become so *different*—had we always been, I wonder, but lacked the experience to see it?—one of us introspective, academic, and disciplined, the other inchoate, nocturnal, uncompromisingly headstrong. How to explain such things, or even to remember them and be honest about them, for memory itself selects and expurgates and diffuses. It was not as fun as it had been.

We bought a farmhouse in the country, even acquired a black Lab puppy to shore up the marriage, and the small-town boy actually joined the anonymous phalanx of Harlem Line commuters in the summer, but the real trouble was just beginning. Doubt is inherent in any reality. She had begun to doubt, and doubt is a contagious hazard, yet the arguments, the insecurities, the melancholies, the insomnias, the inconstancies had to be symptomatic of something deeper, more elusive and mysterious.

All these merged in a daily tangle of hostility and distrust, punctuated by chilly, apprehensive silences. Silence speaks for itself, of course, and there were nights when I did not come home; our precocious love mocked us now, those threads of faded affection seemed frivolous and meaningless, and before our very eyes we had become rivals and antagonists.

The day came when she ordered me from the apartment. Where to go? What to take? I had to escape the city; a confused weekend in Connecticut with friends: "God, you look awful!" The mirror betrayed a complexion sallow as parchment, rings under the eyes like obsidian blisters, and I was developing a wicked little rash about the neck, what we once called *risin's* in Mississippi. Now we were in the deepening maw of divorce, a desolate subterrain all its own. The lawyers, of course, took over—mine a breezy man, cynical and unfeeling, hers hard and professional and unmitigating. Neither she nor I were mavens of heartbreak, and the wound and disarray of "the lawyer phase," as savants of marital rift chose to call it, were as mean and excruciating as anything I had ever known. I felt I was all beaten up. I feared I was losing not only my beloved son, but my pride and dignity, most of my money, my dog, and all the books it had taken me three years to compensate Blackwell's for. The nadir came one wintry night in a dark, cold basement apartment I had just rented downtown. The movers that day had brought a few items of my furniture there, and the utilities were not working, and by candlelight I rummaged through an ancient bureau that had once been my great-grandparents', and I found there a few forlorn mementos of a marriage: letters from her, even then shriveling at the edges, party invitations, a menu from the Ile de France, some of our little boy's toys from Christmases past, a photograph of the two of us holding him for his first glimpse of the Statue of Liberty.

It took me a long time to acknowledge she was truly gone. It was like death, but worse: She was not dead. I tried diligently to consign her to oblivion, but it did not work. I still loved her. There descended on my poor betrayed spirit a bizarre, enveloping jealousy, an acid sexual envy, tortured images of her with other men. The mounting carnage in Vietnam, its headless gluttony and cataclysm, only reinforced my indulgent fever. After the divorce I did not see our ten-year-old son for two months, because I did not trust my bitterness with him, the things I

183

might say. The first weekend he eventually came to spend with me, he rang the bell to my apartment, and when I opened the door he stood there with a shopping bag full of gift-wrapped objects. "Hi, Daddy," he said. "I brought you some presents." When I opened them, they turned out to be *my* Sandburg's *Lincoln,* all seven volumes of it, which he had selected to purloin from my own lost library. Was it an act of forgiving? At least I got my Sandburg back.

I became a weekend father. You saw hundreds of these miserable fellow creatures with their offspring on Saturdays in the Central Park Zoo, or F.A.O. Schwarz, or the movie houses along Broadway or Third Avenue, or the old Palisades in Jersey, all trying to be solicitous, as if to make up for something. Many were the Saturdays he and I would spend all day, breakfast to midnight, in Madison Square Garden, never leaving its splendid interior cosmos for so much as a moment: first the bowling alley, then lunch in the Stockyard, then the Knicks in the afternoon for Bradley, Frazier, Reed, and DeBusschere, later a boxing match in the Felt Forum, followed by a comedy act, then dinner all over again in the Stockyard. And when I safeguarded him the next day to a cab on those poignant Sabbath twilights and he left me, I felt unbearably guilty and bereft and alone.

One day he was to meet me in my office at an appointed hour. A good friend, a noted sportswriter, had arranged to take him onto the field at Shea Stadium an hour before a ball game and introduce him to all the Mets and Cardinals. I waited and waited but he did not come. When I telephoned, it was she who answered. I had not cleared the arrangement with her, she said. She was teaching me a lesson. But to meet the *Mets* and *Cards?* I prayed retribution all over again on my bête noire, the shrink. After that I did not talk to or communicate with her for years.

With divorce one gives up a whole way of life—friends, routines, habitudes, commitments. You are on your own again, and in diaphanous territory, and for a while your most fiendish habits may worsen. Then I told myself I could not *afford* to be deranged. I had a demanding job, after all, and scant choice but to function. The problems of real day-to-day life were easier to deal with than the imaginary ones; I willed my own salvation.

For the longest time I thought I could never love again. I was wary and afraid and remembered too much. Yet as the days slowly pass, on into the years, you discover you *can* love again, and that, of course, is a whole other story. But I shudder now to think what my girlfriend of that time had to live with—and not merely the intolerable acrimony and spleen she was forced to share—for in the nature of it we all subconsciously compare our later loves with the first, no matter the wreckage and flaw.

How could I have known then of the psychic hold she would have on me for the rest of my life? The wisps of memory, the dreams, the tender long-ago assurances. Her ghost would exist till I died.

All that was a very long time ago, and I see now that, as with much of life, this is really a little long-ago tale of time passing, and of vanished grief. So many of our friends of those days are dead now, and others have gone their own way. In the course of an existence, people move in and out of one's life. Often we do not know the *whereabouts* of those once dear to us, much less what they are feeling or remembering. Close relationships oscillate between tranquility and destruction, between fire and ice. Old fidelities wither, and love dies as the lovers go on living. There are a few small islands of warmth and belonging to sustain us if we are lucky. That is how I wish to think of her now, in the days of our happiness.

She became a respected feminist and writer. She subsequently married again, to a distinguished man and old friend. They, too, are now divorced. As for myself, a writing man, I never remarried, although I came close two or three times. Was it fear—of love lost, of love renewed?

Yet the further I grew from those painful moments, the more the bitterness faded; one is left with a kind of mellowing sadness, and recollections of the beginnings of love when one was young, the heightened promise and trust. I also comprehend now that in many ways I grew and developed into the adult I am today, for better or worse, because of her, and of her values. Our son is now older than we were when we married, and I see her in him, in his courage and commitment.

I sometimes ponder the pain I must have caused *her,* the selfishness and doubts: *her* side of the matter. Of course it was not the headshrinker I compelled myself to pursue that faraway Manhattan dusk, for he was only conduit and symbol. I hope he rewrites Freud and makes a million.

In those inevitable moments of despoiling ill temper, we damage what we cherish. All the time we must somehow grow from the sinews of our own experience, learn to conduct ourselves a little more compassionately—for what is intelligence if not the ability to cope with the recurrences of one's existence?

There remains the incontrovertible burden of lost and damaged love. After all the years we never communicated, now there are random notes of congratulation and remembering. Recently I saw a charming letter she wrote a dear comrade of mine here in the town where I live, and the familiar handwriting leaped out at me in a supple rush, and reminded me of the very best she ever was. Finally, I have learned how difficult love is, how hard to achieve and sustain, no matter who the person or how felicitous the circumstance.

In this moment I find myself driving in a Mississippi Delta twilight toward a warm new love, one that matters to me. All around are the landmarks of my own beginnings, the cypresses in the mossy ponds, the lingering woods, the little hardscrabble towns of my youth, the interminable flatness in the burnt-orange glow. The years are passing, and even in this rare twinkling of serenity and happiness and fulfillment I think of Celia, and remember her.

David Van Biema wrote the following article to accompany an extensive photo essay on the creation of life. An ideal model for beginning writers to study, it is notable for its spare simplicity and avoidance of sentimentality, for its use of an unusual technique for creating suspense, for quotations with a foreign accent that show *the enthusiasm and reverence of a remarkable man for his life-long obsession. It first appeared in* Life *magazine, August 1990.*

MASTER OF AN UNBELIEVABLE, INVISIBLE WORLD

David Van Biema

Lennart Nilsson hears the question again and again, at interviews, awards ceremonies, dinner parties, "hundreds, maybe thousands of times," and he can recognize its subtext. When does life begin? the people ask him. *You* must know. You have captured sperm and egg on film, peered into women's uteruses, spent endless hours in operating rooms as tubal pregnancies were being removed, much as great artists before you haunted morgues while preparing to paint their sinewy saints. So tell us: When does human life begin?

Lennart Nilsson, the Swedish photographer, answers by citing Ingmar Bergman, the Swedish filmmaker. Sweden is a small place; the notables tend to know one another. Nilsson, whose close-up photos of a bee pollinating a flower are engraved on the 100-kronor bill, has indeed worked on movie sets with Bergman. "Suppose Ingmar Bergman is doing a story about love," he says, "and you ask him: 'When do you think the hero might . . . when do you think is the moment when he gets in love with the heroine?' He is going to tell you, in one second, 'Look at the movie. Please look at the movie, and you decide. It's up to you.'"

Nilsson looks a little bewildered. He sees no reason why the beginning of life should be nailed down on a collector's board any more than the beginning of love, especially when he is certain that any answer he gives would be drained of wonder and reduced to a legal exhibit in one of humankind's most virulent arguments: the argument over abortion.

Nilsson's position might have been more readily understandable in another century. The linkage between fetal development and abortion is a relatively new concept. Aristotle speculated that a human became human *after* birth. Saint Thomas Aquinas advocated the idea of prenatal "ensoulment"; males got their souls 40 days after conception, females after 80. But neither Aristotle nor Aquinas—nor the Catholic Church—talked in terms of an embryo's right to life. In English and early American common law, the concept of "quickening"—detectable movement in the uterus, usually at about six months—was the standard for determining potential life, but abortion was still more a matter of interrupting the natural order than of killing a human being.

Not until the mid-19th century did the welfare of the fetus even become an issue. At the turn of the 20th century all 45 states had outlawed abortion from conception on, but more in the name of the mother's health than the embryo's. It was the Supreme Court's 1973 decision in *Roe v. Wade,* which established "viability" outside the mother as a legal standard, that inextricably linked the concept of fetal development and the issue of abortion.

And it was around that time when people began posing the question that Lennart Nilsson finds so hard to answer.

He finds it hard because he came to his field from a totally different direction. In 1927, when he was five, Nilsson expressed an interest in the voice emanating from the family radio. His father, a technician with the Swedish railroad, took the radio apart for the child piece by piece, explained it, then reassembled it. That same year Lennart fell through the ice on a lake near his hometown of Strangnas. Family legend has it that when he was pulled out, nearly blue, he calmly said, "I saw some very interesting things down there." The paternal message, obviously absorbed: Behind every familiar surface, be it lake ice or a radio dial, lies what Nilsson calls "the unbelievable, invisible world."

When he grew up and became a photographer, he did books on the world of ants and the world of undersea creatures. But the perfect romance of artist and subject matter began in 1951. Nilsson was on assignment to photograph a professor at Stockholm's august Karolinska scientific institute. He spied a row of tiny bottles, each containing a two-month-old fetus. "I had had no idea the embryo was so mature so early," he says. "In that same second I knew I would concentrate on the early development of the human."

It was the ultimate Nilsson world, familiar as maternity clothes, yet as mysterious as Creation. Now, 25 years after LIFE first published his historic photographs of fetal development, Nilsson has his own office at the Karolinska, where he has assembled a remarkable array of state-of-the-art equipment. His electron microscope, for example, can magnify a sperm cell 400,000 times, then rotate the specimen 360 degrees in any direction. Nilsson can maintain a human egg cell in a climate-controlled box while photographing it under magnification, then return it unharmed to the fertility clinic from which he borrowed it.

From his office have poured thousands of newsmaking photographs—from mosquitoes to hormones to the AIDS virus—that have won the photographer as much respect in the scientific community as he has gained in the more easily impressed journalistic world. But his greatest subject, and his continuing lifetime project, is based on the way he sees a mother's womb—not as a social battleground but as a "very interesting" world in which a magical process occurs.

Oh, he will try to please the questioners, aid in their own, more narrow investigation. Out of sheer civility he will flip once more through his pictures in search of the key moment, but again and again, he cannot choose. There is always another moment, earlier or later in the process, that he loves just as much.

Flip, flip.

"Ah, this is extremely interesting, it is historic," he says, gazing at a photograph of the moment of fusion. The sperm has entered the egg. Their two batches of chromosomes draw inexorably toward one another—like lovers across a crowded room—meet, commingle and create a new genetic combination. A new . . . individual? "Yes, yes," Nilsson says, but he is already moving on, *flip, flip,* toward . . .

Cleavage. Fusion is important, but "if you wait several hours, you see an *unbelievable* creation." Until this moment, the combined cell, for all its uniqueness, has done little. But then it splits in two. "It's like an *explosion,*" crows Nilsson. "Life is stronger than death; it is much stronger, and you see it here. It is the first portrait of us." He pauses, then somewhat apologetically offers: "But you know, this is also something going on with all animals. And even flowers."

Flip, flip.

Now he is muttering. "When does a human life begin? I think it's nearly here, maybe here." He points to a photograph of the embryo landing on the uterine wall—implantation. Until a moment ago, there was only a lonely floating glob of cells, unguessed at even by the mother. Now communications are established. The pregnant woman's antibodies pull away. "We are accepted," says Nilsson, reverently. "We can stay. It is a human, 100 percent." Pause. "But we are not quite sure." For one thing, the glob of cells has no brain.

Flip, flip.

At three weeks there is a primitive heart, even some nerve cells and connections between them. . . . "But you have it also in a rat, a cat," Nilsson says.

Flip, flip.

At five weeks, from the side, it looks like a baby. "Sweet I think," he says. From the front it looks, well, "yes, it looks a little like a rabbit."

Flip, flip.

At six weeks the eyes are forming, at 11 weeks, the fingers.

Flip, flip.

Lars Hamberger, the head of obstetrics and gynecology at Sweden's Gothenburg University, and Nilsson's collaborator on his book *A Child Is Born*, chuckles. "He didn't want to tell you, did he?"

Nilsson: "I cannot tell you. If I told you only ten days, or two days, or forty days, it would be wrong. It would. Look at the pictures. I am not the man who shall decide when human life started. I am a reporter, I am a photographer."

He smiles. "Maybe the first moment of human life, it starts with a kiss."

Which reminds us again of that imaginary Ingmar Bergman film. Perhaps the beginning of life is as complicated and seamless a miracle as falling in love.

*Ja*mes Wooten, *formerly of* The
New York Times *and more recently a Washington news corre-*
spondent for ABC television, spent ten years covering the cam-
paigns of George Wallace. Thus the classic article reprinted
here could be considered an extreme example of saturation
reporting.

Wooten did not set out to become deeply involved with his
subject nor to write extensively about him. As a cub reporter
for an Alabama paper, he was simply given the assignment to
cover Wallace's recuperation from an illness. But the years
drifted on and, though Wooten was later hired by The New
York Times, *his assignment remained the same. Thus he grad-*
ually learned to know Wallace intimately. During those years
fellow journalists described Wooten's feelings about the
Alabama governor as a mixture of grudging affection and
contempt. Then after Wallace retired—a crippled, lonely,
depressed old man—the two met again with Wooten prepared
to despise him more than ever. The article begins at that point.

The account is an interesting revelation of Wooten as well
as Wallace, and is an example of the superb portrait that can
be painted when the writer's collection of data about his sub-
ject has reached the saturation point.

WALLACE AND ME: THE END OF THE ROAD

James Wooten

Just before eight o'clock on the evening of Labor Day, down in Mobile, the long line of people passing by the window of the limousine finally ended, and George Wallace slumped back into the deep-cushioned corner of the backseat, hidden from public view. "Ah sure hope that's all," he sighed wearily, inserting the corpse of a cigar into his mouth, curling his lips into an unintentional but all-too-familiar snarl.

They had spotted the big, black Lincoln the moment it had rolled onto the outfield at the suburban baseball park, and for more than an hour they had trooped through the damp, dewy grass, besieging him for autographs and for pictures of him and them together—and when they were finally gone, he seemed utterly spent. "Ah just don't want to see any more of them," he sighed.

"You want the winduh up?" his old pal Oscar Harper asked solicitously from the other corner of the car.

"Huh?"

"Want the winduh closed?"

"Naw, naw," Wallace mumbled. "They'd just knock 'n' bang on it."

"Well, it's 'bout time fuh you to go anyway," Harper noted, glancing at his watch.

"Huh?"

"Ah said it's almost time to go on up on to the stage, idn't it?"

Wallace did not answer. Tilting his head slightly, he peered through the window of the limousine toward the several thousand people massing behind home plate and along each base line, waiting to hear him address the Labor Day gathering, the oldest annual political rally in Alabama—a sometimes wacky, occasionally volatile, often important, always colorful holiday assemblage that George Wallace had missed only once in the previous twenty-one years, the year Arthur Bremer shot him.

"It's a damned good crowd," Harper suggested.

"What?"

"Ah said it's a good crowd, a nice crowd."

Wallace merely grunted.

"They all gonna be glad to see yuh, Jo'ge."

"Huh?"

"These folks," Harper shouted. "All these folks'll be glad to see you again, Guv'nuh."

Wallace looked quizzically across the impressive width of the car, staring hard at his faithful crony of so many, many years. "Oscuh," he said quite earnestly, "what you don't seem to understand is that most of these folks'll be dee-lighted to git shed uh me." He slumped even deeper into the soft corner of the Lincoln and waved his cold cigar in the direction of the distant crowd. "Yessuh, Oscuh," he concluded in a faint, faraway voice, "they'll be ver-ruh, verruh happy when ol' Jo'ge Wallace is gone."

He is finished now, and it's hard to hate him anymore.

He is fifty-nine years old, a paraplegic, practically deaf, full of bad memories, fairly empty of hope, vulnerable to dangerous infections, prone to periods of deep depression and starving loneliness, worried sick about money, painfully confused about his yesterdays, dreading his tomorrows, haunted by that crackling moment of supreme terror that so thoroughly changed his life, reluctantly retreating cell by cell into himself—and there is about him now such a darkness, such a desperate sadness, that it is nearly impossible to generate any more bitterness toward him. The vivid recollection of what he was blends with the awful reality of what he has become, and the chemistry is so rich that it burns away the rusty, crusty rages of the past. Even the most carefully cultivated anger, generously nourished over the years, shrivels in the stark presence of his brittleness, his fragility, his helplessness, his despair, and is immediately replaced by some unavoidable sense of—of what? Of pity, perhaps, or of simple compassion, perhaps, or—though it is immediately suspect—perhaps of affection?

It was most awkward, most uncomfortable. I had gone back down south equipped with an entirely different set of reflexes, without the old passions that had been burning a hole in my soul for such a long, long time. It was to be a celebratory mission: For the first time since I was nine years old, an election day was dawning in Alabama without George Corley Wallace's name, or a reasonable facsimile thereof, on the ballot. Ever since 1946, when he was fresh out of the Army Air Corps and still having nightmares about his fiery, midnight bombing runs over Tokyo, he had been running, running, running for some public office or another every couple of years—for state representative or Democratic convention delegate or circuit judge or governor or President, and in the process of his constant candidacy, he had come to dominate the state in a way no other man ever had—and I had come to detest every single vestige of his power and prominence.

George Wallace was mean and malicious and malevolent, and he scarred almost everything he touched with his hateful, ugly rhetoric and his bizarre hold on the common folk in the South, but by the end of the summer of 1978, it was clear that the man was finished. He could not succeed himself as governor, and he had chosen not to seek either of the two United States Senate seats available in Alabama. I was glad to hear it—although I had strongly and wrongly told my friends in Washington that he would most certainly run for the Senate—and I wanted very much to be around to witness his departure.

"Oh, Lord, you down heah to write my obituary," he moaned when he saw me that hot night in Mobile, and he was right, of course. I had come back to celebrate his passing, to raise a glass or two in honor of his retirement from the politics and the government and the troubled psyche of Alabama and the American South, and I could hardly wait to watch it happen.

Then on that muggy night in Mobile—on the eve of election day—I crawled into the front seat of the big, black Lincoln and turned toward him and felt his sadness cutting through.

It started with George and me back in early 1967. A failed priest and a miserably ineffective teacher, I was by then a desperate, overage cub reporter for a damned good little newspaper in northern Alabama.

When a colleague became ill, I was temporarily relieved of my daily obituary assignment and hurriedly dispatched down to Montgomery to cover the capital during his recuperation. I'd just climbed the broad marble steps (carefully avoiding the brass star where Jefferson Davis stood when he took the oath of office as president of the Confederacy) and walked into the rotunda when Wallace turned a corner and came click-click-clicking into my life, flanked by two of the biggest state troopers in the entire history of law and order. I'd never seen him before, except on television.

"I'm from *The Huntsville Times,*" I said.

"Well, yessuh, you must be Jim Wooten," he drawled, extending his small, rather delicate hand. "Ah'm Jo'ge Wallace. Used tuh be the guv'nuh. My wife's guv'nuh now, co'se. You gonna cover the legislature? Well, that's good, Jim. You gonna be all right. Ah knew a man once was a preachuh fust 'n' then become a politician. Good felluh, too, so ah know you gonna be all right. You need anything, you just stop by, heah? Co'se, ah don't know much, but ah'll be glad to he'p you anyway ah can."

And then he was gone, his little heels click-click-clicking down the marble corridor, out the doorway, and into the morning sun. He seemed to know exactly where he was going.

It was an amazing performance. Few people were aware of my blighted past—ordained Presbyterian minister, small-town pastor, in Tennessee and Kentucky—and only my editor and family knew I'd be there in Montgomery that day, assigned to cover the legislature. It was a valuable lesson: George Wallace had good intelligence.

"Time to go, Oscuh," he said on that night in Mobile, years later, grasping a ceiling strap and pulling his slight body forward a bit on the seat.

"Yessuh, Guv'nuh," Harper agreed, signaling the two state troopers standing outside the car. "Guv'nuh's ready to go, boys," he said.

Like jaded priests bored with the mass, the troopers went about the practiced ritual of their task— opening the trunk of the limousine, extracting and unfolding the wheelchair, removing its left armrest, and rolling it into place near the right rear door. After one had swung it open, the other laid a thin plastic slab between the backseat and the chair, forming a bridge by deftly inserting it just beneath the edge of Wallace's right buttock.

"You ready, Guv'nuh?" the first trooper asked as he reached inside the car and grasped Wallace's ankles. The governor nodded grimly and took a twofisted grip on the strap. Then, with an enormous surge of pure arm strength, he hoisted himself out of the limousine, across the little plastic slab, and into the lap of the wheelchair while the trooper simultaneously pulled his legs in the same direction, quickly fixing the pristine shoes—their soles shiny, caramel-colored, never having touched the ground—into the metal footrests of the chair and locking the armrest back into place.

It had been a prodigious effort, and when it was done, his head canted terribly to the right, hanging there like a broken marionette, his face gaunt, drawn, pinched by his life. "Ah'll be right back, Oscuh," he said, his voice nearly a whisper. A high school band struck up "Dixie," and a ripple of applause rolled slowly out from home plate down the base lines. He seemed not to notice it was for him. "Ah won't be long, Oscuh," he said. "Ah'll be right back, and then we'll go on home."

It happened very fast.

One day in the summer of '68, I was plugging away on the little Alabama paper, and the next day I was a national correspondent for *The New York Times*. I hardly grasped it myself, so it was no wonder that when I came back down south a few weeks later and climbed aboard his chartered campaign plane—assigned by my new employer and editors to write about his fractious third-party presidential candidacy—he merely nodded at me from his customary seat in the front cabin, assuming I was still one of the local boys sent along to cover another of his wacky forays into the wild and wicked North.

George didn't know I'd been traded to the Yankees.

It didn't take long for word to reach him, though; for moments after we were airborne out of Montgomery that morning, he came lurching rather urgently down the aisle toward my seat, his mouth fiercely clamped around his cigar, his dense eyebrows dancing like nervous caterpillars on his forehead.

"Somebuddy told me you wukkin' fuh *The Noo Yawk Times,*" he accused.

I pleaded guilty.

"Lemme see some foam of identification," he demanded, and when I handed over my shiny, new, laminated press card—duly authorized and signed by E. Clifton Daniel—he turned it over in his fingers and whistled sarcastically through his teeth.

"Whooo-wheee," he said. "This heah's a verruh impo'tant document." He turned in the aisle to the other reporters watching his performance. "Felluhs, this heah's Mistuh Wooten, the gentleman from *The Noo Yawk Times.*" There was laughter all around. "Now, that's the papuh, as you felluhs all know, that called Fee-del Castro the Robin Hood of the Caribbean," he continued, thoroughly enjoying himself.

When the laughs subsided, he turned to leave and then, suddenly, whirled on me for a final thrust. "How much those Yankees payin' you?" he asked.

I shrugged, not about to tell him.

"Well, felluhs," he said, "this just goes to prove what ah've always believed." There was silence in the gallery.

"What's that, Governor?" I finally asked, knowing damned well George never did require a straight man.

"Well, it just proves that evuh man has got their price," he growled. "Yessuh, Wooten, you sure the livin' proof of that," he said, growling and jabbing at me with his cigar. "Evuh man has got their price."

My God, he was something to see in those days: the preeminent hobgoblin of American politics, and for many of those years, I tagged along behind him, nurturing my anger, honing my distaste for what he was and what he was doing. It was me 'n' George sort of wandering around the continent, with him up there in the front of the plane and me back there in the rear and both of us scared to death of flying; him up there on the stage, running for governor or President or standing up for the United States of America or Jesus or Alabama or white people or whatever the hell it was that he was doing, and me away in the back of the hall, all hunkered down, scribbling in my notebook, getting chairs thrown at me and spit spat at me, thinking it was all very important.

Lord, it was a circus. There were the Taylor sisters—Mona and Lisa, emaciated and chemically blond—who warmed up the crowds from Seattle to St. Augustine with the most atrocious country singing ever to escape through two noses; and there was the woman from Indianapolis who latched onto the campaign, claiming at first to be the Dodge girl, later claiming to be his girl; and there were the reporters, constantly debating whether his cockamamy candidacy ought to be treated seriously in their stories; and there was the hulking omnipresence of the state troopers, who loved to talk about their favorite television programs—"Beat the Press" and "Mace the Nation" (one afternoon in Milwaukee, when they were in a playful mood, they hung me by my heels from the seventh-floor window of a hotel); and always, there were the hordes of hecklers waiting for him at every stop, sometimes with eggs, sometimes with rocks, sometimes with bags of shit, and he would sneer at them and snarl at them and play them like Heifetz on a Stradivarius, pitting his folks against them, fomenting more tension upon tension until it inevitably and invariably exploded—and he would step back and say with a thin smile, "Now, now, folks, let's just let the po-lice handle it. They know what they doin'. Just let them handle it, folks."

When it was all over, he didn't seem particularly dismayed that he'd lost. Indeed, he seemed rather exuberant over the fact that he had probably ensured the election of Richard Nixon.

"He's a wonderful man, Jim," he said then. "Co'se, you wouldn't know that or understand it 'cause you a ree-porter."

He asked if I'd enjoyed the campaign.

"Not really, Governor," I lied.

"Well, that's good, Jim, 'cause ah'm fixin' to do it again in 1972."

"Is that a threat or a promise?"

"That, Mistuh *Noo Yawk Times,* is a fact," he snapped. "Co'se it idn't something you can write about. It's off the recuhd, really, 'cause ah got to get mahself elected guv'nuh again befuh ah can run for President again."

He did just that in 1970—with the most blatantly racist campaign in Alabama's recent history—and he did more. He got married again.

The first Mrs. Wallace had succumbed to cancer in May of 1968, not long after the murder of Martin King; a month later, Bob Kennedy was dead. I was assigned to the Poor People's March when she died, and our scruffy cavalcade (with Ralph Abernathy occasionally at the point) had reached Montgomery on the morning of her funeral. I decided to go. I had liked Lurleen. She had been a plain, kind, quiet woman who had fed me supper at the governor's mansion once and had stood at the kitchen sink and washed dishes while I ate at a nearby table and asked her why she had ever run for governor.

"Well, ah guess because Jo'ge told me to," she said. She was already seriously ill when, constitutionally denied a second term, he insisted that she become his surrogate in 1966. The campaign had deeply drained her. She had told him she didn't want to run because of her health, but he would have it no other way. He did not cry at her funeral. I did.

"You met my new wife yet?" he asked boyishly in early 1971, soon after he had begun his new term as governor.

"Yes, I have, Governor."

"Well, whatta yuh think?"

"About what?"

"About my new wife, about Cornelia?"

"Well, she's an awfully pretty woman, Governor," I said.

"Yessuh, Jim," he sighed. "She sure is."

And she was. Cornelia Ellis Snively Wallace was, as Oscar Harper once said, a "smoky woman," with ebony hair, dark skin, and a flash in her eyes that suggested whatever you wanted it to suggest. The niece of Big Jim Folsom, a former governor who was beaten by Wallace in 1962, she had spent part of her childhood in the big, white mansion on Perry Street, in Montgomery. Her mother—

called Big Ruby for her stature and her appetites—had served as her brother's official hostess, and nothing had pleased Cornelia more than to move back into her childhood home with her new husband, George.

"Lots of people don't think of him as handsome," she said one afternoon, a few months after their wedding. "Whatta you think, Jim? Do you think he's handsome?"

"Well, I haven't tried, really, to evaluate him that way," I answered. Of all the things he was or was not, handsome was never, never in the ball park.

"Well, ah sure do," she said. "But he's also verruh strong, you know, and sometimes he's—well, sometimes, he's mean, in a nice way. You know what ah'm talkin about? I don't mean ugly mean. I mean just the kind of mean I like."

I had no idea—but Wallace apparently did, and he seemed inordinately happy about his marriage. She was strikingly attractive, though sometimes a bit flashy, and she was politically savvy most of the time. Most important, she shared his unbounded ambition for prominence and popularity, hungered as much as he did for the crowds and the noise and the excitement and the adulation. It was quite understandable. She was like a daughter to Big Jim Folsom, one of the greatest showmen in Alabama politics, and she'd gone to New York City to become a star; she had to settle for a tour with Roy Acuff and one forgotten recording. Show business is hard to cure, and so off they went onto the brightly lit stage of the 1972 presidential campaign, and once again, it was me 'n' George and, of course, Cornelia too.

"What're you gonna say about the Kennedys, Jo'ge?" she asked as we flew in a tiny corporate jet up to Boston for a campaign speech in April, a month before he was shot.

"Well, ah guess ah'll say they're the most pow'ful political family in America," he answered.

"And what're you gonna say about the Saltonstalls, Jo'ge?"

"Who?"

"The Saltonstalls, you know—"

"Oh, yeah," he said. "Wuddn't that the one let that nigger beat him in the Senate? What was his name?"

"Leverett Saltonstall," I said sitting knee to knee with him in the narrow fuselage. (Saltonstall had actually retired.)

"No, not him, the nigger," he said.

"You mean Ed Brooke?"

"Yeah," he said. "That's the nigger ah mean."

That night, I wrote he had called the only black man in the United States Senate a nigger, and the next day, after it had been printed in *The New York Times* and we had proceeded on up to Michigan and other reporters had begun asking him about it, he vehemently denied he'd ever said it.

"But I heard you," I argued as we walked together out of a press conference up in Bay City.

"No, you didn't," he said. "You was mistaken."

"Well, Mrs. Wallace heard it too," I countered. "Let's just ask her."

"You keep her out of this," he said.

I said nothing as we walked toward his car. He turned to me finally and whispered in my ear. "Wooten," he said, "you're a son of a bitch."

He was changing. In 1968, he would have admitted he'd said it.

I saw him in the autumn of '72, a few months after he was shot. I'd been transferred to Spiro Agnew by then, and the Vice-President went down to Montgomery to pay his respects to Wallace and put another Republican nail on the southern lid. Wallace and Agnew were in a small parlor on the first floor of the mansion (God only knows what they would have had to talk about), and when I was ushered in, Wallace motioned for me to sit next to him.

"You treatin' the Vice-President fair, Jim?" he asked.

Agnew looked pained. I said I was just doing what I always did.

"Well," Wallace said, his voice distant and soft, "that's good, Jim." He turned to Agnew. "Ol' Jim heah, he's all right. Co'se, you know 'bout his newspapuh."

Later, in the dining room, Cornelia told me privately that Wallace was becoming a child again. "The wheelchair is his womb," she said. "He calls me 'Mama,' and he cries a lot, and I don't seem to be able to help him." I suggested that when he got back into the political flow, he'd feel better.

"Well, of course, I want him to run for governor again, but he says he can't do it," she said.

But, of course, he did run, and he won easily in 1974, and then, answering the rooted rhythms and patterns of his life, he could not resist another presidential campaign in 1976. Almost nobody noticed after a while. It was devastating for him. It was the beginning of his new and present retreat.

"The wheelchair did it," he said that night in Mobile. "But ah don't have any regrets whatsoevuh. Why, if it wuddn't fuh me, ol' Jimmy Carter wouldn't be President."

The circus is over now, gone for good from his life, and so is Cornelia. "Ah'm not gonna talk about that," he said on election day in his office at the capitol, where we had met so many years before. "That's personal stuff and ah'm not gonna talk about it. You goin' through a dee-vorce right now, ain't you, Jim? You understand, don't you?"

His intelligence was impeccable—but his spirits were even lower than when I'd left him in Mobile the night before. I'd flown with him that morning over to his little hometown of Clayton, Alabama, to watch him vote, and on the way I'd asked him why he had chosen not to run for either of the U.S. Senate seats being contested that day in the Democratic primary (John Sparkman had decided to retire, and James Allen had died suddenly), and it almost seemed as though the subject itself deeply depressed him.

"Well, ah just got to thinkin' 'bout bein' up theah in Wash'nun, a strange town 'n' all, and with my condition, ah'll tell you the truth, Jim, ah just didn't wanna be up there all by myself," he said.

The two-engine state-owned plane was humming along over a string of hamlets he knew so well—Smut Eye and Jenkins Crossroads and Hector and Blues Old Stand—and he looked down through his plastic porthole and pointed. "Co'se, ah could uh won, you know," he said. "Easy, ah believe. They'd have wanted me to go up there to the Senate, you know, but ah just didn't want to be there by myself."

He signaled for his ever present thermos of ice water, unscrewed the cap, and gulped down several swallows. "Drink a lot of water now, Jim," he said. "Good fuh my kidneys, you know. You ought to drink lots of water yourself 'stead of all that whiskey 'n' stuff. Ah got great kidneys, Jim. Really wonderful kidneys."

The plane droned on toward

Clayton, and he started to speak again, but some involuntary hesitance captured him. His lips opened and shut and came together and lifted again and again, but there was no sound. Finally, he overcame it.

"But ah just didn't wanna go up there to Wash'nun, you know, in my condition, all by myself," he said. "Co'se, ah could uh won, easy."

He does not really believe that, surely, but it is not expected of him to admit otherwise. He would have had one hell of a race either way he went because he would have been unable to reach the black vote in Alabama. He has often spoken of his ability to attract the support of black people, but it is largely a myth, and in a one-party political monolith, their backing is now required for victory.

"That's not true at all," he argued mildly as the plane headed in over peanut fields to a concrete strip outside Clayton. "Besides, ah could uh gotten a substantial po'tion of the black vote. Yessuh, why in 1966, mah wife—that's Guv'nuh Lurleen—she got—" and he was off and running with his familiar spiel about how Alabama's black people have always loved the Wallaces. He does not really believe it, at least not to the extent he was willing to test it with a run for the U.S. Senate.

"Ah just didn't want to go to Wash'nun by myself," he insisted as the plane hit and began to roll. He watched thick stands of pine trees flash past his window, and the slightest wisp of a smile settled itself on his aging face. He was home again, back where he had started, in 1946, so many miles and so many years away from the hot, hard parking lot of that shopping center in Laurel, Maryland.

Something was missing when I went to his office that afternoon. It all seemed the same. He was sitting behind his big desk at the other end of the long room, and as usual, he was surrounded by the trappings of his career—the four furled flags and the great seal of Alabama rising grandly behind him, the array of trophies and plaques from citizens' groups and police associations protecting his flanks, the stack of black-and-white photographs awaiting his signature, the pile of newspaper clippings covering a corner of the table, a multibutton communications console sitting at his fingertips, and two dialless, direct-line telephones—one red, the other black—perching nearby—and it all seemed very much the same.

The difference was that the old George Wallace was missing. In days past, he dominated the dark-paneled salon, filled the room with his presence, despite the extravagant crystal chandelier and the massive conference table. In days past, he was lord and master there—but that afternoon, he was a prisoner.

"C'mon down heah, Jim," he said weakly as I entered, and it was neither invitation nor command. It was, instead, a plea to join him in the thick-walled captivity of his cell.

Still, it is a familiar cell. Robert E. Lee stares balefully down from a magnificent portrait just as he has since it was hung there years before, and from one end to the other, the office reeks with the stale aroma of the governor's cheap cigars—a comfortable, old-shoe odor that he can transfer to any environment when he leaves.

"And ah guess ah'll be able to take some of this stuff too when ah go," he said. "Co'se, then the papuhs'll say ah was stealin' guv'mint property—but they know ah hadn't evuh stole nothin'. They know that. Evuhbuddy knows that."

Indeed, that is the prevailing view of George Wallace around the white domed capitol. It is also firmly believed in the same quarters that many of his close friends did "ver-ruh, verruh well" for themselves during the tenure of his power. "Now, that's not true," he said. "But anyway, ah can't be responsible fuh evuhbuddy, can ah?"

Wallace is worth about $210,000, according to his own accounting, and that includes a few stocks and bonds, an old house in Clayton, a suburban home in Montgomery, and a little savings. He is much worried about money now because of his cost of living. As governor, he has earned only $28,955 annually (the next governor will receive $50,000), but with the state picking up the tab for servants and staff at the mansion and the state troopers and cars required for his mobility, he has been able to survive. He will continue to have two troopers with him when he retires—but that is all. No pension from the state. Nothing else. That has him worried.

"What do you think you'll need to get along?" I asked.

He seemed reluctant to answer.

"Fifty thousand, sixty thousand?"

Still, he would not say.

"Seventy-five?"

He nodded. "And maybe a little more," he said. "But ah can't say that, you know, because of all the handicapped people out there who get along on so much less. Ah don't want them to be discouraged, you know. Ah'm kind of a model, you know, a symbol for a lot of them. They call me up—folks with all sorts of handicaps—they call me up all the time, and ah just try to encourage them, and they always say ah'm such an inspiration to them, you know. So ah can't go 'round sayin' ah got to have lots of money to live now, you know."

He says he does not know what he will do. Perhaps he will join the faculty of one of the state universities. Perhaps he will produce radio commentaries like Ronald Reagan. Perhaps he will write a book or a column. Perhaps he will hit the lecture circuit. His new publicists, Celebrity Management, Inc., of Nashville, speak of a movie about George.

Ah just don't know what ah'm gonna do," he said. "Co'se, ah got to keep active, you know. Ah've always been active. So ah've got to keep on bein' active." But he is deeply afraid that the minimum income he requires will be beyond the reach of the income he can produce, and he inquired urgently about the potential of books and lectures and radio commentary.

"Whatta you figure ol' Reagan makes from that stuff he does?" he asked.

"I don't know, Governor, but I heard it's one hell of a chunk of money."

"Couple hunnert thousand, ah heard."

"Yes, sir, that's about what I remember too."

"Well, you reckon anybody'd want to hear what ah'd say on the radio?"

"I expect a lot of people would, Governor."

"Would you?"

"Well, I don't know if—"

"You wouldn't listen to me, now would you, Jim? Tell the truth."

"Well, I just don't know about every day, Governor," I said.

"Ah reckon ah could get along without you, anyway," he said.

"Yes, sir, I believe you could."

"But what would ah say?"

"What would you say?"

"Yeah," he said, staring hard down at his desk top. "Ah'd have to have somethin' to say, wouldn't I?"

"Well, I'm not sure Reagan has something to say every time he talks."

"Well, that's probably true," he said. "It must be awful hard to have somethin' to say evuh day, idn't it?"

And so we talked on and on into the afternoon, and he remembered how Lyndon Johnson had placed a conference call to him and Hubert Humphrey and Nixon in the campaign of 1968 to brief them on national security affairs; and he recalled how he'd met Jack Kennedy once in Washington at a hotel and how Kennedy had written to him in 1958, thinking George would probably be the next governor of Alabama. "Ah lost, of co'se," he said. "But Kennedy, he knew what he was doin', all right. He was lookin' fuh mah support even then. Ah still got the lettuh somewhere. God, he was a good-lookin' man, wuddn't he?"

The room was quiet momentarily. I asked what he thought about the assassinations—the Kennedys, King, and the attempt on his own life. "Well, ah still see faces," he said.

"Faces?"

"Yessuh," he said. "The faces of the people laughin' after he shot me."

"You think Bremer acted alone?"

"No, no, ah don't—co'se ah can't prove he didn't. It's just that ah can see faces behind it, you know. It didn't make sense without he had some assistance, does it? Ah mean, a boy like that, travelin' all ovuh the country, follerin' me aroun' like a bird dog. No, no, ah still see other faces than him."

It is a subject that fascinates him, on which he dwells for many, many hours with old friends and cronies who come to visit at the mansion or the office. He cannot erase it from his consciousness. The evidence of conspiracy is slim, but the fact of Bremer's bullets is ever present in his daily life. It gnaws at him, taking him back to that last moment before he became the way he is, that last millisecond before the shots, when he was still a hell raiser of a candidate, sneering and snarling and jumping down from the back of flatbed trucks and wading into happy, noisy crowds with his little hands extended, drawing strength and energy from the touching.

"Yessuh," he said that afternoon, "we had some good ol' times, didn't we, Jim?"

"Well, they were exciting, I'll say that, Governor."

"You remember that crowd ah got in Madison Square Garden in 1968? Must of been fifty thousand people theah, wuddn't theah?"

"Well, not that many, Governor," I said. We were reverting back to our traditional campaign argument, waged after each of his appearances.

"How many was theah, then?" he snapped.

"Well, the Garden only holds about twenty-five."

"Uhmmm," he said. "That right? Ah could have sworn there was fifty or sixty thousand people theah—and anyway, though, they liked me, didn't they?"

"Yes, sir, Governor, they sure did."

"Yessuh, ah'd like fuh Lurleen to have seen that," he said. "Like fuh her to have been at the Garden that night. She'd uh sure been proud, ah think."

My grandfather, Jody Wooten, was a southerner who found Wallace's 1968 candidacy much to his liking. He did not like the sound of the times back then—not the kids, not the liberals, not the press, and, of course, not the clamor of black Americans for some slice of the American pie. He was already in his eighties, but he drove his old Chevy sedan in Wallace campaign parades through his little town and manned telephones at the local headquarters, and he put up posters and passed out bumper stickers and laughed at me when I told him that Wallace couldn't possibly win.

Then, one Saturday afternoon, I went to see him and told him how Wallace that week had urged a large crowd in Michigan to show their disapproval of the reporters traveling with him—and they had, certainly with much more fury than even Wallace had expected. They threw metal chairs in our direction (one of Wallace's bodyguards shoved me under a table when the chairs began to fly) and spit on us, threw bottles and cups of water at us—and as I told him the story, he was incredulous.

"You're makin' that up, Jimbo," he said.

"It's the God's truth, Papa."

"And he put them up to it?"

"Yes, sir, he did."

He pondered that, sucking on his empty pipe, and finally he spoke. "Well," he said, "it's all over between us."

"Between us?"

"No, between me and Wallace."

"You're not going to vote for him?"

"No, and I ain't going to work for him no more."

"But why, Papa?"

"Because a fellow ought not to do things like that, that's why," he said. "I don't want to have nothing to do with a fella that will do things like that."

So now, like Papa, I think it is finally over between me and George. For years we served each other, if not well, at least adequately. I was his handy punching bag, constrained always by my reportorial role and my relationship with *The New York Times*. Similarly, he was always there on the outskirts of my consciousness as a convenient object of my general disgust. I detested his every moment of success, gloated over his every defeat, and knew there was nothing he could really do to me.

All of that is finished now. He does not need me anymore—nor any one of us who traipsed around after him for all those years and miles—and I do not further require him as my symbol of southern madness. Since that morning we met in Montgomery, I have discovered other insanities elsewhere, some in myself, most equally as pernicious—and, like him, I've lost a couple of the big ones and knitted guilty wool far into the night after hurting other people. I no longer feel superior to George.

Remembering. This is essentially his life now. There are people around, of course, and there are things happening, of course, but he is still very much alone and very much without anything to do except remember by himself. Lurleen's seventeen-year-old daughter, Lee, is a senior in high school in Montgomery, but her busy teenage life leaves her little time to spend with her father; and the only son, George Jr., is now in his mid-twenties and has his own life around town and around the state; and the oldest child, Bobbi, lives with her husband and children in Livingston. At the mansion with him are two prison trusties who help take care of him, a couple of housekeepers who clean up and cook— and after all the crowds and all the applause and all the lights and all the noise, it is sparse company for him. He has retreated, and he is alone again, as alone now as he felt himself to be in the belly of his B-29 on those terrifying bombing runs over Tokyo, and his world continues to diminish. He will no longer be governor in a few months, and he will have to leave the big white mansion on Perry Street and the limousines and the big rallies—and he will have to make do with his memories.

"But ah don't have no regrets, whatsoevuh," he said.

"What about the divorce?" I asked. "Don't you have any second thoughts about that?"

"Ah'm not gonna talk about the—the you know, uh, the dee-vorce," he said.

He would, of course, be the only one in Montgomery who would not. It was as deep a tragedy as ever befell him, and it was principally of his own making. He was shattered by Arthur Bremer in many ways, but the loss of his lower body seemed most damaging. It propelled him into deeper and darker moods than anyone had ever observed in him, and of course it changed the dimensions of his marriage to the smoky woman. Slowly, he came to believe that she was not a faithful spouse. He was passionately persuaded that she was running around on him—with strangers and friends alike—and so deep was his misery that he shared his imagined cuckoldry with cronies and pals, and they told the stories in their own circles, and soon, it was the hottest gossip item in town. She was, I believe, innocent of such indictments, but she responded by bugging his telephone at the mansion and hearing him say all those things himself—and more. It was 1976 by then. She moved out. Then she moved back in. She'd been divorced once before. She didn't want it again. He still would not accept her as a faithful wife. He drove her out. He had called her Mama and wept in her arms, and she had given him as much as she could—but he would not accept her, and he drove her out.

So now he lives alone in their spacious bedroom in the big white mansion on Perry Street, lives there now with his telephone, his remote-control television set, a little bell for signaling the servants, and the fever shapes of the life he has lived—and he waits there alone for his term to end.

He was right. Every man does have his price, but few have paid so dearly as George Wallace.

In the following article, Beverly Levine begins to create suspense in her first sentence with the ominous word "ordeal." The reader firmly hooked, she never lets the line slacken, steadily dropping details of an ordinary day to heighten the terror to come. As the crisis approaches, she maintains the atmosphere of threat with the dialogue between her and the stalker and by describing her inner thoughts and fears.

This article is unusual in that it is consistently narrative until near the end when Levine shifts into exposition and gives the reader some useful guidelines for traveling alone—safely. This sudden switch could have been startling, but she handles the transition smoothly. Examine exactly how this is done.

TRAVEL
WITHOUT TERROR

Beverly Levine

Always self-confident and sure of myself to handle any situation, I lived through an ordeal which taught me the lesson of forethought and prevention as a female business traveler. I later berated myself for what I could have done differently. It was a lesson hard learned.

It began like many other days, I had no premonition of pending problems. I boarded another plane to another destination without trepidation. Being young and energetic, I did not in the least let the fact that I was alone cause me to modify my behavior or deter me from the things I wanted to do.

My plane arrived late so I rented a car, went straight to my hotel, and surrounded myself with paperwork in preparation for the next day's meetings. Late spring on the Gulf is a glorious time of year so I scheduled my business early to leave myself a luxurious afternoon by the pool.

The day it happened dawned clear and beautiful, with only an occasional cloud to break the monotony of an otherwise depthless blue sky. I was back at my hotel by 2 o'clock, just in time for a late lunch and some sun. My hotel was an upscale highrise, with one side of the building overlooking the pool. I certainly did not give this a thought . . . a thought that a pair of unseen eyes might be looking down on me from the shadows of a room above. The sun blazed, I munched on a salad and sipped a drink, and the afternoon passed with uneventful enjoyment. I read, procrastinated on paperwork, and chatted with the people around me until the sun began to seek refuge beyond the horizon. I then gathered my array of pool paraphernalia and, on the way to my room, gave myself up to thoughts of a sumptuous seafood dinner.

Still warmed by the sun, I decided to take a cool shower and make some phone calls for tomorrow's business. It was past dusk as I walked through the parking lot to my car. I had asked the doorman about nearby restaurants and was told I could not pass up a certain establishment overlooking the bay. Off I went, alone, to dinner and dessert with a view of white lights across the waveless water. Still no intuitional warnings.

A balmy breeze blew as I drove back to my hotel, my windows down and the faint smell of salt hanging in the air. Everything gave the appearance of being perfectly normal as I rode the elevator to the 11th floor and walked the long hallway to my room at the other end.

Ten o'clock was too early to go to bed, and I was not tired anyway. I got undressed and put on a cool nightgown before I turned on the television and climbed onto the bed with my itinerary for the rest of my trip. Two more days and it would be home again to regroup for the next trip.

Close to midnight I felt a chill in the air, not unusual for that time of night. Were my senses more alert than my conscious self? When the phone rang, I jumped as though I had been forcibly struck by the sound. It was beginning.

I said hello a bit tentatively, but I had been called by co-workers that late before. My sensible side said surely it was a call of that kind. The voice which answered me was muffled from the first syllable uttered, yet it was unmistakably male.

"I've been watching you," the voice rasped into my ear.

I froze. "Who is this?" I demanded with more strength than I actually felt.

"I'm going to have you," was his reply.

I slammed down the phone. My thoughts were erratic. Could this man have any idea whom he was calling? Surely not. He must have randomly dialed a number and gotten my room.

Although I did not realize it, I held my breath for several seconds, staring at the phone. I was anticipating another shrill sound to break the silence. When it did not come, I slowly relaxed and took a deep breath. I was right. It was just a crank. He may not even know the number he had dialed.

He waited just long enough for me to let down my defenses. Then the phone rang again. Three long rings echoed in my room before I dared to reach out and pick it up.

"Hello," I said with a false bravado.

My entire body tensed in that second before he spoke.

"I saw you by the pool today. You looked very pretty," he matter-of-factly stated.

I gasped.

"Did you enjoy your dinner? You were gone for a while," he continued with frightening casualness. "I am going to have you," he said with a firmness not before present in his voice.

I finally found my voice. "Who is this?" was all I could think of to say. Fright became a presence right there in the room with me.

His voice turned husky. "You can't get away from me. I want to have you. You know what I mean."

"Leave me alone," I said, partly angry and partly terrified.

The phone dropped to my side. Then I slowly replaced the receiver. I squeezed my eyes shut. "My God," I thought, "please, please don't let this be happening to me."

I was being stalked.

I dialed the front desk. I had never heard my voice sound the way it did at that moment. "This is room 1107. I am getting obscene calls. I'm scared," my voice faltered. This was the last thing the desk clerk wanted to hear. He assured me there was no cause for alarm. I could have slapped him in that instant. I knew this was no joke. He then made the offer to move me to another room if the man called again or if I was bothered anymore. I hung up feeling no more secure than I had before I made the call.

I could not sit still. I paced that room, picked things up and put them right back down, and looked out the peep hole more times than I care to count. My mind was racing.

When the phone rang a single time, it was as though this was some sort of sign sent to me. Yet I could not take any action as a result of a ring. Every light in the room was blazing, including the one in the bathroom, and the television cast a shadow of reality on the room.

Wasn't Johnny Carson continuing to go about his business?

I could scarcely believe it when my room was plunged into darkness and silence in one brief second. I was seized with a terror I had never ever come close to experiencing. Before my eyes could adjust themselves, I had the uncanny perception of being a small helpless animal being tracked. I groped for the curtain to bring even a small amount of light into this hell I had somehow been placed in. The total fear I felt for my life engulfed me like a wave. Nothing, ever, had created even an inkling of the gripping trauma I felt.

I reached for the phone and called downstairs again. I said a silent thank-you that it was working. "The power is out in my room. Is it out all over the hotel?" I knew the answer before I heard the negative response. "Get up here now. I am really scared. The man who has been calling me. . . ." I crumpled. They wanted to know what he had said. "I can't go into it, but he said he is after me. Please hurry!" I was begging. They would send someone right up.

I backed into a corner just as far from the door as I could get. When I heard the thud, my hand covered my mouth to stifle a scream. He was actually at my door. This was real. "I don't want to die," I repeated in my mind again and again. The thud came again. He was trying to break into my room. How could this be happening? I felt like a cowering animal in that corner. The thuds came more quickly but never loudly. "All my dreams. Dear Lord," I prayed, "I am begging you. Please."

Suddenly they stopped. Was this it? My fists were clenched so tightly my nails actually broke the skin in my palms. I was burning on the inside, but outside I was covered with a clammy sweat.

A few seconds later there was a knock on my door. "Security, mam" was the most blessed sound I had ever heard. I rushed to the door and opened it with the chain still on. I somehow had the presence of mind to ask for identification. There were actually two young men outside my door ready to help. Neither had wanted to come alone.

I could not let them in because I was barely dressed. "Let me put something on. But please don't go anywhere," I added pleadingly. As I dressed in the suit I had out for the next day, one of the men checked the breaker box on that floor. The power to my room had been deliberately cut. I had not yet seen the door, but small gashes were there where the stalker had tried to break the lock.

The power came back on just before I let them in. I was weak with relief. Then I saw the mutilated door and almost fainted. How close had I come to the unthinkable?

I told them the whole story. We figured the elevator bell had cued the man that someone was coming.

One man said he checked and the calls to my room had come from within the hotel. There was no way of knowing which room. They were checking out the people on my floor, but it turned out there were only two. Using the service elevator they moved me to the fourth floor to a room with an adjoining room. A security man would stay with me the rest of the night. I felt much better but to say I was back to normal would be far from reality. The entire hotel was searched, but nothing unusual was found. I knew if he had the chance, this man would still be after me. Was I caged?

I sat in that room all night long dressed completely, even my shoes. I was too apprehensive to relax at all. I did not want to be alone for even a second and would not even let the security man staying with me go into the other room. This was a nightmare come to life.

When the sun came up, I felt much better. I had kept the security man up all night long with nervous chatter, but I would be forever grateful.

I was taking the first plane out of this town. They did not tell me until I was almost ready to leave that the front desk had gotten a couple of calls from outside the hotel later in the night. He actually told them he was still planning to get me and that he could wait. This revived everything I had been feeling all night long.

They saw me safely to the airport, where I caught the first possible plane. I have never been happier in my life to return home.

Looking back now, this bizarre event could have turned out much worse . . . or it could have been prevented.

Women in business who travel alone are vulnerable. But when I talked with several people in hotel management, they told me about measures a woman can take right at the hotel to better insure her safety. They also pointed out that I did almost none of these things. Through these discussions and from my own experience, I discovered several ways to lessen the risks. No one should have to go through what I did.

▪ Anytime you travel, keep a flashlight in your suitcase. Even though the circumstances may not be as dire as mine, power outages do happen.

▪ Request a room that is near the elevator. There is more traffic there than any other place on the hall. My room was one of the farthest from the elevator.

▪ While you are making requests, be sure you are on a floor with several other people. Hotels often fill one floor before starting another. At the very worst someone nearby could hear you scream. On my entire floor only two other rooms were occupied.

▪ Never get on the elevator with someone who makes you feel uncomfortable. There is probably no cause for alarm, but do not let being in a hurry cause you to take a chance.

▪ When you get to your room, make sure your phone has been turned on. If the hotel is busy, they may not do this right away. That phone could be your life line; it certainly was mine.

▪ Any time you leave and then return to the hotel, let the valet park your car. A small cost keeps you from having to walk through a parking lot or garage alone. This is an easy way to prevent that possible attack.

▪ Whether eating in the restaurant or out by the pool, it is often better to keep to yourself than to be seen as overly friendly. A simple conversation to one person may mean something different to another. I talked all afternoon with strangers.

▪ Any time you are at the pool or in the restaurant, be sure to conceal your room key with the number on it. It may be all you take with you if you are charging your meal to your room. But this lets any passerby know exactly where you are in the hotel. And it announces the fact that your room is empty for anyone wanting to steal something. This is important. My key sat by my pool chair all afternoon.

▪ Lastly, never assume that just because you have called room service or housekeeping that this is who is at your door. Never open without checking out who is there first.

My experience certainly gave me a new outlook on traveling alone. I still do all the things that I want to do, but I am careful to take precautions when doing them.

A cluster of related images that meander through an article will make a humdrum piece spring into distinction. Such images make abstractions visual or audible or almost touchable. And they channel the various tributaries of the story into one forceful, unified stream.

That is what Nancy E. Davis does with mountain climbing imagery in "The Fall and Rise of Richard Hill." In addition, she nimbly sidesteps some dangerous pitfalls by maintaining a light touch with this technique. The imagery is there and the reader responds to it, but the effect is subtle, never heavy or self-conscious.

The mountain climbing motif is a delightful bonus, but the story itself is paramount. Imagine how different the reader's involvement would have been if the article had merely been an essay on memory loss.

The story is true, but the names have been changed.

THE FALL AND RISE OF RICHARD HILL

Nancy E. Davis

Normally on Friday morning at seven o'clock, Richard Hill would have finished running his mile and a half around the basketball court, lifted weights and ridden the Life Cycle for fifteen minutes, and be heading upstairs for half an hour of stretching and aerobics in the exercise program for the university's faculty and staff. He was in peak condition: the three-times-a-week routine helped him hold his weight at a trim 162, and he looked younger than his 62 years. He liked starting the morning with a workout and enjoyed the camaraderie with his fellow fitness buffs.

But on Friday, February 21, 1986, Richard didn't exercise. He had scheduled quizzes that day for all three of his classes, and he wanted to check the handouts for typos and be sure he had enough copies. So at seven o'clock that Friday morning he was at his office early, preparing to start the day by getting water to make a pot of coffee.

A squeak—really a scream, but he heard it as a squeak—made Richard open his eyes. Above him a blurred white shape gradually resolved into a frightened face. The empty glass coffeepot, unbroken, on the floor beside him—had he set it there as he went down?—and water everywhere. He sat up, his head throbbing, then tried to stand. His foot skidded out, jolting him back to the floor. He touched his shoe and came away with a glob of grease.

Someone, maybe the white face, helped him to his feet. The same person—or someone else?—got him to his office. Through the pounding pain, he thought to call home, but couldn't remember the number. The secretary knows it—she can make the call, he decided.

After a while, a colleague took him home. He directed him without difficulty until they neared the house and Mel asked his address. With a pang, he realized he didn't know that number either. "Just stop at the rusty-looking mailbox," he said. The number's on it, he told himself. That'll remind me. But the mailbox held another shock: the symbols on it might as well have been

Chinese—they were just shapes that had no meaning.

He didn't tell Mel about the numbers. He didn't tell Claire either, when she came out to help him into the house and upstairs to lie down on the bed. Maybe later, he thought. It's just that my head hurts so much and I feel so lousy.

"Later" came at the doctor's office. The nurse took his temperature, his blood pressure, his pulse. And she asked questions: Tell me what happened. Did you lose consciousness? Do you know how long you were unconscious? Have you had any nausea? Are you sleepy? Does light bother you? Show me where you hit your head.

"I've never had a headache before," he said. "If this is what it's like, I hope I never have another one." But even the pain couldn't squelch his scientist's curiosity. "Why does my head ache in front when I hit it in back?"

"It's because the brain is like a bowl of jelly confined by your skull," the nurse explained. "When you hit your head hard, the whole mass in there shifts and slams against the opposite wall of your skull." She recounted the case of a woman whose contusion went undiscovered for days because it was on the opposite side of her head from where she'd been hit. Oh, of course—hydrostatic action, he recognized.

As she turned with her hand on the door to fetch the doctor, he said softly, "There's one more thing. I can't remember my phone number."

Saying it aloud for the first time, he began to grasp the enormity of what had happened to him. His whole body sagged and he dug his palms into his eyes.

Moments later, the doctor—not his regular doctor and tennis buddy, who was retiring soon, but a new young man he'd never met before—gently examined the place on his head: left side, an inch or so above the base of the skull. More questions—following up on the history the nurse had taken, establishing contact.

Then they got to the numbers.

"What's one hundred minus three?" Richard shook his head.

"What's two plus two?" "Two plus two equals four," he recited, but it was just words, like a little poem he'd learned by rote.

"What's two plus three?" No idea. No idea what two meant. No idea what three meant. No idea what plus meant.

"What does this say?" (the device for measuring blood pressure). "Sphygmomanometer." No problem. "And this?" (the gauge). Blank. Zip. Nothing.

The doctor saw the panic. "A bump on the head does funny things to memory sometimes. Don't worry—we won't make you recite the Gettysburg Address or anything." "Four score and seven years ago, our fathers brought forth on this continent a new nation. . ." Words. No problem with remembering words.

Over to the hospital for tests. First the forms: Name—I can do that one. Telephone number . . . address . . . date of birth (April . . .) social security number, for crying out loud. Is *everything* a number? EEG: the technician sandpapering his skin so the electrodes will make good contact—a different pain to distract from the headache. "Any anomalies?" Richard asks afterwards. "No, nothing abnormal." CAT scan: "I should have worn my film badge," he jokes with the technician, letting her know he knows about radiation doses. Bright lights. Motionless on a table, listening to the mechanism clunk as the table advances him by increments through the shiny steel tunnel. General Electric, he reads on the side. Wonder what they're using for a computer, since GE doesn't make them anymore. But mostly he just lies there, eyes shut, and lets the machine shoot its pictures. Afterwards—no anomalies there either. No internal bleeding. No evidence of stroke. No numbers. . . .

Richard C. Hill, Ph.D. in physics, bachelor's degree in mathematics, professor of nuclear engineering at a major technical university. He went home from the doctor and went to bed. Next morning, Saturday, he woke up with the headache and the blank where numbers were supposed to be. Why me? And why *numbers?* I've always had a head like a rock—I've bumped it thousands of times. How am I going to teach my classes? How am I going to do anything?

Enough of that. He'd fallen; how could he get back up? He reviewed his options.

He could put himself into the doctor's hands, let the doctor take responsibility for healing him, for transporting him out of this valley. But he was already getting the feeling that the doctor didn't have a cure.

He could sit around and wait for his head to heal and—maybe—his memory to come back. He'd probably wake up one morning and find himself back at the peak of his mental powers, back where he was before the accident. But the doctor couldn't tell him how long that would take—weeks probably, maybe months. He did say he was sure it would come back. . . .

Or he could climb back up under his own power, relearn what he had forgotten.

After breakfast, he found a calendar and began to study the symbols on it. He knew that they were consecutive numbers and that he must learn their names. He got a blank 4 x 6 index card out of the recipe file and carefully copied each shape, drawing them as if they were Chinese characters. Claire told him the name of each shape, and he wrote it on the card opposite its symbol. He carried the card around with him, taking it out and testing himself every so often.

"I'd better write down our telephone number for you," Claire said. "And our work numbers. I didn't want to risk disturbing your sleep by calling you from work yesterday afternoon—then on the way home I suddenly realized you couldn't have called me if you'd needed me!" She got out another card and wrote the numbers down. He studied them with a frown, then asked, "Are these fours?" With their open, right-angled tops, they looked different from the printed triangular-topped figures he'd copied from the calendar. If he'd been copying Chinese characters, he wouldn't have known what embellishments could be added or changed without altering the meaning. It was the same thing with the numbers.

By lunchtime he could count to 100 by ones. He took a break, then tackled counting by twos, by fives, by tens, by twenties—each step hard-won. He was ready to take a look at money. He emptied his pockets and sorted out the coins, thinking of all the foreign currencies he'd learned over the years and how he'd always scorned the tourists who didn't bother to learn, just sticking out their hands filled with coins and asking the vendor to take the right amount. No shekels or shillings had ever been more unfamiliar than these. He read what each one said—odd, the only numbers on them were the dates. One cent, five cents (Claire told him that one was also called a nickel—he remembered the word, of course), one dime (ten cents—ten of these make one dollar). They worked for an hour—she'd hand him a combination of coins and he'd try to figure out how much they were worth. Bills were easier: "Isn't it clever," he observed, "that they write the amount as a word as well as a number." But he didn't really know what twenty dollars meant. He had no feeling for values, relative or actual—of money or anything else. Suddenly he realized he was soaked with perspiration and exhausted. But he'd made a start, established a base camp for the ascent ahead.

That night they went out to dinner with friends. (He'd wanted to order-in a pizza so he wouldn't have to pay in public. Claire reminded him gently that she could pay the bill. Or, she joked, we could just tell Jim he'll have to pay—you don't do money.) During dinner he was preoccupied. They thought it was the headache, but to their amazement, he came out with what the meal could cost before the bill came. They'd each ordered a meal that cost $9 and change; he knew that if you add enough change to nine, you get to the next number, ten, and he could count by tens. So he pretended each meal was $10, then counted the tens on his fingers to get the total. Somehow, he felt, it would have shamed him not to know how much the dinner cost—even if the $40 he came up with was just more words, not really a meaningful value.

Next day, he thought he could at least work in his shop; there's always something that needs repairing. But when he looked at his drills, he saw a different kind of number that he didn't understand: 1/8, 1/4, 1/2. What did the line between the numbers mean? What did a one mean if it had another number under it like that? He thought it had something to do with measurement. Looking around, he saw a tape measure. He picked it up, pulled out the tape, and examined it. Sure enough, it had those same kinds of stacked numbers. Suddenly he understood how the numbers on it related to each other, how smaller units added up to become larger units. An inch contained eight smaller pieces, each called 1/8. It contained four pieces called 1/4 and two pieces called 1/2. For the first time since the accident, he smiled his old smile.

Acalculia was the name the neurologist gave it. Knowing that his malady had a name and that other people had suffered from it was comforting, made him feel less alone. The doctor gave him an article from a medical journal that described it: an acquired disorder of calculating ability that took several forms. His problem, called anarith-metia, was the rarest—the inability to retrieve learned arithmetic values and/or to manipulate such values. Before examining him, the neurologist asked if he was right-handed or left-handed, then identified the exact spot where Richard had hit his head—the angular gyrus, he called it. (Would it have been on the right side if he'd been left-handed?) Richard looked forward to talking to the doctor again, thinking he must offer an interesting case for study. But when he returned for his appointment the following week, the neurologist looked at him strangely and asked why he was there. "I can't do anything for you," he said. "You'll recover in a month or two. Come back when there's a change." Richard never saw him again.

In the weeks following the accident, Richard practiced combining different denominations of coins until he felt confident enough to pay a bill with change. (He was shaken when he put 50 cents into a soft drink machine—he was sure the coins added up to 50 cents, and he was sure that was what the machine required—and didn't get a drink. Later he learned the price had been raised to 55 cents, but the sign hadn't been changed.)

He bought an almanac and read a few pages each night until he'd read it all the way through. The exercise was tedious, but rewarding. He found that he needed only to be reminded of statistics and dates he'd known before and they were his again. It was as if they were all still in there somewhere, but he had to find new connections to get to them. (He purposely left one date unlearned—his deceased mother's birthday—so he'd be able to tell if his memory came back. No one knew the date but him, he thought. Actually, Claire found it written on a scrap of paper; she hid it without telling him.)

A more difficult task was regaining the ability to manipulate numbers, to calculate. Using his pocket calculator, he generated the multiplication tables up to the fives, then slowly rememorized them, drilling himself in odd moments. From that level, attained after several weeks, he stretched for the sixes, then the sevens, finally the twelves, each ledge a little easier to reach than the one before.

The calculator was an invaluable tool, although at first it contained some mysteries: keys labeled exp, log ln. . . . . He knew they were functions but didn't know how to use them. (He could parrot the words of theories but didn't really understand their meaning, like knowing that boxes were there, but not knowing what was in them.) Still, he was following a trail he'd traveled before; he knew some of the landmarks to look for.

He and Claire set deadlines for his memory's return, moved them,

set new ones: when the headache goes away, six weeks, two months. The headache went away after about ten days; six weeks passed, two months, three. But his memory didn't come back.

Colleagues had administered the quizzes he had scheduled for the day of the accident. He tried to grade the papers. It was much worse than he thought: not only were the students' answers totally incomprehensible, but he didn't have the faintest idea what the answer keys he'd made up were about or any recollection of having written them. He put the tests aside and assessed his ability to teach his classes. Two of them—Materials Science and Nuclear Reactor Technology—were completely out of the question, filled as they were with mathematics and mathematical concepts. But maybe he could handle Fundamentals of Nuclear Engineering, a survey course on nuclear reactors—it was mostly descriptive, a comparison of different nuclear power plant designs.

As it turned out, lecturing on even a plant with which he was very familiar proved impossible—although he could picture it perfectly in his mind, he couldn't say how long the turbine-generator was, how many fuel rods were in a transfer cask. Everything in this business spins on numbers, he realized. Richard faced a crevasse that seemed too wide to cross. He had never been aware of how virtually everything he did revolved around numbers.

He continued to study. Working through his high school math books took only a couple of weeks. (About that time, a mathematician friend asked Claire how he was doing. When she replied, "He's now about at the same level as I am mathematically," the friend blurted in sincere sympathy, "Oh, how terrible!") Above the fundamental level, he had to inch his way along, sometimes running into walls that resisted his best efforts for days. *Introductory College Mathematics* by Milne and Davis, his freshman college math book, became his lucid guide again through the foothills that had led to his profession years ago. (Milne had been his professor; he sometimes prodded himself by picturing how disappointed Milne would be if he could witness his failure to understand.)

Five weeks into his ordeal, toward the end of March, he began to grasp the basics of calculus. Sometimes it took an hour or more to solve a problem, and he had no intuitive feeling for the answer. This lack of intuition he felt most keenly. Nevertheless, he plodded on, reading the textbooks he had used as a student and as a teacher, trying to work the problems, usually succeeding after a time.

Then, after clawing and clambering for three or four months, slowing sometimes, but always continuing, he hit a plateau and stopped. He'd gotten stuck on a concept called partial fractions. For the first time, he despaired of ever regaining his former abilities. He began to plan for early retirement. (Maybe one good thing will come out of this, he thought. This school's been trying to abandon nuclear engineering and hasn't supported us for several years. This could be my chance to get out.)

A psychologist friend recommended a neuropsychologist, a specialist in brain injuries and relearning. "It won't do any good," he told Claire. "He'll be like those M.D.s. How will I make him understand that knowing the calculus is not enough?" But he was desperate, so he went and answered more questions and took more tests. "Could this be psychosomatic," he asked, "a way of getting out of the situation at work?" The psychologist considered it: "We'll know if your memory returns on the day you retire, won't we?"

He reassured him that his months of study had been exactly the right thing to do, and recommended that Richard audit a class during the summer. Richard chose *Advanced Engineering Mathematics,* sat in the back of the room, and worked the problems. Although he felt conspicuous in his gray beard, he had to admit he was helped by seeing the professor work the problems on the board and hearing the class discussion. Once he thought he had hit another snag when he got an answer different from the professor's; relief flooded him when he learned the professor had made a mistake.

The class boosted him over partial fractions, and the fog that had shrouded his goal was dissipating faster now, reduced to occasional wisps. Sometimes he'd reach for a numerical concept—a value, or a size, or an amount—and it wouldn't be there. (He wasn't aware of what he didn't know until he tried to recall it.) He'd go looking for it and, as with the facts in the almanac, once he found it, it was his again.

Fall Quarter he carried a full teaching load. He could grade papers now without spending hours working every problem, and his instinctive feel for a value's correctness gradually returned. The nuclear power plant accident at Chernobyl happened and, after reviewing the specs for a similar plant at Hanford, Washington, he joined a panel of experts who answered questions for faculty, students, and the press about the accident. The Six O'Clock News gave him almost a minute of air time. Only those who knew him well recognized that they were witnessing a comeback.

By Christmas, all vestiges of disability were gone. His memory had returned imperceptibly, its return virtually irrelevant, dwarfed by his personal achievement. No flash of lightning, no flood of total recall, no flag planted on a summit heralded the event. He had found his way back through determination and persistence and drudgery, had re-won the mountaintop on his own. Maybe he would have reached exactly the same place if he'd done nothing, but it was not his nature to do nothing. Like Sir Edmund Hillary, he conquered the mountain because it was there.

Perhaps his mother's birthday hadn't been a good test. He never did remember it.

*In her query letter for the follow-
ing first-person article, Emilyanne Parker (not her real
name) confesses that before she became a law enforcement
officer she had often said, "I hate cops—can't stand 'em!" In
"Officer Survival: The Real Deal" she tells about what it is like
to be one of them—a sheriff's deputy—and about some of the
outrageous situations she encountered after making this surprising reversal in career direction.*

*The article reveals in detail her personal experiences in
entering the predominantly masculine world of law enforcement. As you read this true account, you may understand
why she uses a pseudonym instead of her real name.*

*Also note the value of narrative for holding the reader's
attention.*

OFFICER SURVIVAL: THE REAL DEAL

Emilyanne Parker

It seemed like an ordinary week at first: the sun rose, the alarm clock chirped, and the nine-to-fivers got stuck in traffic. But in retrospect, that week was full of unusual events—at least for me. I had been fingerprinted, photographed, and physically examined. Later, I found myself in a room, a dull, semiglossed-walls-with-no-windows kind of room, with about eight others who were quietly anticipating what would happen next. Then he walked in. The brilliance of his white shirt, the gold, six-pointed star, and the brassy collar insignias announcing "Chief" were hard to ignore.

"Stand up, raise your right hands, and repeat after me," he ordered.

As the sound of chairs dragging across the tiled floor ceased to a silence that seemed to embrace the tension already in the room, and as we found ourselves like human arrows aimed at the chief, I wondered if the others were as doubtful as I was, and if they were preoccupied (as I was) with such questions as, "What am I getting myself into?" Uneasy and almost unwilling, I joined in unison with the others: "I, Emilyanne Parker, do swear that I will faithfully execute all writs, warrants, precepts, and processes directed to me as Deputy Sheriff of this county . . . and that I will support the Constitution of the United States and of this State. SO HELP ME GOD." Gibberish. Jargon. That was the sum total of that oath to me at that time. And though I tried diligently to make sense of what I was saying as I said it, I was somehow thrown by the word "writs" and didn't regain my faculties until "SO HELP ME GOD."

But no one seemed to notice. And whether I understood what I had sworn to didn't seem to matter—it was official anyway. I was no longer just Emilyanne. I was Deputy Parker. And I have since solved more than the meaning of the outlined oath . . . I learned quickly what it meant to be female with the sheriff's department.

First, it meant proving myself to all the skeptics . . . including myself. I have been with my department for a little over four years, and although I didn't know beans about the duties of a deputy beforehand, I have since learned that one of the responsibilities of the sheriff is maintaining the health, safety, and welfare of prisoners. I didn't know that beforehand—but I found out.

My first day on the job was like my first blind date . . . disastrous. I was assigned to the county jail, the night shift (3–11), and the Northeast wing. The county hell was a run-down, dimly lit, two-story dwelling designed to house 800 inmates. The revolting stench within was so gripping that after eight hours there, it was not unusual to discover the stench in my clothes. Moreover, smoke, which filled the halls as densely as the inmates filled the cells, created a haze that compound-ed the lighting problem. Roaches, incidentally, were more numerous than we were, and the floors, walls, and tables (where the roaches were either brushed or crushed) never *looked* clean. The 3–11 shift, I think, had to be the most chaotic of all the three shifts, and the northeast wing was an 18-cell cellblock called "Max"—short for maximum security and "home" to a number of murder-ers, rapists, child molestors, terror-ists, kidnappers, and other high-risk suspects. Each cell, approximately 5' x 17' had one toilet, one sink, and bunk space for four inmates; yet, sometimes there were as many as six or seven inmates in one cell. The extras slept on the cold, concrete floor.

Depressing? Yeah, I thought so too, and to survive the first night, I instinctively blocked the grim reali-ties out of my mind. I told myself that I was going to make it . . . I had to. Otherwise, I'd be out of a job. And, to me, nothing was worse than unemployment—not even this place. So if I was expected to be just as rude and rugged, or just as bold and brazen, or just as calloused and capable as the cops I had seen on TV or on the streets, then I would be. But in actuality, I was none of the above. In fact, I was just a soft-spoken, sweet-natured, church-going, homemaker-type who had no interest in law enforcement other than how fast it could enlarge my net worth. Yet, in spite of my selfish intentions and sweeping inexperi-ence, I had imagined that someone would befriend me, teach me the how to's, and assist me when I seemed to struggle.

Boy, was I wrong. As I sat in the "dayroom" waiting for roll call, the first thing I noticed, after some of the smoke cleared, was how inhos-pitable the atmosphere was. I noticed that not a single staff mem-ber bothered to greet me or say "Welcome"; they just sauntered in, sat down, lit cigarettes, sipped cof-fee, and conversed with one anoth-er. They ignored me just as easily as they ignored the relentless stench. Consequently, I concluded that maybe there was an unwritten rule or code among comrades that pro-hibited fraternization with "new deputies." And I was certainly a new deputy—that was obvious. I had no uniform. (None of the new deputies had uniforms.) And I didn't get one of those taupe-top, brown-bottom outfits until about five months later.

Because I didn't have a uniform, to have one seemed like a mighty big deal. The uniformed deputies seemed to send out a certain signal . . . a signal that boasted, "I have *earned* the honor to wear this." I envied them. Moreover, I didn't like the odd-man-out sensation associated with being ununiformed. Subsequently, I figured that once I proved myself worthy of the honor, I, too, would be just as privileged. But once I became acquainted with the northeast wing, I began to wonder if I really wanted that privilege after all. As a matter of fact, I began to question a lot of things. For example, I wondered why I was assigned alone to a wing where a bunch of suspected felons coexisted. "Don't they know that I don't know what to do?" I thought to myself. I couldn't help but suspect that someone was either plotting my demise, trying to wedge me out, or collecting bets on whether I would last the first half hour. Hence, I set out like a woman with a mission . . . I was dead set on proving that I would be around until *I* was ready to go.

And for eighteen long months, I withstood the wiles and deceptions, the pressures and attitudes, and the gripes and demands of the inmates (and deputies). I was eventually moved from the northeast wing to the east wing where I had twice as many detainees to tend to. But that didn't move me. From time to time, I was assigned to 2F where the female jailbirds were housed. Though I hated working with female inmates, that didn't move me either. Moreover, I worked in the Front Office and the Booking Office where I learned to write bonds, examine criminal records, and manage distressed relatives. Finally, to the surprise of my skeptics and critics, I attained P.O.S.T. (Peace Officers Standard Training) certification. In essence, I had worked throughout most of the entire jail before my seniority dictated that I could transfer to another division.

That moved me—and transfer I did . . . to the courthouse. For the past thirty-one months, I have been serving the courts, and although the pressure to perform is not as high, proving myself still seems to be part of the job. I have accepted that it may *always* be part of the job.

Incidentally, perseverance was not the only ingredient I needed to prove I could maintain the health, safety, and welfare of prisoners. Versatility and training helped. As a turnkey and bailiff, many times I found myself acting as a counselor, a physician, a mediator, a bodyguard, a disciplinarian, a psychoanalyst, and if necessary, a friend.

Sometimes I look back on my turnkey days and wonder how I managed to operate under so many guises before my much-needed training was arranged. And it was in training that I realized just how lucky I had been. Some of the things I did ran totally contrary to policy and procedure, but I didn't know any better since no one bothered to teach me. I was simply given a one-pound ring of brass keys (which were each about five inches long) and told, "Make your rounds." Via the process of elimination, I learned which key unlocked what and what trick proved most effective. And a lot of what I learned came from the inmates, which incidentally, was not always policy. For example, many times inmates would ask me to pass notes, cigarettes, foodstuffs, and other items from their cell to another cell. Being sympathetic to their circumstances, I would oblige them if I had the time. I never bothered to closely inspect what they gave me because I thought they had a right to privacy even though they were locked up. Moreover, I couldn't imagine them having anything suspicious or illegal. But when I learned in the forty-hour Jail Policy and Procedures class that I was never supposed to pass *anything* from cell to cell, I felt like a fugitive myself. And I realized that the little things I didn't think were suspicious (like a pack of cigarettes) could easily have been a cover-up for contraband. Boy, did I feel stupid.

Secretly, I was embarrassed for not even considering the ramifications or breaches in security my actions could have caused. Plus, I was very ashamed of myself—me . . . Miss Conscientious. And as if that wasn't enough, I learned that the inmates knew what the rules were and had used me to their advantage. Consequently, sympathy for them dissipated. Once I learned better, I did better, and security conscientiousness increased.

Security sensitivity came with other lessons. One in particular has stayed with me. It pertained to the dress code. As an ununiformed deputy, I thought it was acceptable to dress comfortably and to accesorize; hence, I wore a blouse with a matching pair of pants, a pair of comfortable shoes, beads, and earrings. Insolently, a uniformed female deputy approached me, stood toe-to-toe with me, glared straight into my eyes, did not say hello, did not introduce herself. She grabbed my beads, twisted them just enough to almost choke me, and held on until she finished scolding coldly: "We do not wear anything around here that inmates can take from us or use against us to cause injury: no sharp combs or hairpins, no scarves, long necklaces, or dangling pierced earrings. Stuff like this (referring to the beads still in her grip) can get you strangled." When she finally freed my beads and me, she briefly searched my countenance for evidence that proved whether I got the message. Indeed I did, but I felt like a little kid who had been bullied by a bigger kid. And as such, I didn't argue or resist. I simply hung my head and surrendered my selfhood to her criticism. The fifteen minutes that followed had me feeling abused, alone, and angry as I replayed her tongue-lashing over and over again in my head. When I recovered, I realized that the stranger didn't hate me but had tried to teach me to safeguard myself first and foremost. Otherwise, I would never be able to protect others.

Once I had proved to all my skeptics and critics that I was competent enough to wear the uniform, the next thing I discovered as a female deputy was how demeaning sexual harassment and sexual discrimination could be. Both sexual harassment and sexual discrimination are illegal, and the ignorant are generally the victims of these injustices. I should know. I have had to contend with both. Regarding sexual harassment, I didn't know it was *illegal*. I just thought it was something I had to put up with working in a male-dominated environment. Moreover, I reasoned that if I complained to my supervisor (who was also a man), he would doubt my allegations, band with the accused, and report me as the troublemaker. Since I didn't want to risk losing my job, and since I was still on probation (all new employees were on probation for six months before

permanency was instated), I silently tolerated unwelcomed remarks about my shapely figure, unsolicited comments about my sex appeal, and certain other unwanted and unmannered advances that offended me tremendously. These insults came from deputies, sergeants, lieutenants, captains, the married, and the unmarried.

When I found out from the AFSCME (American Federation of State, County, and Municipal Employees) that sexual harassment was illegal and defined as "any UNWANTED sexual advance . . . that . . . creates an . . . offensive work environment," I knew that salvation and deliverance had finally come. And although I felt liberated from my fears, I was downright inflamed with all those who had violated me. I determined that hell, and not tolerance, would be the reward of the next man who even looked at me sideways. And the day of reckoning came when a 6'5", 395-pound fellow cornered my 5'6", 127-pound frame near the vending machines during a shift change. Since shift change was always a hectic time, no one noticed the predicament I was in. And even if someone did notice, it was up to me to prove that I could handle myself in tough situations. Consequently, I asked him very politely to excuse me (he was blocking my path), but he ignored my politeness and took me by the hand and the fleshy part of my arm. I had never seen this guy before in my life, so what made him think he could put his hands on me is still a mystery; but when he softly squeezed my hand and arm, I knew I had to do something. I quickly snatched my hand away and snapped that he was never to touch me again. Then I turned and walked away. Stunned, he shouted some stupid remark which I'm sure he thought justified his actions. "Why not? You're a *woman,* ain't you?" he barked. I heard what he said, but I couldn't believe it, and I stopped dead in my tracks. In that instance, I heard "woman" redefined as "female: good for nothing but the whims of a man." Or else he was calling me a lesbian. Seething with insult and outrage, I turned, and with a gaze that coud spear an elephant and a tone of voice that epitomized "hell hath no fury . . . ," I let him have what he had coming. I blasted him with an arctic wind that seemed to crystallize him and everyone else in close proximity: "Yeah, but so is yo' momma!" I retaliated.

When everyone thawed out and assumed the normal routines, I looked back and saw my victim wounded and silenced by my onslaught. Admittedly, I felt sorry for having to chop him down but not enough to tell him so. Wallowing in victory, I marched triumphantly to the northeast wing. My victim? Well, suffice it to say he didn't speak to me again for months, and yes, the sweet, soft-spoken, generally peaceable "Little Miss Parker" gained herself a reputation that day as one female deputy totally intolerant of sexual harassment.

Once the sexual-harassment problem was under control, the other injustice, sexual discrimination, had to be dealt with. If I had a dollar for every time I heard a supervisor exclaim, "We are neither male or female—we're all just deputies," I could probably pay off my college tuition. They like to make such declarations, especially when some of the ladies complain that they don't want to work with male inmates or when they try to act too prissy to do simple tasks like gas the patrol car. I have never had a problem with any aspect of the job, because I know it's all a part of the job. Therefore, I get piqued sometimes when a male deputy with less seniority is chosen over me for an assignment that I am just as qualified for. Obviously, we're *not* all just deputies. The truth of the matter is my law-enforcement brothers (especially the head haunchos) *say* we're all just deputies, but when there's a "man-size" job to do, they become very protective (of the tender gender). Sometimes they become so protective that they are *over*protective, so much so that they are not even willing to give you a fair chance. And no matter how much I insist that I can handle myself, that old, familiar, well-I-don't-know-Parker-I-think-maybe-he-should-go-this-time look comes across the boss's face. Most times I don't waste my time arguing with the boss; I just respect his authority and do as I'm told . . . however menial the task may seem.

But on one occasion, I was almost booted out of an assignment that I was hoping would open up for me. This was no time to back down or shy away. It was time to fight . . . with a major.

I had been assigned to what we call the "late transfer" position by the sergeant in charge of the transfer team. This meant that I would work from 12 noon until 8 p.m., and I would be responsible for assuring that all inmates left at the courthouse by the bus team were transported back to the jail. The major in charge of court operations objected strongly to my having this assignment because of the "possibilities of things that could happen." I was told that if I wanted the late-transfer position, I would have to find a man willing to work with me. "That's funny," I thought, "I don't *ever* remember 'Chuck' having to find a man to work with him when he had this assignment." But that was my ultimatum . . . take it, or leave it.

Needless to say, I was totally outdone by this decision (What? Could "things" not happen to a man?) . . . but I kept my cool. This was no time to get emotional, to cry, or to pout. I recalled and implemented one of my favorite policy and procedure lessons—"write it

up." To elaborate, whenever an objectionable situation arose, deputies were responsible for writing a report which detailed what happened. We are taught "if you don't write it down, it didn't happen."

Hence, I wrote up the major. The memo I wrote was addressed to the major, but the chief and the high sheriff got copies. I explained to them what happened and advised them that I thought the decision was not only unfair and reprehensible, but that it was also illegal. I made no threats or demands. I just told them what I thought. Of course, the major didn't care what I thought and was sure the chief would support his decision. All in all, the major was only trying to protect me. Frankly, I appreciated his concern, but I was tired of being "protected." As it turned out, I received a memo ordering me to report for the late-transfer position. Sweet victory for me . . . bitter disbelief for the major.

Actor Bill Bixby is undoubtedly associated with his role in the syndicated program, "The Incredible Hulk." As Dr. David Banner, he was a compassionate, conscientious, and mild-mannered human being. Whenever he became angry or outraged, however, he would be physically transformed into a brawny and uncontrollable human beast. Normalcy returned when the beast calmed down. The metamorphosed state plagued the good doctor, and he spent a lifetime trying to find a cure that could tame the beast within. And as David Banner was troubled by his physical transformations, I, too, am disturbed by the mentally-metamorphosed monster I have become. When I joined the sheriff's department, I had my own opinions about different subjects, a set of morals I strictly adhered to, and a personality that was recognizably my own. Most importantly, I liked *me*. But somehow, as a sheriff's deputy, I was transformed, to some degree, into a mental carbon copy of my colleagues. Though I tried to protect my personality from erosion as the Ancients had tried to preserve the dead from decay, I could not resist the change. Hence, I still have some definite opinions about certain subjects, but my attitude, personality, and morals have changed noticeably. Whereas I used to get indignant and incensed with my co-workers when I saw them treat people as if they were subhuman, I don't get that way now. Whereas I used to want to avenge the defenseless or get into bitter disputes with deputies who were blatantly discourteous to our public or the inmates, now I refuse to fight anybody's battles but mine. And though I have not been reduced to treating anyone less than human, I am not proud of how calloused, uncaring, and brazen I have become. I think the change was a matter of survival. Hopefully, I will find a "cure" for my beast within . . . SO HELP ME GOD.

Overall, my experience as a female sheriff's deputy has been one I'd never trade. Though I constantly have to prove myself to my superiors, and though sexual harassment and sexual discrimination may always be a problem, and though I really hate the mental metamorphosis I have experienced, it has all been a real challenge, and now I *know* that the best way out of any hardship is through it. Through my experiences, I have become more sensitive to self-security; I have become wiser to the ways and wiles of the world, and I have a greater appreciation for the men and women who enforce the law.

❑ SOURCES ❑

CHAPTER 1

Dylan Thomas, "Notes on the Art of Poetry," *About Languages: Contexts for College Writing,* n.d.

Benjamin Stein, "Nothing Concentrates a Worker Like Living on the Edge," *The Wall Street Journal,* April 3, 1989.

CHAPTER 2

"Torture and Torment," *Newsweek.* Copyright February 4, 1991, Newsweek, Inc. All rights reserved. Reprinted by permission.

A. M. Rosenthal, "Learning on the Job," *The New York Times Magazine,* December 14, 1986.

"When Fred Astaire Leaves the Room," Editorial, *The New York Times.* Copyright 1987 by The New York Times Company. Reprinted by permission.

Richard Burton, "Elizabeth Taylor," *Meeting Mrs. Jenkins,* William Morris, New York, 1965. Also appeared in *Vogue,* March 1, 1965.

Annie Dillard, "The Stunt Pilot," *Esquire,* January, 1989. Copyright 1989 by Annie Dillard.

Henry Woodhead, "Stalking the Wild Orthographers," *The Atlanta Weekly.* n.d. Reprinted with permission of the author.

CHAPTER 5

Hank Ernst, Jr. "A Journalist Intern in New York." Copyright 1991. Printed with permission of the writer.

Annie Dillard, "Introduction," *Best American Essays 1988.* New York: Houghton Mifflin Company, Tichnor & Fields, 1988. Reprinted by permission of the publisher.

Elfriede Kristwald, "What's Love Got to Do With It?" *The Boston Globe,* February 11, 1990. Reprinted by permission of the writer.

George Leonard, "The Case for Pleasure," *Esquire,* May, 1984. Reprinted by permission of George Leonard.

Edward Coleman Hosch, "Rocky Road." Printed with permission of the writer.

Shawna Vogel, "Lighting Up the Body Clock," *Discover,* December, 1990. Copyright 1990 Discover Publications. Reprinted by permission.

CHAPTER 6

Mitchell J. Shields. Letter in response to a student's query. Printed with permission of the writer.

Leigh Hilliard. Query letter printed by permission of the writer.

Helen M. Friese. Query letter printed with permission of the writer.

Jennifer A. Cogelia. Query letter printed with permission of the writer.

McCall's. Response to student's query letter. Reprinted by permission of *McCall's* magazine. Copyright 1978 by the New York Times Company.

CHAPTER 7

William Zinsser, "Shanghai Blues," *Willie and Dwike: An American Profile.* New York: Harper & Row, 1984. Copyright 1984 by William K. Zinsser. Reprinted by permission of the author.

Rick Reilly, "The Nifty Fifty: Fifty Reasons Why Golf Is Cool Again," *Sports Illustrated,* July 2, 1990. Reprinted courtesy of *Sports Illustrated* from the July 2, 1990, issue. Copyright 1990, The Time Inc. Magazine Company. All Rights Reserved.

Gary Smith, "Ali and His Entourage," *Sports Illustrated,* April 15, 1988. Reprinted by permission of author.

Richard Daigle, "A Former Iranian Hostage Looks Back," *The Retired Officer,* November, 1990. Reprinted by permission of the writer.

Frida Ghitis, "Confronting Fear," *Creative Loafing,* May 28, 1988. Reprinted by permission of the writer.

Thomas M. Disch, "The Death of Broadway," *The Atlantic,* March, 1991. Copyright 1991 by *The Atlantic Monthly Co.* Reprinted by permission of Thomas M. Disch.

CHAPTER 9

Budd Schulberg, "A Fighter, Not a Hater," *Parade,* October 27, 1991. Reprinted with permission from *Parade,* Copyright © 1991.

Ken Metzler, *Creative Interviewing.* Englewood Cliffs, N.J.: Prentice Hall, 1977.

Tom Wolfe and E. W. Johnson, *The New Journalism.* New York, Harper & Row, 1973.

Edwin Reingold, excerpt from "Letter to the Publisher," *Time,* September 17, 1973. Copyright 1973 Time Warner Inc. Reprinted by permission.

CHAPTER 10

Arnold Schechter, "Moving Hazards at the Northernmost U.S. Golf Course," *Sports Illustrated,* May 3, 1982. Reprinted by permission of the author.

CHAPTER 11

Brad Darrack, "Kirk Douglas," *People,* Oct. 3, 1988.

Sarah Mixon, "Death Detested." Printed by permission of the writer.

Katherine Griffin, "Good Earth," *In Health,* May–June, 1991.

James Shreeve, "Machiavellian Monkeys," *Discover,* June, 1991.

Carla Rapaport, "Why Japan Keeps on Winning," *Fortune,* July 15, 1991. Reprinted by permission.

Larry L. King, "Hurtin' Good," *The Washington Post Magazine,* n.d.

Paul West, "Portrait of the Artist as a Lion on Stilts," *TriQuarterly,* Number 75 (Spring/Summer), 1989. Copyright 1989. Reprinted by permission of the author.

CHAPTER 12

James Dickey, "The Delights of the Edge," first printed in *Mademoiselle,* June, 1974. Reprinted in *Night-Hurdling,* Bruccoli Clark, 1983.

Ken Auletta, "Profile: Governor Mario Cuomo," *The New Yorker,* April 9, 1984. Reprinted by permission; Copyright 1984 Ken Auletta.

Pat Conroy, "A Southerner in Paris," *The Atlanta Weekly,* March 29, 1981.

Joe Kane, "Officer Hicks, Gay Cop," *Esquire,* June, 1985. Reprinted with permission of the author (who wrote *Running the Amazon.*)

Michael Pollan, "Why Mow? The Case Against Lawns," *The New York Times Magazine,* November 5, 1989. Copyright 1989 by Michael Pollan.

William Zinsser, "Venice," *Willie and Dwike.* New York: Harper & Row, 1984. Reprinted by permission of the author.

CHAPTER 13

Vladimir Nabokov, "Mademoiselle O," *The Atlantic,* January, 1943.

"Translation Quiz," *Eternity,* October, 1978.

Louis Milic, *Stylists on Style: A Handbook with Selections for Analysis.* New York: Scribner, 1969.

Vivian Moss, "Film Producer Sees Embryo Inside Womb," *The Lutheran Standard,* October 3, 1978.

Pat Conroy, "Shadows of the Old South," *Geoliving,* May, 1981.

Richard Selzer, "A Mask on the Face of Death," *Life,* August, 1987. Copyright 1987 by Richard Selzer.

CHAPTER 14

Annie Dillard, "The Stunt Pilot," *Esquire,* January, 1989.

CHAPTER 15

Stuart Culpepper, "Fear and Loathing on the Streets of Atlanta," *Atlanta Magazine,* October, 1979. Reprinted by permission of the author. Copyright 1979 by Stuart Culpepper.

CHAPTER 16

Suggested Letter of Agreement, American Society of Journalists and Authors. Copyright 1991. Reprinted by permission.

CHAPTER 17

Edward Jay Friedlander and John Lee, *Feature Writing for Newspapers & Magazines.* New York: HarperCollins Publishers, 1988.
"The Business of Writing," *Writer's Market.* Cincinnati, Ohio: F&W Publications, 1991.

APPENDIX

Willie Morris, "Here Lies My Heart," *Esquire,* June, 1990. Reprinted by permission of the author.
David Van Biema, "Master of an Unbelievable, Invisible World," *Life Magazine,* August, 1990. Copyright 1990 The Time Inc. Magazine Company. Reprinted with permission.
James Wooten, "Wallace and Me: The End of the Road," *Esquire*, November, 1978.
Beverly Levine, "Travel Without Fear." Copyright 1987. Printed with permission of the writer.
Nancy E. Davis, "The Fall and Rise of Richard Hill." Copyright 1987. Printed with the permission of the writer.
Emilyanne Parker, "Officer Survival: The Real Deal." Copyright 1991. Printed with permission of the writer.

❑ SELECTED BIBLIOGRAPHY ❑

INTERVIEWING

Biagi, Shirley. *Interviews that Work: A Practical Guide for Journalists.* Belmont, California: Wadsworth Publishing Company, 1986.

Brady, John. *The Craft of Interviewing.* Cincinnati: Writer's Digest, 1977. A comprehensive and informal book on interviewing: how to get, prepare for, handle, record, and end interviews with celebrities and authorities.

Killenberg, George M. and Rob Anderson. *Before the Story.* New York: St. Martin's Press, 1989. No-nonsense discussion of interviewing techniques and their complexity: reading body language, handling conflict and anger, and detecting deception.

Metzler, Ken. *Creative Interviewing.* Englewood Cliffs, N.Y.: Prentice-Hall, 1989. Helpful advice on how to overcome being intimidated by authorities, how to prepare different types of creative questions in advance, and how to handle the unexpected in an interview.

Mitford, Jessica. *Poison Penmanship: The Gentle Art of Muckraking.* New York: Farrar, Straus and Giroux, Inc., 1988. Mitford's most famous investigative magazine articles, with her entertaining comments on how she exposed corruption, "tracing and destroying the enemy." Includes description of her own ingenious interviewing techniques.

LIBRARY RESEARCH SOURCES

American Library Directory. New York: Bowker. Published annually. A geographic list of libraries in the United States and Canada, including the special collections each maintains.

Biography and Genealogy Master Index. Detroit: Gale Research. Cumulations published every five years, providing a single source for concise information on any notable person of any nationality, living or dead.

Biography Index. New York: Wilson. A cumulative index to biographical material in books and magazines, diaries, memoirs, obituaries, fiction, drama, and so on. Includes individuals both living and dead, past and present, national and international. Indexed by profession and name.

Business Information Sources. Los Angeles: University of California Press, 1985. A selected, annotated list of business books and reference sources with an emphasis on recent material published in the United States. Examples of subjects covered: investments, computers, insurance, real estate, marketing, production management.

Business Periodicals Index. New York: Wilson. Published monthly, except August. A subject index to business magazines in such fields as accounting, advertising, banking, public relations, economics, and also specific businesses and trades.

Current Biography. New York: Wilson. Published monthly, except December. Best single source of biographical data on newsworthy contemporary persons in all fields of achievement and of many nationalities. Extensive and interesting coverage, often including a portrait. Contains a classified list by occupations.

Dictionary of American Biography. New York: Scribner's. A multi-volume biographical dictionary of deceased Americans who made distinguished contributions to the development of the United States. Each article written by a scholar.

Encyclopedia of Associations. Detroit: Gale Research. Revised about every two years. Descriptions of national and international organizations of every conceivable type. Includes addresses and officers.

Facts on File. New York: Facts on File. A weekly world news digest with cumulative index.

Guide to Reference Books. Sheehy, Eugene P. Chicago: American Library Association, 1986. Brief descriptions of thousands of reference books on almost every conceivable subject. Extremely useful to novice researchers unaware of the staggering amount of information available, even on esoteric topics.

Humanities Index. New York: Wilson. Published quarterly with annual cumulations. Supersedes in part the Social Sciences and Humanities Index. An author and subject index to periodicals devoted to such studies as folklore, history, literature, the performing arts, and so on.

Library of Congress Subject Headings, 8th ed. Washington: Library of Congress, 1975. Provides access to the card catalogs of libraries that use the Library of Congress subject headings when the researcher cannot think of the proper key word for a heading (see pages 77–78 of this book for fuller explanation).

The New York Times Index. An exhaustive index to perhaps the world's best newspaper. A rich mine for various kinds of information: obituaries of almost all noteworthy persons, full texts of Presidential speeches, sports events, reviews of plays and books, and so on.

Public Affairs Information Service Bulletin. Published weekly with periodic cumulations. A selective subject listing in the areas of economic and social conditions, international relations, and public affairs in English-language publications throughout the world.

Readers' Guide to Periodical Literature. New York: Wilson. A cumulative index to selected popular magazines of a general nature. Entries listed by author and subject.

Search Strategies in Mass Communication. Ward, Jean and Kathleen A. Hansen. New York: Longman Inc., 1987. Excellent instruction in how to conduct research in the new age of electronic information storage and retrieval.

Social Sciences Index. New York: Wilson. Published quarterly with annual cumulations. A subject and author index to selected scholarly periodicals devoted to the social sciences—anthropology, criminology, psychology, political science, and so on.—listed by author and subject.

Subject Guide to Books in Print. New York: Bowker. Published annually. A companion to *Books in Print*, listing under subjects the books still in print in the English language published in the United States.

Thomas' Register of American Manufacturers. New York: Thomas. Published annually. A directory of manufacturers listed by names of companies, products and services, and brand names, with useful information on each firm.

Who's Who in America. Chicago: Marquis. Published biennially. The standard dictionary of contemporary biography, including "the best known men and women in all lines of useful and reputable achievement."

Who's Who of American Women. Chicago: Marquis. Published biennially. A biographical dictionary of notable living American women.

Who Was Who in America. Chicago: Marquis. Sketches of individuals related to the history of America from the founding of the Jamestown Colony to the date of publication.

MARKET SOURCES

Gale Directory of Publications. Philadelphia: N.W. Ayer and Sons, 1869. Alphabetized list of publications for all major and most minor population centers in the United States. Facts, maps, and charts concerning circulation, personnel, publication dates, market area, rates.

International Directory of Little Magazines and Small Presses. Paradise, Calif.: Dustbooks. Annual. Information on little-known or new publications, many of which seek freelance articles but offer no payment. Descriptions of types of material used, with cross indexes.

Literary Market Place. New York: Bowker. Published annually. A selective list of magazines "to help writers seeking to place their output in the right medium." Names of editors, addresses of magazines, circulations. Many unfamiliar titles included. Lists conferences, writers' associations, events.

Magazines for Libraries. Bill Katz and Berry G. Richards, eds. New York: Bowker, 1982. Valuable for freelancers because of its evaluations and descriptions of 6,500 periodicals. Description of *The New Yorker*, for example: "the best general magazine in the world."

The Writer's Handbook. Burack, S. K., ed. Boston: The Writer. Annual. Useful list of potential markets and a section of articles written by professionals on how to write and sell nonfiction.

Writer's Market. Cincinnati: Writer's Digest. Annual. A list of more than 4,000 magazine markets, categorized and alphabetized, that use freelance material. Descriptions of desired material and fees; names and addresses of editors.

MASS MEDIA LAW

Nelson, Harold, and Dwight Teeter. *Law of Mass Communications*. Mineola, N.Y.: Foundation Press, 1989. One of the most authoritative and comprehensive undergraduate texts on journalism law. Contains detailed explanations of the law of copyright, libel, and right to privacy.

Overbeck, Wayne and Rick D. Pullen. *Major Principles of Media Law*. New York: Harcourt Brace Jovanovich College Publishers, 1991 Edition. An *annual* media law textbook revised each summer so that college students in the fall will have current information on evolving legal issues.

Pember, Don R. *Mass Media Law*. Dubuque, Iowa: Wm. C. Brown Company, 1989. A readable book for laymen with examples that help clarify the intent of mass media law.

USAGE

Bernstein, Theodore M. *The Careful Writer: A Modern Guide to English Usage*. New York: Atheneum, 1978. A witty handbook on usage by the late consulting editor of *The New York Times* that can help clarify the differences between such troublesome words as *affect* and *effect, which* and *that, less* and *fewer.*

Kessler, Lauren, and Duncan McDonald. *When Words Collide*. Belmont, Calif.: Wadsworth Publishing Company, 1988. Based on the philosophy that "learning grammar is the first step to writing well." Excellent sections on spelling and punctuation.

Hodges, John C., ed. *Harbrace College Handbook*. New York: Harcourt Brace Jovanovich, 1990. A compact reference for common usage problems and compositional skills. Describes "the usual practice of good contemporary writers." Especially helpful sections on punctuation, agreement, and effective sentences.

WRITING

Brooks, Terri. *Words Worth*. New York: St. Martin's Press, 1989. A lively, informal book on freelancing with an especially good section on voice (or tone).

Fensch, Thomas. *The Sports Writing Handbook*. Hillsdale, N.J.: Lawrence Erlbaum Associates, 1988. Slanted toward newspaper journalism, but much of the material is applicable to magazine writing. Practical and informal with an especially helpful chapter on leads of every conceivable kind.

Murray, Donald M. *The Craft of Revision*. Fort Worth: Holt, Rinehart, and Winston, 1991. Based on the belief that good writing evolves from a series of carefully written drafts and from the surfacing of subconscious ideas brought about by the writing process.

Fontaine, Andre and William A. Glavin. *The Art of Writing Nonfiction*. New York: Crowell, 1989. An exploration and description of the process of interpretive journalism. Discussions of different kinds of writing—"dramatic, descriptive, explanatory, and emotional." Leisurely, anecdotal approach.

Rico, Gabrielle Lusser. *Writing the Natural Way*. Los Angeles: J. P. Tarcher, 1983. How to enhance your creative power with specific techniques based on brain research.

Strunk, William, Jr., and E. B. White. *Elements of Style*. New York: Macmillan Publishing Company, 1979. A classic rulebook for common usage problems in which each rule is phrased so as to illustrate the principle involved. Superb section on style.

Zinsser, William. *On Writing Well*. New York: Harper & Row, 1980. Notable for its wit and informal style. Stresses the importance of intimacy and simplicity in writing.

Zinsser, William. *Writing to Learn*. New York: Harper & Row, 1988. Directed to people who are afraid of writing of any kind: letters, memos, reports, and subjects like math and science "that we don't think we have an aptitude for." Examples of graceful writing on subjects ordinarily considered too technical for the average reader.

INDEX